DISCOVERING THE WORLD OF THE ANCIENT GREEKS

DISCOVERING THE WORLD OF THE ANCIENT GREEKS

ZOFIA ARCHIBALD

Facts On File
New York • Oxford

A QUARTO BOOK

For information contact:

Facts on File Limited   or   Facts on File, Inc.
Collins Street   460 Park Avenue South
Oxford OX4 1XJ   New York NY10016
UK   USA

A British CIP catalogue record for this book is available from the British Library

A United States of America CIP catalogue record for this book is available
from the Library of Congress.

ISBN 0-8160-2614-9

Facts On File books are available at special discounts when purchased in
bulk quantities for businesses, associations, institutions or sales
promotions. Please contact the Special Sales Department of our Oxford
office on 0865 728399 or our New York office on 212/683-2244
(dial 800/322-8755 except in NY, AK or HI).

This book was designed and produced by
Quarto Publishing plc
The Old Brewery
6 Blundell Street
London N7 9BH

Senior Editor Sally MacEachern

Editor Helen Douglas-Cooper

Index Hazel Bell

Designer Graham Davis

Cartography Lovell Johns

Illustrator Stephen Conlin

Picture Researcher David Moncur

Assistant Art Director Philip Gilderdale

Art Director Moira Clinch

Publishing Director Janet Slingsby

Typeset by ABC Typesetting Limited, Bournemouth
Manufactured in Singapore by Chrome Graphics (Overseas) Pte. Ltd
Printed by Leefung-Asco Printers Ltd, Hong Kong

10   9   8   7   6   5   4   3   2   1

CONTENTS

TIME CHART

c.6500–2900 BC

c.6500-2900 BC

Domestication of animals and plants creates basis for settled community life in the Neolithic period.

c.2900-2000

Early Aegean Bronze Age cultures.

c.1930

First palaces on Crete.

1700

Cretan palaces destroyed and rebuilt.

1550

"Shaft Graves" at Mycenae; overseas expansion of Minoan culture.

c.1450

Destruction of Cretan palaces.

c.1375-50

Appearance of Mycenaean customs and administration on Crete (introduction of Linear B script).

c.1200

Destruction of level viia at Troy ("Priam's city"?), and some years later of many Mycenaean centres; population shifts.

c.1050

New burial customs and community traditions; heralding "Geometric" styles. First great Greek migration to west coast of Asia Minor.

c.850-700

Development of distinctive regional cultures around the Aegean.

776

First Olympic Games (conventional date).

by 750

Phoenician script adapted to create Greek alphabet; Greek trading posts in east and west Mediterranean.

735-700

First Greek colonies in Sicily.

later 8th century

Homer's epic poems, the *Iliad* and *Odyssey*, written.

730

c.730-710

Spartans conquer south-west Peloponnese in First Messenian War.

late 8th century

Lelantine war in Euboia – first inter-state conflict in Greece.

c.700

Hesiod, epic poet, of Boiotia.

c.650-600

Earliest written law code from Dreros, Crete.

621

Drakon's law code at Athens.

c.561-528

Peisistratos tyrant three times in Athens.

540

Anaximander died (wrote first philosophical treatise and made first map of the known world).

c.530

Pythagoras fled from Samos to Kroton, southern Italy.

515

Birth of Parmenides, first philosopher to contemplate the meaning of being; framed laws for Elea (Velia).

510

Tyrants expelled from Athens.

499-494

Ionians revolt against Persian Empire.

490

Greeks, led by Athenians, defeat Persian army at Marathon, Attika.

c.484

Birth of Herodotos, the "father of history", at Halikarnassos.

480

Spartans defeated at Thermopylai. Persians sack Athens. Athenian navy soundly defeats Persians in sea battle of Salamis Bay.

479

479

Remaining Persian ground forces defeated at Plataia.

478

Delian League founded under Athenian leadership to carry on the war against Persia by land and sea.

472

Aischylos tragedy, the *Persians*.

471

Themistokles ostracized from Athens.

468

Sophokles' first tragic victory, using three actors and a chorus.

461

Radical democracy introduced at Athens under, Ephialtes and Perikles.

461-446

"First" Peloponnesian War between Athens and Sparta.

458

Aischylos' *Oresteia*.

449

"Peace of Kallias": a recognition of mutual spheres of influence, though the Ionian Greeks remained in an ambiguous position.

447-432

Major programme of public works on the Athenian Akropolis.

441

Euripides' first victory with a tragic play.

438

Consecration of the Parthenon Athens. Death of the distinguished lyric poet, Pindar.

431

431-405

"Second" Peloponnesian War between Athens and Sparta.

431

Euripides' *Medea*. Distinguished historian Thukydides begins to record his account of the War.

427

Sophist Gorgias visits Athens. Birth of Plato.

425

Aristophanes' *Acharnians*.

421

Temporary Peace of Nikias.

415-13

Disastrous Athenian expedition to Sicily.

411

Anti-democratic coup of the Four Hundred at Athens, followed by that of the Five Thousand.

410

Return of democracy.

406

Athenian victory at the Arginusai islands. Deaths of Euripides and Sophokles.

404-403

Tyranny of the Thirty at Athens, followed by restoration of full democracy.

399

Trial and execution of Sokrates.

387/6

King's Peace between the Persian King Artaxerxes and the Greeks.

386	336	229	149

386

Plato founds his Academy.

384

Birth of orator Demosthenes and Aristotle.

371

Spartans defeated by Thebans at Leuktra; beginning of irreversible Spartan decline.

362

Rivals for leadership of the Greek world – Sparta, Athens and Thebes – reach stalemate in the battle of Mantineia.

359

Philip II king of Macedon.

357/6

Philip captures Amphipolis in north Aegean, at the same time as important allies of Athens oppose her in the "Social War"; war between Athens and Macedon.

356

Birth of Alexander the Great.

355-46

Third Sacred War embroils Greek states in more factional fighting, enabling Philip of Macedon to intervene in Greek affairs.

338

Philip defeats Athenians, Thebans and their allies at Chaironeia.

337

League of Korinth founded by Philip to provide inter-state forum for the Greeks. Philip on behalf of the League declares war on Persia. Death of Hippokrates of Kos.

336

Assassination of Philip II; Alexander assumes leadership of crusade against Persia.

331

Foundation of Alexandria in Egypt.

323

Death of Alexander at Babylon

322

Deaths of Aristotle and Demosthenes; restricted constitution introduced at Athens following unsuccessful Lamian War against Macedon. First war of the Successors.

285

Lighthouse off Alexandria built.

280-75

Campaigns of Pyrrhos of Epiros in Italy and Sicily.

279

Gauls invade Macedon and Greece as far as Delphi.

c.267-2

Athens fails to throw off Macedonian control in Chremonidean War.

c.268-215

Hieron II king of Syracuse.

251

Aratos frees Sikyon from tyranny; Sikyon joins the Achaian League in the north-west Peloponnese.

243

Aratos and the Achaians capture the citadel of Akrokorinth from the Macedonians.

c.240

Former Seleucid province of Baktria becomes independent under King Diodotos I.

229

King Kleomenes III of Sparta opposed by Achaia League but succeeds in effecting radical reforms at Sparta.

224

Earthquake shatters the Colossus.

215

Philip V of Macedon allies with Hannibal in the Second Punic War.

214-205

First Macedonian War between the Romans and Philip V.

197

Defeat of Philip V by the Romans at Kynoskephalai.

196

Roman general Flamininus proclaims the "freedom of the Greeks" at the Isthmian Games.

c.197-50

Construction of Great Altar, Pergamon.

192-188

War between Antiochos III of Asia and the Romans.

168

Revived Macedon under Perseus defeated at Pydna. Macedon divided into four republics.

175-64

Persecution of the Jews by Antiochos IV; rising of the Maccabees in Palestine.

150

Achaian hostages since Pydna freed, among them Polybios, whose *Histories* described how the greatness of Rome overcame the Greeks.

149-46

Creation of a Roman province in Macedonia, and the dissolution of the League.

88-86

Athenians, siding with the uprising of King Mithridates VI of Pontos, crushed by Sulla.

AD

54

St Paul preaches on the Areiopagos hill, Athens.

after 120

Death of Plutarch of Chaironeia, philosopher and author of the *"Parallel Lives"* of famous Greeks and Romans.

143

Athenian Herodes Atticus, Roman senator, holds the consulship.

150-60

Travel writer Pausanias of Lydia tours Greece and begins his *Guide*.

267

Goths (Herulians) sack Athens, Sparta and Korinth.

330

Foundation of Constantinople by the Emperor Constantine at Greek Byzantion.

529

Philosophical schools of Athens closed by order of Justinian.

later 6th century

Greece overrun by Slavs.

ANCIENT GREECE

ADRIATIC SEA

YUGOSLAVIA

BULGARIA

ALBANIA

THRA

Nestos

Philippoi

Strymon

Abdera

Pella

Amphipolis

Axios

MACEDONIA

Thessalonika

CHALKIDIKE

Methone

Akanthos

SAMOTHRAC

Haliakmon

Pydna

Aigai

Potidaia

GREECE

Dion

Torone

Mende

LEMNOS

Olympos ▲

Myrina

Bouthroton

Ossa ▲

Kérkyra

Dodona

Larissa

Acheron

Krannon

EPIROS

Peneios

Pherai

HALONNESOS

Kassope

THESSALY

Pagasai

Iolkos

Ambrakia

Pharsalos

SKIATHOS

AEGE

SPORADES

SEA

AKARNANIA

Histiaia/Oreos

LEVKAS

Stratos

AITOLIA

Thermopylai

Acheloos

PHOKIS

Parnassos ▲

LOKRIS

EUBOIA

Amphissa

Delphi

Orchomenos

Chalkis

Oiniadai

Pleuron

Kirrha

Chaironeia

Eretria

ITHAKA

Naupaktos

BOIOTIA

Tanagra

Leuktra

Thebes

GULF OF KORINTH

Plataia

Oropos

ACHAIA

Eleusis

Marathon

Kithairon ▲

ATTIKA

Kephisos

Elis

Sikyon

Megara

Athens

Peneios

ARKADIA

Stymphalos

Korakou

Salamis

Piraeus

ANDROS

Phlious

Korinth

Olympia

Orchomenos

Nemea

Zygouries

Aigina

KEOS

Alpheios

Mantineia

ARGOLID

Epidauros

ZAKYNTHOS

Argos

Tiryns

KYTHNOS

SYROS

Lerna

Tegea

Troizen

DELOS

PELOPONNESE

Megalopolis

SERIPHOS

PAROS

IONIAN

Ithome ▲ *Pamisos*

SEA

Messene

Eurotas

SIPHNOS

MESSENIA

Sparta

SYKINOS

LAKONIA

MELOS

Gytheion

THERA/

CYCLADES

SANTOF

MEDITERRANEAN

SEA OF CRETE

SEA

KYTHERA

Knossos

M

Phaistos

Kommos

Gortyn

BLACK

SEA

SEA OF MARMARA

Ainos

Kyzikos

Abydos

Skamander

Assos

TURKEY

Methymna

Pergamon

Mytilene

LESBOS

Kaikos

AIOLIS

Kyme

Phokaia

Magnesia

Hermos

Sardis

Smyrna

Erythrai

Klazomenai

IOS

Teos

IONIA

Kaister

Kolophon

Ephesos

SAMOS

Magnesia

Maiander

Priene

Miletos

Didyma

KARIA

Halikarnassos

KALYMNOS

AMORGOS

Knidos

DODECANESE

RHODOS

Zakros

NAMES ANCIENT AND MODERN

In many cases, ancient sites are now known by their modern Greek or Turkish names, making them difficult to find on a modern map. In some cases, sites are known by their ancient names, but are very close to a modern town, making it easier to identify them by the modern town name (e.g. Oropos is near the modern town of Skála Oropoú). The listing below is designed to help the reader locate the sites mentioned in the book.

Ancient names with modern names in italics.

Abdera *Ávdira*	Halikarnassos *Bodrum*	Pherai *Velestínon*
Abydos *Çanakkale*	Histiaia/Oreos *Istiaía*	Phokaia *Foçe*
Aigai *Vergina*	Iolkos *Volos*	Piraeus *Piraievs*
Aigina *Aíyina*	Kérkyra *Corfu*	Plataia *Plataiaí*
Ainos *Enez*	Korinth *Kórinthos*	Potidaia *nr. Néa Potídhaia*
Akanthos *Ierissós*	Kythera *Kíthara*	Salamis *Salamis*
Ambrakia *Árta*	Kyzikos *nr. Bandirma*	Samothrace *Samothraki*
Amphissa *Ámfissa*	Lesbos *Lesvos*	Sardis *Sartmustafa*
Argos *Árgus*	Magnesia *Manisa*	Sikyon *Sikíon*
Athens *Athinai*	Megalopolis *Megalópolis*	Skiathos *Skiathos*
Bouthroton *Butrint*	Megara *Mégara*	Smyrna *Bayrakli, nr. Izmir*
Chalkis *Khalkis*	Messene *Messíni*	Sparta *Sparti*
Chios *Khios*	Miletos *Milet*	Taras *Tarentum*
Delphi *Dhelfoí*	Mytilene *Mítilini*	Teos *Sigaçik*
Eleusis *Elevsís*	Oropos *nr. Skála Oropoú*	Thebes *Thívai*
Ephesos *Selçuk*	Pagasai-Demetrias *nr. Volos*	Thera *Santorini/Fira*
Eretria *nr. Néa Psará*	Pergamon *Bergama*	Thessalonika *Thessaloniki*
Gytheion *Yíthion*	Pharsalos *Fársala*	

PREFACE

Marble slab inscribed with a law (*c.* 420–400 BC) regulating the manufacture and export of wine on the island of Thasos in the north Aegean. The oldest known Greek law concerning wine and vinegar comes from Thasos (*c.* 480/70 BC). In the 2nd century BC the middle of the stone was recut and a law on wills was inserted.

On being asked by a ship's captain why his master, Lord Byron, had undertaken the journey to a country like Greece in 1809, William Fletcher is said to have replied, "Bless you! There is very little country. It's all rocks and robbers. They live in holes in the rocks and some come out like foxes. They have long guns, pistols and knives. We were obliged to have a guard of soldiers to go from one place to another." His further comments on the lifestyle he and his master endured are even less encouraging: "(they lived) like dogs, on goat's flesh and rice, sitting on the floor in a hovel; all eating out of one dirty round dish; no knives, and only one or two horn spoons. They drink a stuff called wine, but it tastes more of turps than grapes, and is carried about in stinking goatskins, and everyone drinks from the same bowl; then they have coffee, which is pounded, and they drink it, dregs and all without sugar."

Byron, who overheard the conversation, was evidently unimpressed by his servant's lack of appreciation. He wrote elsewhere of Fletcher's incapacities and intolerance of foreign ways. Byron himself was impervious to such trifles. He was fit enough later in the following year to swim the Hellespont in an hour and ten minutes.

This encounter reveals the gulf that separates the inspired idealist from the casual but detached observer. The English nobleman's visionary eye was already contemplating the tragic servitude of Greece under the Turkish yoke, while his servant was expecting a home from home.

Today foreign travel may be far better adapted to the tourist, but a spirit of adventure is still needed to transform buried stones into peopled landscapes. This book is about visions, past and present, of the Greek world, a world with a perceptible heart in the Aegean Sea, but one whose boundaries were constantly shifting. Every traveller carries his or her own intellectual baggage which weights impressions in one or another direction. Byron was altogether exceptional in his enthusiasm for the liberation of contemporary Greece. He was certainly galvanized by the achievements of the ancient Greeks, but was not particularly interested in the surviving antiquities.

At the beginning of the 19th century, Greece was rather off the beaten track for tourists. Since the collapse of Constantinople in 1453 only occasional and particularly determined travellers had seen anything of its monuments. This situation changed gradually during the 18th century, as central authority in the Turkish empire weakened, and was reversed after the Napoleonic Wars. The

French Revolution and the military struggles that followed it made ordinary travel to France and Italy hazardous and Greece, together with other Turkish provinces, began to be considered as serious alternatives, albeit for pioneers rather than dilettantes. As we have seen, Greece was still a difficult country to cross.

In an age of electronic transmission and video cameras we might be tempted to think that the mysteries of the past have been stripped away and converted into archaeological theme parks. This is not so. To have seen the sites is only the first step to understanding why they exist and what they mean. Even the most popular and well known sites remain enigmatic. Few have been extensively excavated, so conclusions about their character and populations are necessarily based on limited evidence. This is not as difficult as trying to reconstruct Parisian life from the *Place de la Concorde* and *Etoile,* plus some patrician apartments from the *Faubourg St. Germain.* The centres of ancient cities were far smaller than modern ones and surviving texts, especially Pausanias' *Guide to Greece,* as well as inscriptions, give a reliable idea of what we might have seen.

The monuments provide information about Greek architecture and technology. In order to find something out about the users we must get involved in the detective work of archaeology, tracking down suspicious conflagrations, turning out waste tips, checking teeth and bones. The most exciting forensic work is only just beginning. Until the middle of the 18th century there were no accurate visual records of Greece. There were descriptions, sometimes quite detailed, of places and habitats; sketches of individual monuments. After the liberation of Greece in 1834, artists and architects flooded in to draw and paint, not only the remains of famous ancient sites but also contemporary ones. Although buildings still dominate our vision of the ancient past, the quantity and quality of everyday objects and the ever growing numbers of written documents give us the ability to reconstruct, in considerable detail, the 2,000 years of Greek society between the rise of the Middle Bronze Age Palace civilizations and the Roman Empire.

In the early decades of excavation the most famous Greek sites and their monuments, as described by ancient writers, received the most attention – the home of the Olympic games, Olympia ABOVE and Korinth LEFT among them. Today classical archaeologists are concerned with all aspects of ancient society and country as well as "city".

INTRODUCTION

Sun, sea and rocks – those features which most attract visitors today – have never provided an easy living. The Greek peninsula is a mountainous limestone outcrop, pitted with fertile patches around river estuaries and narrow coastal plains. The Pindos mountains form the peninsula's spine, climbing to between 7500ft and 8500ft (2280–2584m), and dividing the wetter, western side from the drier eastern one. The Aegean is a geologically active region and serious earthquakes are still common. The plains, where many of the earliest human settlements were situated, are most extensive in the north (coastal Macedonia and Thessaly), in central Greece – the area known in ancient times as Boiotia ("Cowplain") – together with western parts of the Peloponnese and the plain of Sparta.

The evolution of society in the Greek peninsula is connected both with developments within the continent of Europe and with the Near East. At some point early in the history of post-glacial Europe, Greek speakers became a distinct group within the Indo-European family, and by the Late Bronze Age were dispersed throughout the Greek mainland. But the inhospitable nature of the landscape meant that the easiest method of communication was by sea, from mainland to islands and from the islands to the mainland of Asia Minor (modern Turkey).

Early geographical knowledge was entirely coastal, so that even the southern-most shores of Turkey, Cyprus and the Levant were more familiar to mainland Greeks than the Pindos mountains. As a result, Greece was the first region of Europe to benefit from the developments in early farming and stock raising which took place in western Asia during the Neolithic (Old Stone Age) around 5200–3000 BC, and the Greeks may also have learned something about the techniques of casting copper and bronze from the neighbouring peoples of western Asia Minor in the third millennium BC.

THE EARLY BRONZE AGE

During the Early Bronze Age (c.2900–2000 BC) the most significant developments in farming and technology took place not on the mainland, as had been the case in the Neolithic, but in the islands, particularly the Cyclades ("the encircling ones" around Delos). Vines and olives were added to the diet of wheat, barley and legumes, established in the Neolithic period. Before the development of bronze metallurgy, the most important raw material for making tools was a volcanic glass called obsidian, which is plentiful on the island of Melos in the Cyclades. Stone

The temple of Pythian Apollo near the theatre and stadium, Rhodes. Most daily activities in ancient Greece, sacred as well as secular, took place out of doors. Temple buildings provided welcome shade as well as the appropriate symbolism for ritual. Unlike churches and mosques, they were built to be seen first and foremost from the outside. The interior chamber(s) were for a long time treated as little more than strongrooms.

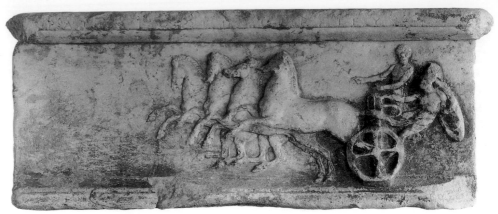

Marble base RIGHT which once carried a prize won in the Panathenaic games (early 4th century BC). The race illustrated on the relief may have very ancient origins. It involved jumping in full armour from a moving chariot and then remounting. Chariot warfare was last practised in Greece in the Late Bronze Age.

The Egyptian god Bes ABOVE standing on the shoulders of a flute player. This humorous bronze figurine is one of many exotic dedications – from as far afield as Caucasus, Georgia and Mesopotamia – to have emerged in the last 20 years from excavations at the sanctuary of Hera on Samos. Some were probably made by Greeks who had travelled widely, others by visiting foreigners.

cutting tools were gradually replaced by bronze ones. At first copper alone was used, but experimentation showed that its functional properties were improved in the presence of certain other metals, especially tin. It now seems likely that the extraction of silver from silver-bearing lead ores may have come first. Lumps of lead can be reduced from their ores even in a simple camp fire, whereas the most obvious sources of copper, the lovely green malachite and azurite ores, require higher temperatures.

Once regular bronze production was established around 2500 BC, contacts with other parts of the Aegean, in terms of the export of products and ideas, seem to have spread rapidly. Substantial architectural structures, ornaments made from precious metals, metallic vessels and elaborately painted pottery are characteristic of the Early Bronze Age not only in the islands, including Crete and Lesbos, but at Troy and in parts of mainland Greece.

THE MIDDLE BRONZE AGE

On such foundations arose the Minoan civilization of the Middle Bronze Age (c.2000–1450 BC), centred on great palatial complexes, which served as central redistribution stores as well as foci for the exercise of power and ritual. The Minoans were successful traders and craftsmen, learning new techniques from Egypt and the Near East, and developing them to extremely high standards. Traces of their presence have been found in the western as well as many parts of the eastern Mediterranean.

Around 1500 BC a cataclysmic volcanic eruption on the island of Thera reverberated throughout the southern Aegean. Within 50 years a second disaster followed, this time destroying virtually every major structure on Crete. However, after a lapse of some decades, these Minoan sites were reoccupied by Greek-speaking mainlanders from the Peloponnese, whose authority was centred at Mycenae.

THE LATE BRONZE AGE

The Mycenaeans transformed and expanded Minoan horizons in the Late Bronze Age (c.1450–1200 BC). They became great seafarers like the Minoans and utilized many common artistic and architectural forms. But the ethos of their culture was self-consciously martial. A combination of circumstances, perhaps including conflicts between different centres of power as well as invaders, led to the demise of this extraordinary era.

THE ARCHAIC AND CLASSICAL PERIODS (8th–4th CENTURY BC)

There is no simple dividing line between the Mycenaean Bronze Age and the period, beginning in the 8th century BC, from which historical documents survive. Many characteristic features of later Greek civilization, including some major divinities, the taste for narrative representation in art, and the fascination with realistic detail, were already present in the Bronze Age. However when, in the 8th century, Homer attempted to recreate in epic mode a heroic age, he had no notion of the complexities of Mycenaean administration. His heroic world does not reflect their social distinctions or the realities of daily life. Neither is there any hint of their high-

level, inter-state contacts with Anatolia, Egypt and the Levant; for in the intervening centuries, the language of royal diplomacy had perished with its few high-ranking practitioners.

During the "Dark Ages" the break-down of former principalities into smaller units was accompanied by significant shifts of population, evidently into safer and more remote regions. The new culture which emerged in the 10th century BC was differently organized and materially quite distinct, not least because tools and weapons were now being made of iron.

The first Greek historians of the 5th century BC reconstructed their history back to the 8th century BC. Although the accuracy of such early dates is disputable, it seems clear that fundamental changes in Greek society did occur at this time. Both history and archaeology indicate that the nuclei of later Greek city-states, or *poleis,*

The main burial ground of Athens between the late 12th to 4th century BC was situated north-west of the city, near the potters' quarter, the *Kerameikos.* The full range of burial customs throughout this period can be seen there. The Street of the Tombs was planned early in the 4th century as a series of family plots.

arose during the 8th century BC. Nucleated settlements, centred on an open meeting space, and community shrines began to appear all over the Aegean, at the same time as the earliest examples of vernacular writing and the crystallization of a remarkable epic tradition. The earliest Greek overseas settlements, around 770 BC in the Bay of Naples, are contemporary with the earliest conventional date for the foundation of the Olympic games (776 BC).

THE POLIS

"City-state" is not a convenient term for the Greek *polis*. *Poleis* were not cities in our sense of the term, at least not until the Hellenistic age after the death of Alexander the Great, and even then they retained an intimate relationship with the surrounding land. When Aristotle said, at the beginning of the *Politics,* that man was

The largest, unfinished Doric temple at Segesta, north-west Sicily, dominates the surrounding plain. Segesta was the capital of the Elymi, the most northerly of the three ethnic groups which occupied Sicily before the arrival of Greek colonists. By the 5th century BC the Segestans had adopted a Greek script and Greek architectural forms, but viewed their neighbours, the Megarians of Selinos, as rivals. However, the prevailing influence in this part of Sicily came from the Carthaginians, who subdued the region from the late 5th century.

a political animal, he did not mean that man or woman were city dwellers. He meant that it was natural for them to form autonomous communities, that civilization was about organization, because it was only in community life – within a legal and judicial framework – that people could aspire to their real virtues and capacities. What we find in the earliest days of the Greek *poleis* fits in rather well with Aristotle's much later analysis. Those items which had previously been buried with individuals (and especially rich aristocrats) – armour and weapons, bronze cauldrons, elaborate dress pins and ornaments – were now more usually dedicated at civic sanctuaries.

The earliest *poleis* were concentrated in central Greece, the eastern Peloponnese and on the opposing coast of Turkey, mainly between the islands of Lesbos, Chios and Samos. These were the sites which dominated Greek history for the next 500 years. Apart from foundation legends, the first detailed historical reports are all concerned with armed conflict – the wars between the Spartans and their western neighbours, the Messenians; the confrontation between the cities of Chalkis and Eretria, which sucked in allies from Samos and Thessaly on the one hand and Miletos on the other. Less dramatic episodes, such as the conflict between Korinth and Megara, or Thebes and Orchomenos in Boiotia, set a pattern of opposition which became endemic. Border disputes were still common even in the Roman period, and outsiders found it difficult to understand just how deeply entrenched these attitudes were. The scarcity of good agricultural land is one obvious motive. However, these conflicts also tended to attract their own mythologies, particularly

Aristotle (384–322 BC), the son of a court physician in Macedon, inherited the intense curiosity in natural phenomena shown by the Ionian philosophers. His greatest contributions to science and philosophy were his classification of knowledge into disciplines, discussions on how to conduct an effective argument; his pragmatic interest in society, its development and institutions; and especially his biological and zoological treatises. He was interested in poetry and drama, geology, meteorology and chemistry. His most ambitious enterprise was the launching of a huge research programme in various subjects, including the constitutions of Greek states, the creation of a zoological museum and histories of previous philosophical ideas.

Attic Red Figure *kalyx krater* of the late 5th century BC, showing two members of the chorus of birds from Aristophanes' play of the same name (produced in 414 BC). The fluteplayer between them would normally have led the chorus into the theatre.

when sanctuaries (often major ones at that) were deliberately set up in peripheral territories to assert the authority of one city.

The *poleis* were governed by established aristocratic clans (often former royal dynasties), which also constituted the most important group of landowners. The gap between these traditional office holders and, most frequently, the majority who were excluded from office, became a source of great tension. This dissatisfaction sometimes erupted in the overthrow of the traditional order by an outsider, often called a "tyrant", who was nonetheless usually an aristocrat. Sometimes this occurred by due legal process (where the means already existed), otherwise by a straightforward coup. The second half of the 7th century was dominated by tyrannical regimes which rarely lasted beyond the second generation. The original causes of these coups – problems of representation, economic rights, and, above all, rights to land, largely remained.

CONFLICTS

During the 6th century BC, the Spartans, who were at that time the only truly professional soldiers in Greece, became the acknowledged leaders of the Greek world. After the Persian Wars (492-479 BC) the Athenians, who had served with distinction by land and sea, emerged as a rival power and soon began to acquire an Aegean empire. Tension over mutual spheres of influence led to open battles in the 450s and eventually to the Great Peloponnesian War (431-405 BC), which the Spartans won with the help of a fleet financed by Persian money and an exceptionally able general, Lysander.

An aristocratic Persian tomb monument near Phokaia (Foça) in western Turkey. From the later 6th century onwards, Persian noblemen were given estates in the river valleys of the Hermos and Maiander and set a new model of affluence and behaviour for wealthy Greeks of the coast.

19

View from the lower crags of Mount Parnassos at Delphi. The main sanctuary enclosure lower down the slopes, with its landscaped terraces and polished stone, stands in marked contrast to the wild, untamed beauty of the mountain.

In the next century, the traditional enmities that existed among the *poleis* of mainland Greece continued. Small states struggled to remain independent against a background of complicated ideological disputes. Cities were riven by democratic and oligarchic factions, the democratic parties tending to seek alliance with Athens, and later Thebes, while oligarchs favoured Sparta. Philip II of Macedon (359–336 BC) took advantage of this factionalism to create a network of loyalties to Macedon, the new champion of freedom from the oppression of the three great contemporary powers, Athens, Sparta and Thebes. If his son, Alexander the Great, had any ambitious plans to bring an end to civic strife, it was by bringing the whole of Greece under his direct control, together with parts of Europe and Asia. His early death in 323 BC nipped any hope of unification in the bud.

THE HELLENISTIC WORLD (323–31 BC)

After Alexander's death, his territorial conquests – including Greece, Egypt, Syria, Persia, Asia Minor and India – broke up into separate kingdoms, each ruled by one of his former Macedonian generals (the Successors). The Greek *poleis* were absorbed into the Successor kingdoms and lost their independence, although they continued to conduct their internal affairs with a considerable degree of autonomy (provided that the regime was favourable to the monarch).

Throughout the Successor kingdoms many new cities were created which attracted large numbers of Greeks. In the new kingdoms of Asia and Egypt, Greeks held privileged positions not shared by the majority of the indigenous inhabitants. Anyone with enough talent and determination could seek his fortune, and many did. Artists, architects, engineers, surveyors, map-makers, philosophers and poets

The Athenian *Agora* in the 2nd century AD, viewed from the east. In the foreground are two late additions – the *Odeion* (concert hall) of Agrippa and the 5th century BC temple of Ares. Behind, the Tholos, Council House, temple of Apollo, Stoa of Zeus and Royal Stoa along the west side, all date from 5th–4th centuries BC.

were in demand at the royal courts of Pella, Alexandria, Antioch, Hieron II's Syracuse and Pergamon. There was also a huge demand for ordinary colonists, particularly in Asia. Civic institutions and amenities increased enormously during this phase. Ambitious public building programmes, sponsored by wealthy citizens as well as the Kings, changed what had previously been open meeting places around the civic sanctuaries into paved piazzas with covered halls (stoas), around which further complexes – gymnasia, shopping malls and purpose-built administrative buildings – were arranged.

The situation on the Greek mainland was less dynamic. Rather than dissolve or simplify the divided loyalties of earlier centuries, Macedonian rule merely

Alexander the Great of Macedon confronting Darius III at the battle of Issos, 333 BC. Detail of a mosaic from the House of the Faun, Pompeii, laid in the second half of the 2nd century BC, and perhaps copied from a famous painting by Philoxenos of Eretria c. 300 BC.

entrenched resentment, and states formed themselves into federations to counteract the influence of the Successor kings, particularly the Antigonid dynasty which now ruled Macedon. Two such federations, the Aitolian league in west-central Greece and the Achaian League in the northern Peloponnese, were equally opposed to Macedonian encroachment. The pragmatic *rapprochement* of the Achaian League with Macedon in the time of Antigonos Doson (229–221 BC) soon led to an active confrontation between the two Leagues (219–217), during which the new Macedonian king, Philip V, invaded Aitolia. This provided the opportunity for a new power – Rome – to intervene in Greece. The Romans concluded an alliance with the Aitolians in 211 BC. Although the mainland Greek states were nominally

Aerial view of Pella, the capital of Macedon from *c.* 400 BC, which lost its importance after the defeat of Macedon by the Romans in 168 BC. Recent excavations at Pella and Vergina, the old capital of Aigai, are providing extensive new data on Macedonian culture and institutions.

"freed" from Macedonian domination, in effect they passed through a series of administrative reorganizations under the patronage of the Roman Senate. Foreign policy was, from the beginning, a matter of deference to Rome. In 146 BC Macedonia and the former territories of the Achaian League in the Peloponnese were formally incorporated into a new Roman province. Other cities remained technically independent until the creation of the Empire in 27 BC.

CLASSICAL GREECE FORGOTTEN

Under Roman rule the *poleis* survived as administrative structures and many continued to flourish, under the generous patronage of emperors and senators. The growing gap between the burgeoning cities of Asia Minor, the Levant and Alexandria in Egypt on the one hand and mainland Greece on the other, already apparent in the Hellenistic period, became ever greater, despite the public works showered on Athens, still a city of learning, and Korinth, the new capital of the Roman province of Achaia. But invasions by the Goths in the 3rd century AD and the Slavs in the 6th century resulted in large-scale destruction which was rectified only with difficulty and in piecemeal fashion.

More significant for the cultural status of the ancient sites were the edicts of successive late Roman Emperors. Theodosius I prohibited the celebration of pagan festivals in AD 393, having already suppressed the oracle at Delphi. Wilful destruction of pagan relics was approved and officially encouraged. Earthquakes and invasions did the rest. The advent of Christianity as the official religion of the Roman Empire under Constantine brought a change in outlook, but there were still many other factors which contributed to the decline of the ancient sites and the activities carried on in them. However, Greek language and learning were preserved, enthusiastically, in the capital, Byzantion, although the remoteness of Byzantion from western centres of learning meant that this knowledge lay dormant until it was actively sought out again in the Renaissance of the 15th century.

Aerial view of the citadel at Mycenae. The community which continued to exist in the vicinity during succeeding centuries lived in the shadow of its Bronze Age predecessors; the "Tomb of Agamemnon" became the site of a cult to the legendary hero. The centre of the community underwent something of a revival in the Hellenistic period, with the appearance of new civic buildings and the repair of old ones.

Syracuse, the north side of the Duomo seen from the east, showing the Doric columns of the 5th century BC temple of Athena around which the Christian cathedral was built. Many Greek temples (and other antiquities, including tombs and slabs of masonry) have been preserved by their use for new purposes.

THE ARCHAEOLOGICAL STORY

From the 2nd century BC, when the Romans began ransacking Greece for works of art, until well into this century, knowledge of Greek culture was restricted to art and literature. The development of archaeological methods from the late 19th century onwards has opened a window into the Greek world.

DIVIDED LOOT

Between 200 BC and AD 200, wealthy Romans acquired Greek works of art

and studied the best Greek writers. This vogue for things Hellenic was to have

a profound impact on European civilization.

Silver jug, allegedly from Lebanon, with trefoil lip. The handle terminates in a Seilenos head in low relief, similar to those found on bronze and silver jugs of the 4th century bc. Probably a copy, made in the Augustan era, of a Hellenistic Greek original. This was acquired with a silver sieve and silver drinking cup that may be genuine "antiques" of the 4th century bc, to which the jug was added to make a set (h 21.5 cm/8½ in).

The Roman poet Horace commented in a letter to a friend, "Greece the captive enthralled her savage captor". He was referring to the way in which Greek art and culture came to dominate Roman fashions after Greece was subjected politically to the Romans in 146 bc. Moreover, the artists and architects who were invited to celebrate Rome and the Romans were with few exceptions Greeks.

The Romans, like their Macedonian predecessors, claimed that they were liberating the Greeks. However, a rapacious zeal for Greek art and luxuries was evident from their earliest interventions. The mainland Greeks did not learn from the example that had been made of the Greek colonists on neighbouring Sicily during the Punic Wars between Rome and Carthage. During the Second Punic War (218-201 bc) Syracuse was captured and looted by the Romans. Vast quantities of booty, including many works of art, were brought back to Rome by the victor, Marcellus, who boasted that he had taught the Romans to admire Greek art. In 209 bc, Fabius, the general who had recently defeated Hannibal in the Second Punic War, had the colossal statue of Herakles by the renowned sculptor Lysippos transferred from

Tarentum to Rome (though he left his Zeus). A famous statue group by the same artist, showing Alexander the Great and those of his friends who were killed at the battle of the Granikos river, was displayed in a specially-built portico. This was to be the pattern later in the 2nd century bc, after the final capture of Greece, when the movement of art works from Greece to Rome became a torrent.

The sheer quantity of art imported in this way transformed Rome into a huge gallery of marbles and bronzes. Lucius Scipio brought back 138 statues, numerous pieces of embossed metalware and coins from Asia in 188 bc. In the following year Marcus Fulvius Nobilior took 285 bronzes and 230 marbles from the city of Ambrakia alone. But there were far richer prizes to be won. Lucius Aemilius Paullus, the victor of the battle of Pydna, Macedonia, in 168 bc, displayed 250 *cartloads* of statues, paintings and metal vases in his triumphal procession, while further orgies of looting followed the sack of Korinth in 146 bc. In addition, the collections of the Pergamene kings were bequeathed by their ruler, Attalos III, to the Roman people in 133 bc because he had no heirs. The continuing appeal of such luxuries is reflected in Cicero's harangues against the extortions of Gaius

Verres while proconsul of Sicily in 73–71 BC, although this was not the first time that such excesses had been attacked.

THE FASHION FOR COPIES

The early trophies had been dedicated in Roman temples, but in the last third of the 2nd century BC new temples began to be built to Greek designs, supervised by Greek architects. Occasionally, imported Greek marble was used, though sparingly. This was paralleled by the new vogue for copies of ancient Greek works of art, which could now be made mechanically. Numerous marble copies of statues were produced, often from bronze originals, as well as various pastiches. A popular form of portrait was to

The "dancing faun" satyr, LEFT, (h 1.43 m/4 ft 5¾ in), a restored marble copy in the Uffizi Gallery, Florence, perhaps made in the early 3rd century AD, of a Hellenistic Greek bronze. The original figure was probably snapping his fingers in the direction of a seated nymph. A more energetic satyr ABOVE at the entrance to the painted room in the Villa dei Misteri, Pompeii.

The ruins of temple G at Selinos, western Sicily, from the west. This was the northernmost of a group of temples built on a spur east of the city. It was perhaps overambitious and was never finished (second in size only to that of Olympian Zeus at Agrigento). Each column drum weighed more than 100 tons.

Pluto abducting Persephone; detail of the chamber painting in Tomb II, the "Great Tumulus", Vergina, Macedonia ABOVE. The framed pictures which appear on the wall schemes of Roman houses utilize many Greek technical and compositional features. Dirce RIGHT being tied to a wild bull as a punishment for her cruelty (House of the Vettii at Pompeii) echoes the pose of Persephone.

combine a draped Greek statue from a standard repertoire with a personalized head. Again, the sculptors were virtually all Greeks.

The stylistic preferences of contemporary Romans are reflected in a spate of rhetorical and prose works. The most useful account of the development of ancient art is to be found not in any Greek work but in chapters 35 and 36 of the compendious *Natural History* by Pliny the Elder (24/3 BC–AD 79). This, together with digressions in Cicero's treatises *On The Orator* and *Brutus* show a clear hierarchy of styles. The acme of Greek art was considered by the Romans to have been the age of Perikles (*c*.460-*c*.430 BC), supremely represented by the artist Pheidias, whose cult figures of Zeus at Olympia and Athena Parthenos on the Athenian Akropolis fascinated generations of Roman tourists. The proliferation of copies of athletic statues by a near-contemporary of Pheidias's, the Argive sculptor Polykleitos, includes two fine bronze copies, one from Pompeii, the other from Herculaneum. Archaic Greek art was considered immature, although there was a taste for garden sculpture and minor statuary in an archaizing style.

Contemporary Hellenistic painting and statuary had a much more profound and lasting influence on the development of Roman art, not least because the practitioners were themselves Greek. There is a clear generic relationship between, for example, the figures from the Great Altar of Pergamon or Pergamene statue groups of defeated and dying Gauls on the one hand, and sculptures commissioned specifically for a Roman audience, such as the Laocoön group now in the Vatican. The contribution of Hellenistic painting to Roman art has for long been suspected, but its extent has only recently been revealed. Few Greek originals were known to exist until the discovery of some marvellous examples on the walls of Macedonian tombs at Vergina and elsewhere.

Aristocratic Macedonians were often buried in monumental chamber tombs with architecture that is reminiscent of domestic or palatial structures. Between the plastered columns, or on the interior walls, large-scale figural paintings have been found, depicting mythological scenes. Among the most interesting is the series of murals from three tombs inside the Great Tumulus at Vergina (the ancient Macedonian capital, Aigai). The style and subject matter of many Roman wall paintings, particularly some of those made to look like pictures on a wall, reflect the continuity of this artistic tradition.

CONSTANTINOPLE

The transfer of the Roman Empire's capital to Constantinople in AD 330

also shifted the storehouse of the Greek cultural tradition back to its original

homeland, preserving Hellenic civilization for the next thousand years.

Detail of a 2nd-century AD papyrus roll of Homer's *Iliad,* known as the "Bankes Homer" after its discoverer, William John Bankes. Greek papyri were virtually unknown to scholarship before the middle of the 18th century.

Greek works of art, literature and philosophy continued to be popular throughout the history of the Roman empire. Greek rhetoric and philosophy were considered fundamental to a good education and Greek was the official language of the eastern provinces. The political importance of these regions was to reassert itself during the 3rd and 4th centuries AD.

When Constantine moved his capital to Byzantion on the Hellespontine Straits and renamed the new, expanded city which arose Constantinople (AD 330), he was confirming a territorial division between the eastern and western parts of the Roman Empire established by the Emperor Diocletian in AD 284. This division was further enhanced by their very different subsequent histories.

The Eastern Byzantine Empire remained largely intact until the Fourth Crusade was diverted there in 1204. Among the notable antiquities still to be seen at that time was a colossal bronze armed statue of Athena by Pheidias. Between the 13th and 16th centuries, the Franks and the Venetians became the effective rulers of Greece, and in theory ancient Greek works of art may have found their way west during that time. However, very little is known about such a trade.

Italian artists such as Niccola Pisano (c.1225-c.1284) and Donatello (c.1386-1466) might have drawn inspiration from imported antiquities, Greco-Italian objects excavated in Italy, and Byzantine objects, which were still strongly imbued with Classical traditions.

GREECE DISTANCED

The revival of interest in the land of Greece, albeit stimulated by the acquisitiveness of the Crusaders, was cut short by the expansion of the Turks, who overran the mainland and Peloponnese within a few years of the capture of Constantinople in 1453. Although the Venetians held on, mainly in Crete, Cyprus and Rhodes, for another century or so, and the Florentines established a commercial base in Constantinople, access to Greek antiquities was to remain limited until the 19th century.

Despite the vagaries of political power, Rome remained the centre of the western world as the seat of the Vicar of Christ, and it was entirely through the ecclesiastical connection that Rome continued to embody the ancient past and preserve its legal, administrative and linguistic traditions. Cathedrals and monasteries became the repositories of ancient treasures, texts and the sources of know-

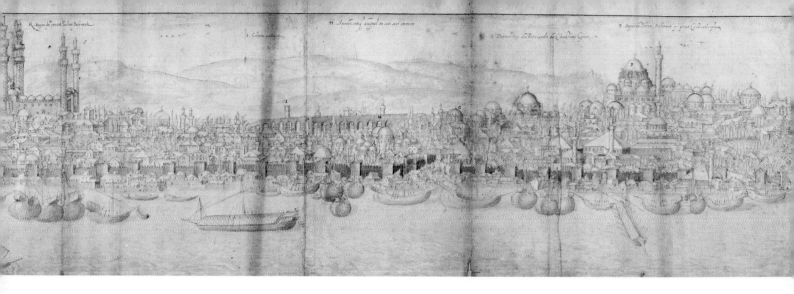

ledge about the past. The most widely read works were Roman: Cicero's treatises *On Friendship, Old Age, Invention, Offices,* and some of his letters; Seneca's *Letters,* Pliny's *Natural History,* the *Memoirs* of Valerius Maximus, the *Attic Nights* of Aulus Gellius: the *Saturnalia* of Macrobius. Of poets there were Virgil and Horace, the *Satires* of Juvenal and Persius, Ovid's *Metamorphoses* and Claudian, the last representative of the Classical tradition in late 4th-century Rome. This random collocation could give no coherent view of ancient Rome. Many fundamental texts, whether historical or literary, languished forgotten in the recesses of monastic libraries.

THE SURVIVAL OF GREEK TEXTS

Greek authors were virtually unknown except for a small number of Platonic dialogues translated into Latin, although Greek texts continued to be copied and annotated by successions of dedicated Byzantine scholars. In 1354 the Byzantine emperor's envoy to the papal court at Avignon presented Petrarch with a copy of the *Iliad,* although the poet could not read a word of it and began learning Greek very late in life.

The pace of transmission of Greek culture was stepped up towards the end of the 14th century, once a new generation of Florentines began to learn Greek from a Byzantine scholar, Manuel Chrysoloras. Early in the 15th century, Lorenzo Valla began the long task of translating Homer, though the text was completed only after his death. The first western scholar to rival the Byzantines in their knowledge of ancient Greek was Politian (1454-94). Meanwhile the initiates were keen to acquire new texts. The Dukes of Florence promoted the search by sending envoys to Greece. The most celebrated of them, Janus Lascaris, brought 200 volumes from Mount Athos to the Medicean Library in 1491. However, this interest in Greek texts did not as yet extend to Greek antiquities.

A 16th-century French panorama of Constantinople ABOVE. The former Byzantine domes are dwarfed by the great Suleymaniye mosque with its four minarets, which was built for Sultan Suleiman the Magnificent in 1550-7, and that of Mehmet II, who captured Constantinople in 1453.

The mosque of Sultan Ahmed, (1609-16) BELOW, also known as the "Blue Mosque" because of its blue tilework. Although architecturally the Suleymaniye mosque was much influenced by the Byzantine Haghia Sophia, the new technique of painted tiles completely altered the inner appearance of 16th-century mosques.

THE ITALIAN COLLECTORS

Ancient Greek art was far less influential than Roman art during the Middle

Ages. But the growth of humanism, particularly in Italy during the 15th

century, sent scholars and artists in search of the "lost" Greek culture.

Although the subject matter of ancient literature was familiar to Medieval scholars, it was not until the 15th century, when there was a renewed interest in the representation of nature, combined with a conscious search for antiquities, that the themes and images of the ancient world began to regain some perspective. The beginnings of a systematic return to lost texts and lost worlds began in Padua, and was taken up in Florence. The sculptor Donatello may well have encouraged the banker Cosimo de' Medici to begin collecting antiquities. By the end of the 15th century, the Medici collection of Lorenzo the Magnificent was the finest in Italy, and included coins, gems, glass and sarcophagi as well as statuary.

EARLY RENAISSANCE SCHOLARSHIP

The term "humanist" in its Renaissance sense was coined by the poet Francesco Petrarca (Petrarch) (1304-74). Cicero had described the Greeks as the "most human people", insofar as they established an education for culture. Petrarch was convinced of

Herakles choosing between Vice and Virtue. Cameo in blue and white jasper ware by Wedgwood and Bentley, 1777 (h 25.4 x 33 cm/ 10 x 13 in). Herakles gained a place among the gods for his feats on behalf of humanity, although his all-too-mortal weaknesses often got him into trouble. The intellectual nuances of the hero's moral struggles were more sharply appreciated in the 18th century than his swashbuckling adventures.

Herakles wrestling with the giant Antaios LEFT. Reverse side of a bronze coin from Alexandria. The group may reflect a full size Hellenistic bronze sculpture. A fine marble copy of this type was acquired by the Medici Duke Cosimo I of Tuscany from the Vatican collections and is now in the Pitti Palace in Florence.

the moral values as well as wisdom to be derived from the study of ancient literary works. His approach to the sources was original and imaginative, and it was he who began the great search for lost works of antiquity in the monastic libraries of Europe. His Florentine followers referred to his endeavours as *studia humanitatis* – the study of humanity, or what it is to be human – and so the Classics remained well into the 19th century.

Early Renaissance scholars were aware of the acknowledged debt to Greek letters paid by the Romans, but knowledge about Greece itself continued to be filtered through Latin sources. "It was all Greek to me", the phrase Shakespeare put into the mouth of Julius Caesar, was true of all but a tiny minority, and so it remained. Until the middle of the 18th century, Greek antiquities were also viewed almost wholly through the medium of Roman taste, whether in writings about art, copies of antique sculpture, or paintings.

COLLECTIONS IN ROME

Jacob Burckhardt's *Civilisation of the Renaissance in Italy* (1860) was the first major work by a modern historian to present the 15th and early 16th centuries as the rebirth of Rome – the spirit of antiquity embodied in a new Italian form. In the middle decades of the 15th century, the historian Flavio Biondo of Forli wrote two major works, *Roma triumphans* and *Roma Instaurata*, commemorating those monuments of antiquity then known to have survived, but referring also to vanished ones. The rebuilding of Rome began under Pope Nicholas V (1447-55) who founded the department of Classical manuscripts in the Vatican and began the construction of what was to be the first great sculpture museum in Rome, the Palazzo dei Conservatori, though it became famous only after Pope Sixtus IV (1471-84) donated a unique (Italian, not Greek) collection of large-scale ancient bronzes to it, specifically intended for public display.

His successor, Pius II Piccolomini (proud of his reputedly ancestral names, Aeneas and Silvius) had an avid personal interest in Roman antiquities, tirelessly exploring the ancient cities, roads and aqueducts, and of course, collecting interesting pieces. In 1503 a new Pope, Julius II della Rovere, commissioned the architect Bramante to modify a small villa at the back of the old Vatican Palace with the aim of installing in it a collection of sculptures. The villa, known as the Belvedere, was connected to the Vatican by two long covered hallways.

A marble statuette ABOVE of Herakles leaning on his club from the island of Delos is a popular version of a famous bronze statue made c320 BC by the artist Lysippos. The best known copy is a colossal marble made for the Baths of Caracalla in the 3rd century AD (now in Naples).

THE BELVEDERE
AT THE VATICAN

The Belvedere in the Vatican was the name originally given to the villa built by Pope Innocent VIII in 1485 on higher ground above the Vatican Palace. Later the name was extended to the courtyard (Cortile del Belvedere) adjoining it after Bramante had redesigned the area for Julius II. The courtyard was planted with orange trees and adorned with fountains, while the sculptures were arranged in niches around the enclosing walls. At the time of its construction, Julius owned only one of the sculptures which was to find a place in the Belvedere court. This was a statue of Apollo which was to become, as a result of its exposure here, one of the best-known ancient pieces in Europe.

The Apollo was soon followed by the chance discovery of the Laocoön group in 1509, immediately recognized as the work singled out by Pliny as the most admired of sculptures in Rome. It was bought by Julius II soon afterwards and installed in a niche of the Belvedere court. Full-size copying of the Laocoön provided leading Italian sculptors of the day with a superb technical challenge, since the reproduction of large-scale statuary was not yet regularly practised. A further development was the reproduction of sets of statues from antique originals, pioneered by the Italian Primaticcio in the 1540s for Francis I of France (who already owned a marble copy of the Laocoön) and intended to decorate the king's new palace at Fontainebleau.

The statues selected for the Belvedere reveal just how prestigious the collection was becoming despite its diverse character. Alongside the Laocoön, which can be considered Greco-Roman, there were four statues which are thought to be good copies of late Classical or Hellenistic originals: the Apollo; a reclining draped woman, then identified as Cleopatra; an important tableau of Herakles grappling with the giant Antaios (later given to Duke Cosimo I of Tuscany), and a male nude with a portrait head of Hadrian's lover, Antinous. There was also an indifferent, and to modern eyes, extremely coy Venus, a full-size statue of the Emperor Commodus as Herakles, and two symmetrical reclining river gods.

The Trojan prince and priest Laocoön LEFT, suffocated with his sons by giant snakes for being suspicious of the wooden horse. Cleopatra sleeping TOP drawing from the school of Raphael of the Vatican marble. Athletic torso CENTRE signed by the Athenian, Apollonios, son of Nestor. Because Michelangelo set so much store by the principles he claimed to have discovered in it, the torso was known as the "school of Michelangelo". Apollo the archer BOTTOM.

Besides the Vatican, there were five other major collections belonging to noble Italian families, all of which had strong connections with the papal court – the Farnese, the Medici, the Borghese, the Ludovisi and the Barberini. These represented the premier league among Italian collectors. Their superior wealth and access enabled them to acquire collections few others could rival, collections which dominated the growing number of prints and drawings of ancient art circulating in Europe.

The first comprehensive compendium of statues in Rome appeared in 1556, but gradually the scope of published drawings was reduced and in 1645 François Perrier's selection of less than one hundred of the most celebrated works appeared. It was this selection, reproduced by other artists, which constituted the canon of artistic taste for the next 200 years. Following Francis I's example, sets of copies from among the most celebrated works were commissioned a century later for Charles I of England, Philip IV of Spain, John III Sobieski of Poland and Louis XIV of France, followed in the 18th century by the major and minor nobility of England, the German principalities, the Russian palaces of St Petersburg and the Academies of Fine Art in New York and Pennsylvania.

THE MEDICI COLLECTION

By this time the Medici collections in Florence had begun to rival, if not supersede, Rome as the focus of antiquarian interest. In the mid-1550s, Francesco, a son of Grand Duke Cosimo I of Tuscany, began to convert the upper floors of the civic offices of Florence in the Uffizi palace into an art gallery. The crowning feature was an octagonal room known as the Tribuna, which was in every sense a jewel-box. Although various features of the decoration and contents changed, this room was made the show-case of the Medici collections. During the 1670s many of the best-known Medici sculptures in Rome were moved to the Tribuna. At the same time, Florence became the centre of the market in copies,

Small versions of famous statues of Aphrodite were very popular in the Hellenistic period; Aphrodite unbinds her sandal in preparation for the bath ABOVE; bronze statuette from Paramythia, north-west Greece. Marble Aphrodite from Delos RIGHT, modelled on a famous bronze made c340 BC by Praxiteles.

Praxiteles' famous bronze Aphrodite on Knidos ABOVE RIGHT (right) was much admired and copied in Hellenistic and Roman times (drawing from the school of Raphael). A coy version of the Knidian, with both hands raised to her body and the mantle dropped, was bought for the Capitoline Museum in Rome by Pope Benedict XIV in 1752 RIGHT (h 1.78 m/5 ft 7 in). Similar statues with the mantle raised were also known ABOVE RIGHT (left).

although the collection of copies acquired by the French Academy in Rome (founded by Louis XIV in 1666) remained unrivalled.

THE GRAND TOUR

The increasing prestige of the Tribuna coincided with the expansion of the Grand Tour, a kind of upper-class finishing school for the young men of Europe, but especially popular with the British. It is somewhat ironic that artists of modest means in more distant parts of Europe had access neither to the copies and occasional ancient works in princely private collections, nor to adequate numbers of casts in the various Academies which followed the examples of Florence and Rome. On the other hand, superannuated would-be landowners were fitted out with every kind of sketch book and equipment to study not just the antiquities of Italy, but the flora, fauna, climate, crops and manners of the inhabitants.

The Tribuna in the Uffizi Gallery, *c*1772, by Johann Zoffany. Not all the sculptures known to have been on display are shown in the painting, and some which were housed elsewhere in the Medici collections are included. Most of the portrait figures admiring works of art are British tourists and diplomats who visited Florence in the 1770s.

WINCKELMANN

Enthusiastic collectors rediscovered many Roman copies of Greek works of art. However, no criteria existed for analysis or dating until an 18th century scholar and pioneer in art history laid down definitive guidelines.

The art historian Winckelmann ABOVE relied on notes by the Scots architect Robert Mylne for his own 1759 account of the Greek temples at Agrigento. The first tourists who recorded Sicilian sites, (including Selinos, Temple E, BELOW) were the philosopher George Berkeley in 1717, and John Breval in 1725.

W hy did these sculptures in the Vatican, the private collections in Rome and the Uffizi in Florence attract so much interest, as well as money? In part the answer lies in the artistic pre-occupations of the day. Sculpture had played a central role in Renaissance art. By the mid-18th century neo-Classicism had become the fashion in Europe and auction houses in London were capitalizing on the latest peccadilloes of the landed classes – the acquisition of antiquities. But it is important to realize that these objects were perceived as pieces of history, the only available large-scale works apart from architecture which were connected with historical individuals.

The emergence and tenacity of a narrow artistic canon was due as much to the possessiveness of the richest collectors as to any intrinsic aesthetic value in the sculptures themselves. The criteria by which they might be judged had not yet been developed, and ownership inevitably affected the status of a particular piece. Restorations were normal, and often considered to enhance the original – and originals they were for a very long time thought to be.

It was not until the 19th century that the Apollo Belvedere was recognized as a copy of a lost Greek bronze original, perhaps by the celebrated 4th-century BC sculptor Leochares, who also made a group of portrait statues of Philip II of Macedon, Alexander and other members of their family at Olympia. It now seems extraordinary that in one half-century the French philosopher and polymath Diderot had called the Herakles Farnese, the Belvedere Venus, Apollo, Antinous and the much admired Torso, the Laocoön and the like "apostles of good taste among the nations" (1763), and Stendhal the novelist complained that so prosperous a nation as the American possessed not a single copy of the Apollo Belvedere (1819); or that Hippolyte Taine, the French critic and historian, found the Apollo a rather well-bred god who had servants at home, while the American painter Benjamin West thought him very like a Mohawk. The artist John Flaxman even considered the Apollo Belvedere superior to the "Theseus" from the Parthenon. Such differences of opinion illustrate how much was yet to be learnt about the gulf between Greek works and Roman copies, concerning both the technical adaptations of copyists and their aesthetic considerations. The problems of identification and attribution were seen as the real challenge for art historians.

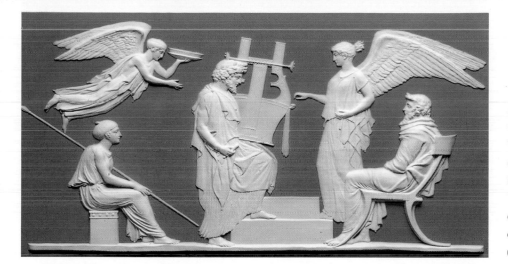

Apotheosis of Homer LEFT: blue and white jasperware relief by Wedgwood and Bentley, 1779. The design was copied from a vase in Hamilton's collection. During the 18th century, Homer began to be appreciated not just as a great ancient poet, but as a writer of universal importance.

The man who showed the way forward was Johann Joachim Winckelmann (1717-68), who in 1763-4 published the first systematic account of ancient art, presenting a chronological survey beginning with Egypt, the Etruscans and going on to divide Greek art into early, middle and late phases. He was the first to argue in detail (though the suggestion had already been made elsewhere) that many Roman sculptures were in fact copies of Greek works, and that Greek art of the pre-Roman period was superior to anything produced in subsequent centuries. Naturally, these views did not go unchallenged, but what made his arguments ultimately persuasive was his meticulous, almost microscopic, attention to detail.

Winckelmann had studied not only Greek and history, which provided him with the textual sources of Greek art, but also mathematics and medicine. As librarian to the mercurial Cardinal Albani and Prefect of Papal Antiquities, he had almost unrivalled access to the finest collections. His eye was as keen as that of a forensic scientist; not for him the empty platitudes of an aesthete, but the size of a nipple or the flare of a nostril. This intense preoccupation with detail helps scholars to recognize the characteristic techniques of individual artists, and was a foundation stone of art history (ancient and modern).

The study of ancient sculpture is sometimes seen as an antiquarian throwback to a pre-scientific age. In fact, plaster casts are still used to piece together statues dispersed in different museums and old casts are sometimes valuable as unique copies of sculpture which has been destroyed or damaged (as in the case of those Parthenon carvings which remained *in situ*). It is easy to forget that the halls of marbles in international museums are jigsaw fragments, separated from their original context and thus divested of their power. We have to read the descriptions of Plutarch to understand why the colossal Olympian Zeus of Pheidias created an extraordinary sense of awe in the observer, or why Praxiteles' Aphrodite of Knidos, the first frankly erotic nude of antiquity, became so famous. From now on it was the context which was to play an increasingly significant role in the study and understanding of Greek sculpture, and antiquarianism began to develop into a mature archaeology. Sculpture was such a significant feature of the Greek landscape that it would be a mistake to see it as a mere appendage; on the contrary, it was the focus of a huge amount of technical, intellectual and emotional endeavour.

Apotheosis of Homer ABOVE: commemorative marble relief by Archelaos of Priene, 2nd century BC (h 1.145 m/3 ft 6¼ in). Homer, is crowned by Ptolemy IV (222-204 BC) and Queen Arsinoe III of Egypt. Others include Zeus, the Muses, Myth and History, Poetry, Tragedy, Comedy, and a child as human nature.

THE BAY OF NAPLES

Despite the enthusiasm for antiquities, there was little effort to reconstruct

the past in its original setting. But in 1738 digging below Mount Vesuvius

began to reveal the well-preserved remains of an entire city.

Sir William Hamilton, from the studio of Sir Joshua Reynolds, 1777. Lying open on his knees is one of the lavishly illustrated volumes of his first collection of vases, whose publication inspired contemporary artists, particularly in the decorative arts, to employ Classical motifs.

Although many great discoveries were made in the 16th century, it was not until the 18th century that they began to reacquire a historical context. Nevertheless, it should be emphasized that most of the 16th-century finds came from sites of known ancient importance. The villa and gardens of the Farnese family were on the Palatine hill, seat of many Roman imperial palaces, while that of the Ludovisi was reputedly situated over the Gardens of Sallust – all well known for their celebrated statues, many of them imports from Greece. The most important site outside Rome was at Tivoli, where Hadrian had once had a sumptuous villa built and filled with copies of many famous Greek works. However, the clandestine investigations made there from the 1550s were of little significance until large parts of the extensive site were sold off early in the 18th century. Spectacular discoveries began soon afterwards, fuelling the interest of European (and particularly English) tourists.

Among the more serious European collectors was Charles Townley (1737-1805), whose impressive collection of statues, portrait busts and marbles was eventually bought by the British Museum after his death. Another was Sir William Hamilton, who was sent to Naples as British envoy in 1764. His interest in painted pottery vases (at first called "Etruscan" because so many were discovered in Etruscan tombs, but later identified as Greek) amounted to an obsession. His second wife, Emma, was said to have caught his attention because she exhibited the same grace as figures on his vases. She made a virtue of necessity and presented Grecian "attitudes" as party-pieces. Hamilton sold part of his collection of vases, bronzes and other antiquities, to the British Museum in 1772. A later consignment, which was as interesting, if not as valuable as the first, was wrecked off the Scilly Isles, although parts of it were retrieved by divers in 1975-7.

POMPEII AND HERCULANEUM

By the middle of the 18th century Naples, capital of the Bourbon kingdom of the two Sicilies and the largest city in Italy, was attracting as much attention as Venice, Florence and Rome. Not least of the attractions were the new excavations at Herculaneum and Pompeii, begun in 1738 and 1748 respectively. The architect Robert Adam, who visited the sites in 1755, recalled the tunnels dug through the warren of streets and ransacked for valuable objects, wall paintings and mosaics. At Herculaneum the 25m (80ft) thick mantle of rock was pierced by shafts and tunnels, so that by 1765 a rough plan of the city was available.

For the first time two genuine ancient cities had been unearthed, complete with their petrified inhabitants, equipment and homes. Their impact on later scholars was profound. In 1860 Giuseppe Fiorelli became director of excavations at Pompeii. He instituted a highly ambitious programme of research aimed at discovering everything, however seemingly insignificant, there was to be known about the city. Fiovelli pioneered the method of pouring plaster into hollows formed when organic material disintegrated. He invited international scholars to a new Scuola di Pompeii, founded to co-ordinate expertise. These two sites demonstrated dramatically the wealth of information which could yet be retrieved about the ancient world, and gave clearer hints about the relationship between Greek and Roman culture.

Red Figure volute *krater* RIGHT made in Apulia (south-eastern Italy) *c*380-70 BC, showing offerings being brought to a hero's shrine. Many of the vases Hamilton acquired were of this type.

Emma, the second Lady Hamilton, as the spirit of Comedy BELOW. In the exuberant and uninhibited atmosphere of Naples, Emma could mirror Classical poses without offending the sensibilities of polite society.

The temple of Concord, Agrigento, *c*430 BC, BELOW. This is the best-preserved of all Greek temples, except the Athenian Hephaistion, and was restored in the 18th century.

The temple of "Neptune" (probably Hera) ABOVE is the smallest and latest (*c*450 BC) of the three best-preserved at Paestum. Not only is the full exterior height virtually complete, but the two tiers of interior columns inside the sanctuary are unique.

FINDING AND RECORDING

During the 17th and 18th centuries, more travellers visited Greece, making

notes and drawings of sites described by Classical writers. These preliminary

efforts were the first steps towards scholarly methods of archaeology.

The marriage of Zeus and Hera on a metope slab from Temple E at Selinos, *c*470-60 BC. A 15th-century Dominican priest had described the marvels of Greek architecture in Sicily. By the middle of the 18th century scholarly tourists had multiplied. One of the best-documented tours was that made in 1777 by an amateur artist, Richard Gore, the German painter Jakob Philipp Hackert, and the dilettante Richard Payne Knight.

Removing antiquities from their findspots without regard for the details of their whereabouts and associations destroys much of their original significance. This factor does not deter treasure hunters today any more than it did their predecessors over the centuries. What the treasure hunters forget is that all such objects had a purpose and without information about their context their real significance is lost. Only by excavating a designated area in a methodical way can any vestige of this original function be reconstructed. This is why accurate records are fundamental to archaeology and why serious scholars have to visit the site and muddy their boots.

Johann Winckelmann had long toyed with the idea of going to Greece. He made an expedition to Paestum, south of Naples, and was greatly impressed by the Greek temples, still among the best preserved in the Greek world. He also supervised the visit of a protégé, the young German aristocrat Johann Hermann Riedesel, to Sicily and southern Italy in 1767. But fate intervened and Winckelmann was murdered in Trieste in the following year. He had ample opportunities to go to Greece and was encouraged by friends, but he clearly felt that to confront the contemporary reality would be a betrayal of all that the Hellenic ideal stood for. Besides, he had everything he needed in order to study Greek art (or so he thought) in Rome. He was by no means unique; it can hardly have been accidental that so few Germans visited Greece before 1800. One exception was Georg Transfeldt, who correctly identified the colossal ruins of the temple of Olympian Zeus in Athens (misnamed by others as the "Palace of Hadrian") and a 4th century BC victory monument named after its dedicant, Lysikrates.

DIPLOMATIC OPENING

Both politics and ideology influenced people's decision to go to Greece. Relations between Christian Europe and the Ottoman Turks were at best formal and, as the Turkish empire expanded during the 17th century, increasingly strained. The English and the French had stronger overseas interests at the time than the Germans, and tended to travel more widely. French diplomacy favoured good relations with the Sublime Porte and Russia against the German states. Poland and Austria were the countries most acutely affected by Turkish encroachment. The British, on the other hand, were more interested in Mediterranean commerce than the power

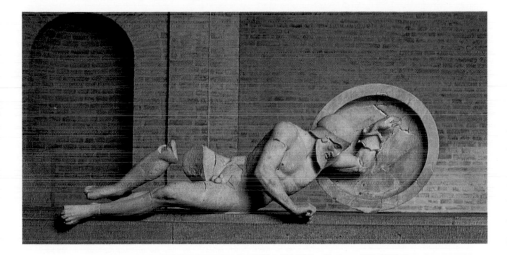

Dying warrior LEFT from the corner of the east pediment of the Aphaia temple, Aigina, *c*480 BC (h 0.64 m/ 25⅕ in). Both the west and east fronts showed Greeks fighting Trojans with Athena in the centre, though the east end is later both in style and composition.

politics of the French, but both nations sent out Consuls regularly to Constantinople. The French also had diplomatic representatives in Athens, and the British had a Consul in Smyrna (modern Izmur), the principal port of the Anatolian seaboard and the seat of the Turkey Company. These diplomats were often keen antiquarians themselves (e.g., the Comte de Caylus, Marquis de Nointel, Comte de Choiseul-Gouffier) and could provide the necessary papers or secure Turkish *firmans* (permits) for visitors.

Even if Winckelmann had gone to Greece, it is difficult to imagine what his response would have been, notwithstanding his enthusiasm for Paestum. Even Paestum took some getting used to for the unpractised eye of

James Stuart sketching the Erechtheion on the Akropolis at Athens, 1751 BELOW. This light-hearted parody of the contemporary romantic approach to Greek landscape is nevertheless a historical record of the Turkish minders sent to keep an eye on him.

Goethe in 1787, when at first sight the magnificent colonnades looked squat, cramped and oppressive. This was despite the fact that many French and English travellers of the 17th and early 18th century had already done a great deal to make the antiquities of Greece known in Europe.

RICHARD CHANDLER'S EXPEDITION

In 1764, an expedition under the auspices of the Society of Dilettanti (founded in 1732 to promote the fine arts) and led by a young Oxford graduate of 26, Richard Chandler (1738-1810), accompanied by the architect Nicholas Revett and a promising artist, William Pars, were delegated to discover and identify Classical sites, to take careful note of their geographical location, make detailed plans and take accurate measurements of any structures identified, draw any sculptures and observe any curiositie. in a daily journal. The expedition took almost two years, beginning at Smyrna and progressing through Greek Asia Minor, including the Troad and Hellespontine Straits, Miletos, Klazomenai, Teos, Priene, Laodikeia, Sardis, Philadelphia and Magnesia. They then sailed to Aigina, past Sounion to Athens. At Athens they supplemented the work that had already been carried out by Revett and James Stuart between 1751 and 1755, made some excursions into Attika itself, then crossed to the Peloponnese via Epidauros, Nauplion and Tiryns, to Korinth. They then recrossed the Korinthian Gulf to Delphi and back to Patras, continuing along the coast into Elis as far as Olympia.

The itinerary was a familiar one, and many of these sites had already been explored by others. What made this expedition unique was its scientific nature and the professionalism with which it was carried out. Chandler used the information of his predecessors to verify what he saw, and in his notes he often quoted extensively from earlier works, as well as from the principal ancient sources, Pausanias' *Guide to Greece* and Strabo's *Geography*. Among his predecessors were Jacob Spon (1649-85), and George Wheler (1650-1723), who had met in Rome and were later joined by Francis Vernon (?1637-77). These three travellers were the last to see and record the Akropolis monuments in Athens (1676) before the disastrous explosion of 1687. The temple was being used at the time by the Ottomans as an ammunition store, and blew up destroying much of the north and south flanks as well as the pediments of the Parthenon. The Parthenon sculptures had been drawn in 1674 during the investigations carried out on behalf of the Marquis de Nointel, Louis XIV's ambassador at Constantinople. Some 55 drawings were made, of which 35 survive, and are usually attributed to Jacques Carrey, although Cornelio Magni, who published the results of Nointel's expedition, claimed that the artist was Flemish. Accurate if uninspired, they are nevertheless all that we are ever likely to know of the complete sculptures, particularly the two pediments – the most prominent parts of a Greek temple where the principal sculptures were usually located.

Of later travellers who made major contributions to Chandler's enterprise, two in particular deserve mention – Joseph Pitton de Tournefort (1656-1708), a Professor of Botany sent by the French Government to

Edward Lear, Choropiskeros, Corfu. Lear (1812-1888), funded by the Earl of Derby, visited Albania and Greece in the late 1840s and 1850s. The result was a series of landscape paintings and two illustrated travel books, *Journals of a Landscape Painter in Albania* (1851) and *Views in the Seven Ionian Islands* (1863). They are remarkable for their detailed descriptions.

THOMAS BRUCE,
EARL OF ELGIN

1766-1841

Thomas Bruce, 7th Earl of Elgin (1766-1841), was His Majesty King George III's Ambassador to Constantinople between 1799 and 1803. The architect Thomas Harrison requested Elgin to use his influence there to obtain casts of famous sculptures. Elgin did far better than that, he obtained the Grand Vizier's permission to remove anything and everything he might wish from the Parthenon, as well as making casts, measurements and drawings of the entire building. Large parts of the cornice were destroyed in the process. Elgin's officials fell to plundering the *Propylaia* (the colonnaded gateway) as well as the exquisite miniature temple of Athena Nike (Athena of Victory). They also removed pieces from the Erechtheion though only one of the female figures, known as Karyatids and acting as a support in place of columns, was taken. (It is now in the British Museum.) Later, one of the transport ships, the *Mentor*, was wrecked off Cape Malea and it took three years to recover its precious cargo. After a trail of vicissitudes, the marbles were eventually sold to the British Museum for £35,000 in 1816.

The sale of the marbles caused much controversy at the time, not least because of the cavalier manner in which they were taken down. Even today Greek governments have sought the return of the marbles. Moreover, there were "experts", such as the artist John Flaxman, who had a very poor opinion of the Parthenon sculptures. This reflects the comparatively low appreciation, at the beginning of the 19th century, of genuine Classical Greek originals as opposed to Roman copies, notwithstanding Winckelmann's observations about the way famous sculptures had been reproduced.

Three figures (K, L, M) from the east pediment of the Parthenon. TOP LEFT. Detail ABOVE RIGHT from the frieze decorating the wall of the sanctuary, showing the Panathenaic procession. Thomas Bruce, Earl of Elgin LEFT. Horseman from the frieze, carved *c*440, BELOW.

47

Thomas Howard, 14th Earl of Arundel and Surrey, the "Collector", and his wife, the Countess Alatheia, by Sir Anthony Van Dyck RIGHT.

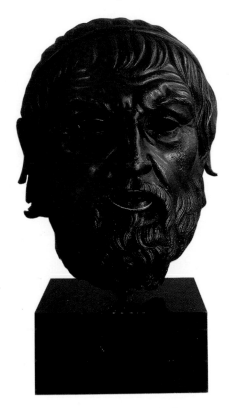

The Arundel *Homer*, one of the very few surviving Hellenistic bronze portrait heads, acquired by the 14th Earl of Arundel around the 1630s and by the British Museum in 1760. Modern scholars prefer to identify the portrait as that of the 5th-century BC tragic poet, Sophokles.

describe the natural resources and monuments of Greece in 1700-02, and Robert Wood (*c.*1717-71), antiquary and later Under-secretary of State to William Pitt. Tournefort's account, *Relation d'un voyage du Levant* (1717), was more widely read than any other 18th-century travel work and contained a great deal of useful background material as well as observations on the ruins. Wood made two major visits to Greece, one in 1742-3, the other beginning in 1749, and his *Essay on the Original Genius of Homer*, first published in 1767, made a huge impact, particularly in Germany. This was not simply a description but a critical polemic, arguing that an understanding of the ancient world was greatly enhanced by knowledge of the places referred to by Classical writers. He was especially interested in Homer's language, but made interesting observations on Homeric customs, comparing, for instance, the patriarchal traditions of the Bedouin (his earlier visits had taken him to Syria and Egypt) with those of Homer's heroic dynasties. Wood met Stuart and Revett in Athens and was largely responsible for formulating the principles of Chandler's expedition.

Stuart and Revett's architectural studies, employing the same principles of exactitude, were published by the Society of Dilettanti as the *Antiquities of Athens* in three folio editions in 1762, 1788 and 1790. Revett's sections and elevations are still an important source of information, particularly on those monuments which have disappeared (such as the temple on the Ilissos river) and for features which have been eroded or lost. Chandler's journey was published separately in the *Ionian Antiquities*, which were enlarged to five volumes between 1769 and 1915, and included the work of later travellers, such as William Gell.

The new preponderance of the scientific over the sentimental was, nevertheless, a long time taking root – the desire to possess was still stronger than the desire to know. Casts of sculptures were popular because they were next best to the "original". However, although genuine antiquities from Greece did not, curiously, have the same buying power as the Roman versions until the impact of the Parthenon and other architectural sculptures had been felt, there were some avid collectors of original Greek antiquities in Europe.

THOMAS HOWARD, EARL OF ARUNDEL

Among the earliest known big collectors was Thomas Howard, Earl of Arundel (1585-1645), who amassed some 37 statues, 128 busts and 250 inscriptions and sarcophagi during the 1620s and 30s, through the good offices of Sir Thomas Roe, James I's ambassador to Constantinople, but chiefly through his own chaplain, William Petty. The collection was dispersed after Arundel's death, but some pieces (including the celebrated date chart known as the *Marmor Parium*) were acquired by the University of Oxford through the intervention of the diarist John Evelyn, and in due course were edited by Chandler.

Through activities such as these some sites, like Smyrna and the island of Delos, became virtually denuded of sculpture. Foremost in the race were the French ambassadors, the Marquis de Nointel and the Comte de

Excavation of an antique building, discovered in a cellar of the Villa Negroni, Rome. "An Antique Building", by Thomas Jones (dated 1779).

Choiseul-Gouffier, the latter instructing his agents to take away anything they could lay their hands on, sparing "neither the dead nor the living".

THE BASSAE RELIEFS

The story of the Bassae reliefs is not unlike those from the Akropolis. The temple of Apollo Epikourios (the Helper) at Bassae, Arkadia, in the centre of the Peloponnese (designed by Iktinos, the architect of the Parthenon)

had been discovered in 1765 by a French architect, Joachim Bocher, who reported it to Chandler. The site was visited by a number of travellers involved in topographical work in the early years of the 19th century, including Edward Dodwell and (Sir) William Gell. In 1811, a party of antiquarians headed by Charles Cockerell, who was later to become one of the great classical architects of the century, and including two Danes, Bröndsted and Koes, Baron Otto Magnus von Stackelberg, the Swabian painter Jacob Linckh and the Nürnberg architect, Haller von Hallerstein, had started a joint project which began at the so-called temple of Zeus (in fact, Athena Aphaia) on the island of Aegina.

The magnificent late archaic pedimental sculptures disinterred there were bought by King Ludwig I of Bavaria and have since been on display in Munich. The party then moved on to Bassae, where the temple was first measured and drawn, then the relief sculptures and the cult statue removed with the permission of the governor of the Morea (Peloponnese), Vili Pasha. Both the cult statue and the Korinthian column from the interior (the prototype designed by Iktinos) were lost or abandoned during the proceedings. In 1815 the sculptured frieze from the interior was bought by the British Museum. The next year they were joined by the Elgin Marbles (see box, p. 47).

MORAL DILEMMA

Aesthetic considerations were uppermost in the minds of the parliamentarians who voted to buy the sculptures for the nation. Yet, in the case of the marbles, the sale aroused a

The temple of Hephaistos LEFT (begun in 449 BC) by the architect, George Ledwell Taylor, c1818-19. The temple was converted into the church of St George, probably in the 7th century AD. It was last used in 1834 when King Otho entered Athens.

continuing controversy. There are strong arguments both in favour of returning them to Greece (the original sale was made by an occupying power; the exceptional status of the Parthenon in the history of Greek art and architecture) and against it (the British Museum is not the only major European collection which possesses fragments from the Parthenon; there would be serious repercussions for a host of international collections which have antiquities acquired prior to Greek Independence; there is no convenient location for the marbles on the Akropolis, while many millions of people can view them with ease in the Duveen Gallery).

GREECE ROMANTICIZED

These first excavations of Greek sites reflect the ambiguity of such enterprises when no legal safeguards existed for the protection of historic buildings. The members of the expedition were serious scholars, who left detailed and well-illustrated accounts of their activities. A study tour of Greece was already becoming *de rigueur* for any aspiring Classical architect and the greatest number of drawings and paintings of Greek sites and Greek landscapes by Europeans date from the first half of the 19th century. What is immediately clear

from such landscapes is their emotional quality; a ruined edifice rising weed-bound from a grassy bank: the colours are suffused, the light muted, quite unlike the deep colours of a genuine Greek view, and the Greeks, when they appear, are poised romantically between an inscription here or a pillar there. They continue the sentimental, patronizing tone of the early travel writers, who felt that the modern Greeks were unworthy of their glorious past. Tournefort was the archetypal French intellectual as his eye rested on the inhabitants, Greek or Turkish: "virtually their whole lives are spent in idleness; to eat rice, drink water, smoke tobacco, sip coffee – there's the life of a Muslim". The frontispiece to Choiseul-Gouffier's *Voyage pittoresque* shows Greece as a woman in chains, surrounded by the tombstones of long-dead champions of freedom such as Miltiades, Themistokles, Epaminondas, Demosthenes, Phokion and Philopoimen – a roll-call of the heroes from the best years of Greek history. Meanwhile, distant German poets like Herder and Hölderlin read up Tournefort and Choiseul-Gouffier (in a tendentious translation) and gave a more stylish expression to the view that the great past of Greece had gone forever, while the spirit was reborn on German soil.

Charles Robert Cockerell, "Excavations at the temple of Aphaia in Aigina", 1811 ABOVE. Greek antiquarianism in the early 19th century was first and foremost the study of architectural remains. More architects visited Greece than Classical scholars. Among the first were the leaders of the "Greek Revival" in architecture, William Wilkins (1801) and Robert Smirke (1803).

ARCHAEOLOGICAL METHODS

A structured approach is crucial to recovering information about past civilizations. Archaeologists today have to follow rigorous methods in discovering and uncovering sites and analyzing what they find there.

A lighthearted view of excavation (or how not to conduct a dig!) as seen by Audrey Petty (Corbett); holding the large pot in the foreground is a distinguished woman member of the British School at Athens, Ann Jeffery.

Archaeology as a scientific discipline involves three principal activities: fieldwork, excavation and post-excavation analysis.

FIELDWORK

Fieldwork is a preparatory technique that includes getting to know the geography and geology of a given area and the ancient remains in it from what can be detected at ground level, before excavation begins. It requires the ability to read maps, to identify any correlations between the incidence of plant species and man-made features, to recognize field monuments (ancient banks, ditches, settlement mounds) and to record them using surveyors' equipment. Laser- and computer-assisted mapping techniques are now becoming available but are not yet in general use.

Other preparatory techniques include *aerial photography* and *geophysical prospecting*. In Greece aerial photography was pioneered by John Bradford, a former RAF pilot, after 1945. Bradford's photographs revealed not just the layout of ancient cities such as Rhodes beneath the modern street plan, but also a great deal of information about land use on the peripheries of the cities. Geophysical survey involves sweeping a designated area with a proton magnetometer or similar equipment which registers how underground material resists an electric current. Any underlying shallow features will show much greater resistance.

FIELD SURVEY

Field survey is a method of intensive field-walking specially adapted to the recovery of less obvious data. Its purpose is to examine a designated land area as a whole, rather than to pinpoint sites where one might expect to find relevant data. A small team systematically combs the mapped area with boards in hand, ready to note down any surface finds – potsherds, building stone, terracing or any other evidence of older land use. The kind of data obtained is, of coure, multi-period, and provides the most detailed overall picture of how intensively units of land were utilized over many centuries. In Greece this kind of study is particularly useful for recording evidence outside the urban centres, where most archaeological investigations have been concentrated.

EXCAVATION

Excavation of a site consists of far more than just digging a hole in the ground. The site is first assessed in a general way (is it a recognized type? anomalous? unique?), and this assess-

Archaeologist using a resistivity meter (proton magnetometer) during the initial survey of a site. An electric current passes through the soil due to trapped salts and moisture; impermeable objects will resist the current. The great advantage of this method is that currents tend to pass from one electrode to the other in deep arcs.

ment determines how the excavation is carried out, time and funds permitting. Small exploratory trenches may be dug to assess the overall character and intensity of occupation. (Different criteria apply in the case of cemeteries). The position of the full-scale excavation, and its purpose, is then decided on, and a site grid is drawn up on an appropriate map scale. The existence of building structures plays a large part in determining how the digging in small areas should proceed, although it is vital to keep the relationship between the interior and exterior history of a building clear. Each designated area within the site grid (e.g., pit, house interior), the appearance of the soil and any features, have to be described in as complete detail as possible and the exact loca-

tion of the excavators' finds recorded.

Once digging has started, one of the main problems is to control the vertical and horizontal planes of the excavation simultaneously. Only by comparing the vertical profile (stratigraphic section) with the horizontal layout can the site be reconstructed.

POST-EXCAVATION ANALYSIS

Post-excavation analysis includes conservation, cleaning, numbering and drawing the finds, and applying the information gained thereby to an interpretation of the whole site. Specialized scientific methods can help to date both organic and inorganic material, but the greatest challenge lies in understanding how the various excavated details fit into a coherent development of the site.

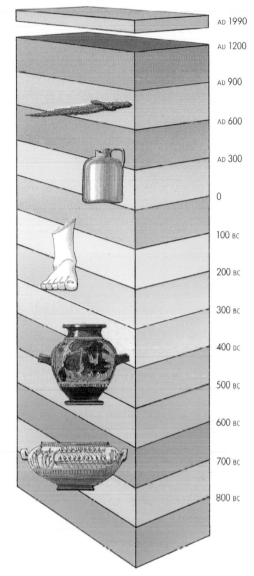

An archaeological level represents a specific phase in a community's life. The structures and rubbish of that phase are sealed by any new phase with its own, slightly different features.

The excavation of a many-layered site such as a *tell* LEFT requires very careful recording of each new level. This is identifiable by differences in the character of the soil. Each level is numbered and the objects found in it given matching numbers.

MYTH INTO HISTORY

The ancient Greece investigated by scholars was a legendary one. However,

Greeks searching for a national identity during their struggle against the

Turks were acutely aware of the symbolic power of their past.

Samothrace: the "Hieron" (sanctuary), a Doric temple ABOVE, and a view over the precinct from the south BELOW. The Great Gods, also known as the *Kabeiroi,* were of non-Greek origin, and "mysteries" were celebrated at the island sanctuary. Most of the excavated structures date from the late 4th and 3rd centuries BC, when its patrons were the Macedonian kings.

With the Greek War of Independence, which broke out in 1821, began a new phase. The ancient past was, from the beginning, closely associated with modern independence. Independence was seen first and foremost as revival, a necessary renewal of identity; but the Greeks were well aware of the fact that it was the romanticized past which had won it the support of the European powers. The new state created in 1828 was a truncated Greece – Thessaly, Epiros and Macedonia were not yet part of it and German influence was strong under the new King Otho, son of Ludwig I of Bavaria.

Ludwig Ross was appointed Ephor-General (Director) of a new Department of Antiquities in Athens and given the task of executing surveys of all archaeological sites. His work was assisted by the admirable topographical studies of Colonel William Martin Leake (1777-1860), who had visited Greece between 1800 and 1810, mapping region by region using professional surveying methods. Leake's map of Athens correctly identified the major civic areas, including the Agora (the political centre of ancient Athens), the chief highway northwards out of Athens, the Diplyon Gate, and the adjacent potters'

quarter and burial ground, the Kerameikos. Moreover, the French expedition which had occupied the Peloponnese from 1829 to 1832 conducted a scientific survey of the peninsula modelled on Napoleon's Egyptian one. In 1834 a law was passed banning the illicit export of antiquities; two years later a Greek, Kyriakos Pittakes, became the first Greek Ephor-General of Antiquities in Athens and in 1837 the Greek Archaeological Society was formed.

The immediate task of archaeologists in Athens was to divest the Akropolis, for centuries a Turkish enclave, of its Turkish fortifications and other accretions. It began with the uncovering of the Parthenon's foundations and the clearing of the bastions built into the *Propylaia*. In the process, an older temple underlying the Parthenon and an older gateway were discovered, as well as important inscriptions relating to Athens' greatest years of power. Equally significant fragments of pottery were found among the sculptural debris left by the Persian sack of the Akropolis in 480 BC. Lack of money has always been one of the biggest challenges to major archaeological work and subscriptions, both public and private, played a very major role throughout the 19th century. The Frenchman,

East pediment RIGHT of the Siphnian Treasury (strong-house for votive offerings) at Delphi, c525 BC, showing Zeus separating Herakles, right, and the twins, Apollo and Artemis, left, as they wrestle over the sacred tripod on which the priestess sat to prophesy.

Ernest Beulé made it possible to have the late Roman gateway made from reused Classical masonry (later named after him) reconstructed in front of the Akropolis. The Turkish fortifications were not finally cleared until 1877, an operation financed by Heinrich Schliemann. Excavation of the Akropolis as a whole began in the 1880s under the Greek archaeologists Stamatakis and later Kavvadias.

THE FRENCH SCHOOL

Systematic excavations in the rest of Greece did not really get under way until the 1860s and 1870s. In 1860-62 Paul Foucart and Karl Wascher, members of the French Archaeological School (founded in 1846) sank preliminary trenches at Delphi, though full excavations could not proceed until the whole village of Kastri, overlying the ancient site, had been expropriated. When there was talk of an American donation to cover the compensation costs, the French government offered the Greeks half a million francs in exchange for exclusive French rights to excavate and publish on the site. The terms were accepted and Delphi has formed the principal focus of the French School ever since. In 1856-7, Léon Heuzey, another member of the French School, had travelled about the far

western corners of the mainland, Akarnania, conducting a thorough investigation both of the antiquities and of the contemporary inhabitants. In 1861, he was joined by Honoré Daumet and together they toured Macedonia, discovering the first vaulted Macedonian tombs as well as many inscriptions.

AUSTRIANS AT SAMOTHRACE (1873)

In 1863 the French Vice-Consul Champoiseau discovered on the island of Samothrace in the north Aegean the marble statue of Victory alighting (whence it was conveyed to the Louvre). Alexander the Great's father Philip II of Macedon had reputedly fallen in love with Olympias (Alexander's mother) at the renowned sanctuary of the Great Gods on the island, the centre of a mystery cult. Full excavations were undertaken there by an Austrian mission led by Professor Alexander Conze of Vienna, beginning in 1873, which revealed a Doric temple, a unique rotunda dedicated by Queen Arsinoe II of Egypt, as well as the actual precinct in which the Victory had originally been housed. The site publication, in which each structure was assigned to a different author, was a pioneering work, accompanied not only by plans and detailed drawings but also photographs.

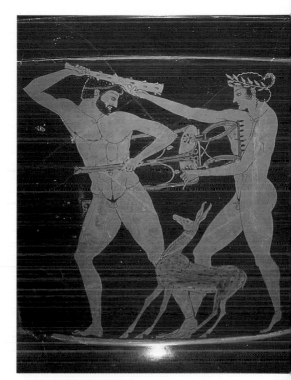

Herakles and Apollo fighting over the Delphic tripod on an Athenian Red Figure wine mixing bowl c490 BC found at Vulci, Etruria. This minor legend may have been a popular theme on Athenian vases because of its non-serious nature, whereas a political meaning (connected with the First Sacred War) has been suggested for its appearance on the Delphic Treasury.

THE GERMANS AT OLYMPIA

Classical scholarship became an aspect of power politics and national prestige

during the last half of the 19th century, and Germany in particular kept up

an unstinting effort to achieve first place among its rivals.

Unlike many of his colleagues, who were Classicists or art historians by profession, Wilhelm Dörpfeld had trained as an architect. His outlook and approach were pragmatic and scientific. He was not concerned with the rediscovery of famous works of art but with the development of a new discipline – excavation.

In 1874, a German Archaeological Institute was opened in Athens modelled on the recently re-constituted Roman one. The new Chancellor, Count Otto von Bismarck, had been influential in creating the Roman Institute as an independent government-funded research institution in the belief that German Classical scholarship would enhance the position of Germany as the leading cultural nation in Europe. In the following year began the first series of annual excavations at Olympia, the site of the ancient Olympic games, and, next to Delphi, the most prestigious ancient sanctuary (1875-81). Winckelmann had considered such a project, as had Ross, but it was Ernst Curtius (1814-96), a distinguished Classical philologist and historian, who finally succeeded, after 23 years, in persuading both the German government and the Crown to fund the project.

This was the first great planned excavation of a complete site. For eight months in the year a team of 300 workmen under the overall supervision of Curtius and the architect Friedrich Adler began digging out the built monuments, starting with the temple of Zeus (identified by loose architectural sculptures) and fanning outwards, using the detailed topographical account given by the second century AD writer, Pausanias. Although a diary was kept and all structures were drawn at the time of excavation, the working procedure was not based on the identification and removal of each layer of soil and all its contents. The "stratigraphic" method, which is still the most fundamental archaeological technique, was in its infancy in the 1880s and 1890s. At Olympia there was almost too much information, with buildings and styles dating from the Archaic period well into the Byzantine Empire, the later ones overlying earlier structures. This is where the documentary evidence which could be related to specific structures proved so useful at the time.

In the first two seasons the temple of Zeus was excavated, followed by the older temple of Hera, the Metroon (sanctuary of the Mother of the Gods) various statue bases in front of the temple of Zeus, a Byzantine church on the south-west, parts of the "Gymnasium" (palaistra), a battery of treasuries dedicated by various cities of the Greek world, the rotunda known as the Philippeion (sanctuary dedicated by Philip II) and entrance to the stadium. A marble statue of Hermes carrying the infant Dionysos, identified as the work of the celebrated

Olympia LEFT; view of the main road entering the site, looking north. On the left, the Doric colonnade of the exercise yard, with remains of the surrounding rooms in the foreground. In the distance are the hills of Elis.

The Aphaia temple, Aigina LEFT; reconstruction after Fürtwangler and Fiechter, 1906. Column drums from the temple of Zeus, Olympia ABOVE, and the top step (stylobate) on which the columns originally stood.

4th-century BC sculptor Praxiteles admired by the Roman writer Pausanias in his *Guide to Greece*, was found in 1877. By the time the excavations were closed in 1881 the area uncovered had been extended to include the "hotel" (Leonidaion) and a number of important administrative buildings (the Bouleuterion and Prytaneion, and the South Stoa). In addition some 130 sculptures, 400 inscriptions, 1000 terracottas and 13,000 bronze objects had been unearthed.

Olympia was a huge undertaking. A five-volume publication of the principal remains duly appeared, with major contributions by two exceptional former apprentices, Adolf Furtwängler (1853-1907) and Wilhelm Dörpfeld (1853-1941). It is not really surprising, however shocking to modern ears, that pottery was given short shrift and packed away uncatalogued, although this would not have happened on a professionally excavated site after 1900.

EXCAVATION OF CLASSICAL SITES

The methods promoted by Dörpfeld at Olympia and elsewhere had a major

impact on excavation in Greece for many years to come. In the final decades

of the 19th century the amateur scholar became a professional archaeologist.

The fundamental methods of archaeological excavation were developed in the 1880s and 1890s, when Mediterranean archaeology was very much in the forefront of investigation. Men like Heinrich Schliemann and Arthur Evans were real pioneers of the discipline, not only from a technical point of view but also as men who made archaeology a subject of general interest. In the Greek world at this time stone monuments, their plan, elevation and construction methods were the most absorbing projects. Dörpfeld's work at Olympia was highly influential in this respect. He had shown how to distinguish different phases of a building by examining architectural details such as the profile of a column capital or base, the size of different members and the type of lead clamps used to join masonry.

It now became possible to compare these findings with other sites. The Akropolis at Athens and Delphi have already been mentioned. Dörpfeld himself was active on the Akropolis, and had excavated the theatre of Dionysos and the area between the Pnyx (where the Athenian Assembly met) and Areiopagos hills. The French School under Théofile Homolle began to explore the sanctuary of Apollo on Delos between 1877 and 1894, though a systematic programme was not carried out until 1906. Meanwhile, Maurice Holleaux examined another sanctuary of Apollo (Ptoion), centre of a somewhat less pretentious, local but well endowed cult in Boiotia where a large number of marble kouroi (youths) and bronze tripods were recovered. At Nemea, another of the inter-city sanctuaries, the temple of Zeus was uncovered in 1885. In the

A *herm* (statue of Hermes) ABOVE, erected in 341 BC at the entrance of the precinct of Apollo on the island of Delos. These images consisted of a bearded head and genitals fixed to a pillar. Theatre (the largest in Greece) and meeting hall (Thersilion) at Megalopolis RIGHT, one of Arkadia's two main urban centres in the 4th century BC, excavated by the British School in 1890-93.

Telesterion (Hall of Initiation) at Eleusis LEFT, where the famous Mysteries sacred to Demeter were performed. The Hall was one of the major projects commissioned by the Athenian statesman, Perikles.

late 1880s and 1890s, the French continued to explore Akarnania with its early Hellenistic walled centres (Stratos, Oiniadai and Pleuron) as well as some of the principal Peloponnesian *poleis* (Mantinea and Tegea; Troizen).

Preliminary investigations were carried out by the Greek Archaeological Service at three other important sanctuaries: that of Zeus at Dodona, in north-west Greece, by Karapanos (1876); of Demeter and Kore at Eleusis, north-west of Athens (1882-95, renewed between 1917 and 1945); and of the hero Amphiaraos at Oropos on the eastern border between Athens and Boiotia (1884-1929). A new and trend-setting cult place of the Classical period, dedicated to Asklepios at Epidauros on the north-east Peloponnesian coast, was cleared by Kavvadias (1876-77 and 1881-1903). Ancient ship-sheds were discovered at Piraeus, the harbour of Athens, in 1885, with slipways hollowed out in the rock face just above the water's edge, separated into bays by limestone columns. Dörpfeld's hand and counsel was felt at numerous sites, from Eleusis to Piraeus and Sounion, from Korinth to Epidauros. But sites of the Classical period represent only one aspect of his career. No less important were prehistoric ones.

Terrace of the Lions, Delos ABOVE, which led up to the precinct of Leto. Five, perhaps half the original number which once faced onto the Sacred Lake, are still in place. The theatre at Delos LEFT, built during the 3rd century BC, had an unusual scene building with porticoes on three sides.

SCHLIEMANN AT TROY AND MYCENAE

While Classical Greece was gradually being uncovered the more distant past

remained hidden. It took a gifted amateur, with the determination and self-

confidence of the fanatic, to uncover the most famous ancient city of all.

The main thrust of antiquarian and later true archaeological interest was directed towards the recovery of Classical antiquity. Prehistory was inaccessible before the development of excavating techniques. Thanks to the vision and determination of Heinrich Schliemann, a German commercial traveller, and to his success in persuading Dörpfeld to join him (albeit at a late stage) in his endeavours, Greek prehistoric archaeology evolved from an amateur gold-digger's mecca to a recognized branch of Mediterranean studies. For a world which was still absorbing the implications of Darwin's *On the Origin of Species* (1859) and was still quite uncertain how to classify prehistory (a term coined at least as early as 1833), Heinrich Schliemann's excavations at Troy and Mycenae were quite simply earth-shaking.

Some of the criticism vented in his direction was clearly motivated by professional jealousy. Schliemann was an outsider, a very successful businessman who had trespassed into archaeology because he could finance excavations out of his own pocket. But he was a romantic. Having started a Classical education, he was obliged, at the age of 11, to change to a technical one because of reduced family circumstances. Yet, he later claimed, throughout his career as the overseas agent of a Dutch company, he dreamed about his first vocation and especially Homer. It was not until 1866, after numerous travels which took him from Moscow to America and Japan that, at the age of 44, he settled down to Greek studies in Paris. In 1868 he made his first visit to Greece and the Troad. There Schliemann met the American Consul Frank Calvert. Calvert had examined the topography of Troy, and may well have put Schliemann on the right track. In his first serious publication, *Ithaca, the Peloponnesus and Troy* (1869), Schliemann made two principal claims: that Homer's Troy was located

Heinrich Schliemann (1822-90), the pastor's son whose energy, intelligence and business acumen enabled him first to retire early as a very rich man, then to apply his commercial panache to the discovery of Greek prehistory. He spoke eight European languages and later added Greek to his school Latin.

Sophia Schliemann played an active part in her husband's excavations. Here she is seen wearing jewellery from the "treasure of Priam" (*c*2200 BC), which was lost after World War II.

on the Hissarlik hill near the coast, in other words on the same site as the Classical and Roman city of Ilion, not further inland as some scholars had argued; and (on the basis of Pausanias' descriptions) that the graves of Agamemnon, the leader of the Greek host in the *Iliad,* and other members of his family were not to be located in the beehive tombs found around Mycenae (which had been ransacked for treasures by the Turks), but inside the citadel itself. In the following year Schliemann set out to prove his case.

TROY

Full permission was needed for any large-scale work, so excavations did not begin until October 1871. The first finds were, naturally enough, Hellenistic — inscriptions, and the Council House. The complexity of the site soon meant that the original area had to be reduced in order to reach prehistoric levels.

Between 1871 and 1873 Schliemann managed to lay bare what looked like three superimposed cities. In the very last month a remarkable discovery was made. Schliemann described how he and his second wife, Sophia, (though an independent account puts her in Athens at the time) had called the workforce to an early lunchbreak. He had detected a copper bowl with what turned out to be an unparalleled collection of treasure inside — gold

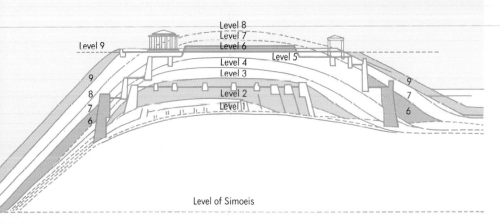

One of the most prominent features of Troy's archaeological remains, the north-east tower of the 6th citadel ABOVE, rising to 9 m (30 ft) and double that in breadth. On the left in the foreground is a deep well or cistern which was probably the fortress's chief water source.

Level 8
Level 7
Level 9
Level 6
Level 5
Level 4
Level 3
Level 2
Level 1

Level of Simoeis

Roman age (level 9)   Age of Mycenae (level 6)   Pre histrical age (level 2)

Grave Circle A RIGHT, on the citadel of Mycenae, where Schliemann found the first elite Mycenaean burials. Deep shafts were dug on the citadel *c* 1600 BC, the tombs marked at ground level by standing stones. In the 13th century BC these were enclosed in a stone circle and the fortress wall was built around it.

Heinrich and Sophia Schliemann viewing the circle of stones inside the Lion Gate at Mycenae in 1876 ABOVE. Six shafts containing 18 or 19 prestigious burials were found that year, dating from the 16th century BC. A slightly older grave circle (B) was disclosed by the Greek archaeologist Papadimitriou in 1952-4, lying west of the citadel.

ornaments, gold, silver and bronze vessels, tools and weapons – "Priam's treasure" as it was immediately dubbed. It is now unfortunately lost.

MYCENAE

The sensational findings at Troy were immediately published (1874), but Schliemann was already busy with his next project, at Mycenae, where full excavations began in 1876. Digging just inside the still prominent Lion Gate, he found sculpted gravestones, and beneath them a series of rich burials, of both men and women, known henceforth as the Shaft Graves. Schliemann meticulously recorded thousands of objects from these tombs – jewellery, sheet gold ornaments, gold plate, crystal sceptres, bronze spear-heads and swords with gold ornaments on the hilts.

Schliemann's progress reports to the London *Times* in the autumn and winter of 1876 caused a sensation. *Mycenae* (1879), published in London and New York, followed by a French edition the following year, made him notorious. Everyone had a theory about the incumbents of the Shaft Graves. Curtius even called the gold mask of "Agamemnon" a Byzantine Christ. There was just no context for these finds, though Schliemann was confident that he had revealed a Bronze-Age civilization equal in importance to Homer's heroic world.

FURTHER DISCOVERIES AT TROY

Schliemann returned to Troy, making a brief foray to Ithaka on the way, where he hoped to find the palace of Odysseus on Mount Aitos. In 1878-9 the "second city" of Troy was fully exposed, along with the "palace of Priam", a series of larger inter-connected rooms. This was followed by excavations in central Greece that uncovered another surviving structure with strong mythical associations, a beehive tomb near Orchomenos in Boiotia, thought to be the tomb of the

A *tholos* (beehive-shaped) stone tomb LEFT and BELOW, lying just outside the Lion Gate at Mycenae and dubbed the "Tomb of Klytaimnestra" (the legendary wife of Agamemnon) was excavated by Sophia Schliemann in 1876. The interior had already been robbed by a Turkish official. Vili Pasha.

legendary King Minyas.

In 1882 Schliemann was joined by Dörpfeld, who helped him to reinterpret the stratigraphy of Troy (now found to be seven, not four cities) and to excavate the citadel of Tiryns, another "Homeric" site in the Peloponnese not far from Mycenae. This turned out to have a palace like that of Troy in plan, centred on a large hall with an axial porch, but there was a bonus: a series of plastered walls were recovered decorated with the first "bull leaping" fresco, a procession of ladies, and hounds hunting a boar, as well as purely abstract motifs including dolphins and octopusses.

Schliemann died suddenly in 1890 after an operation in Naples, too soon to see the fruits of his work mature. Dörpfeld went on to discover the walls of Troy VI, and another series of interconnecting halls of *megaron* type, though the likeliest candidate for "Homeric Troy" was identified as the materially impoverished Troy VIIa by the University of Cincinnati expedition (1932-38) under Professor Carl Blegen. The amateur Schliemann may have horrified his professional counterparts with his native enthusiasm and impatience but it was he (and later Dörpfeld) who had taken the bull of stratigraphic excavation by the horns.

Interior of the "Treasury of Atreus", called after Agamemnon's father, the finest and maturest example of the false vault in Bronze Age architecture ABOVE. The carved half-columns and lintel blocks of green limestone which originally adorned the entrance were for the most part removed by Lord Elgin and are now in the British Museum.

KNOSSOS

Schliemann's work in the Troad and Argolid raised the possibility that there

might be some historical reality behind the most famous Greek myth. Further

evidence of the prehistoric past came with archaeological work on Crete.

"Sir Arthur Evans" by Richmond. Evans rediscovered the Minoan civilization of Bronze Age Crete and throughout his life remained an enthusiastic supporter of the notion that the ancient legends about the power of King Minos and the mysterious Labyrinth at Knossos did have some historical basis.

The 1890s were a momentous decade for Greek prehistoric studies, culminating in the discovery of the Middle Bronze Age palaces at Knossos and Phaistos. Two major synchronisms with Egyptian chronology were made soon after Schliemann's death. Ernest Gardner, the second Director of the British School at Athens (founded in 1884), persuaded William Flinders Petrie (1853-1942), the Egyptian archaeologist, to look at the material from Mycenae. At Naukratis in Egypt and Tell el-Hesi in Palestine, Petrie had had to contend with much more fundamental technical problems than the excavations of Olympia. There were no recognizable structures to disinter, only layers of earth deposit enclosing different kinds of pots. Petrie developed his own methods of identifying the pottery types in each stratum. Unlike Classical archaeologists such as Furtwängler, who was beginning to isolate painted pottery into groups, Petrie had to rely entirely on intrinsic features of the fabric and the type of glaze. At Tell el-Hesi he was able to synchronize some layers with Dynastic dates.

At Mycenae in 1891 he recognized Egyptian features and actual imports dateable to the 18th Dynasty of Egypt. In the following year he found Mycenaean pottery comparable to that from Dörpfeld's excavations at Troy VI and Tiryns in the palace of Akhenaten at Tell el-Amarna in Egypt. This provided the first absolute date for the Mycenaean period in the first quarter of the 14th century BC. Petrie had also some odd sherds from Kahun, a village built to house the pyramid builders of Sesostris II's (1906-1888 BC) tomb. These sherds turned out to be "Kamares ware", a distinctive type of painted vase named after the cave sanctuary on Mount Ida in central Crete where they were first found. Similar vases also emerged in Sir Arthur Evans' "first palace level" at Knossos, providing a date around 2000 BC for the beginning of the Minoan Palace civilization.

THE AEGEAN BRONZE AGE

Knossos was to be the crowning point of a series of Aegean prehistoric ventures. The French School had taken an interest in the island of Thera since the 1860s and well-preserved complexes of rooms had occasionally been found there during quarrying operations, which intensified with the bulk transport of pumice to make cement for the Suez Canal. In 1880 a beehive tomb at Menidhi in Attika was found to contain Bronze Age burials.

In 1886, Christos Tsountas excavated an undisturbed beehive tomb at Vapheio, south of Sparta, containing a magnificent warrior's outfit and many precious gems and vessels, including the celebrated pair of gold cups with bull scenes in low relief. In the following years, Tsountas unearthed 52 chamber tombs outside Mycenae and went on to investigate hundreds more in the Cyclades and Peloponnese. The fruits of his research on Mycenaean sites were published as a major study in 1893.

What was needed to make some sense of the Aegean jigsaw was a well stratified site which would show how the evidence found in the burials could be matched up against a sequence of superimposed levels to form a relative chronology. Phylakopi on

Minoan painted terracotta statuette with arms raised, c1400 BC, probably representing a worshipper.

The Grand Staircase of the Palace at Knossos ABOVE LEFT during excavation, c1905 and BELOW the restoration as it looks today. Evans, dressed in white and wearing a pith helmet, stands in the centre with the archaeologist who supervised the dig, Duncan Mackenzie, on his left. The workmen in the foreground were replacing wooden props with iron girders, and restored columns can be seen on the original sockets.

Alan Wace (1879-1957), the English archaeologist noted especially for his work on prehistoric Macedonia (the book he published with M.S. Thompson in 1912 is still a fundamental handbook).

Cretan women washing potsherds in the Central Court of the Palace at Knossos, outside the porch of the Throne Room, BELOW. As many as 300 workmen and women were employed on the site.

the island of Melos, excavated by the British School between 1896 and 1899 filled this gap. On the earliest level was an open village with pottery of the same type as that found in many of Tsountas' cist graves (stone-lined pits). This was succeeded by a fortified settlement where copper, bronze, the native obsidian (volcanic glass) and marble were in use, together with locally made and imported Middle Bronze Age pottery, and Minoan-style frescoes. In the third phase the settlement acquired further Minoan characteristics, as well as a small Mycenaean palace.

WORK BEGINS ON CRETE

In 1899 the President and Secretary of the thriving collection of antiquities at Candia (Heraklion), Joseph Hatzidhakis and Stephanos Xanthoudides, were instrumental in the passing of new legislation which enabled the foreign schools to participate in an intensive study of Crete. Arthur Evans, a vociferous and effective supporter of Balkan countries' independence from Austria and Turkey in the 1870s, won the affection of Cretans by his fundraising activities during the troubled years leading up to Cretan independence (1898). This genuine concern undoubtedly opened doors for Evans; without local backing he would have failed in his ambition to buy the Kephala hill-site, still known locally as Knossos (perhaps the land which Schliemann had tried unsuccessfully to acquire in the late 1880s). He had a first-rate team of specialists, while his labour force included, quite deliberately, Turks as well as Greeks. Within the first nine weeks the "palace of Minos" was unearthed, together with a Neolithic *tell* 6.5m (21ft) thick.

While Evans dug into the palace, David Hogarth of the British School investigated the town and nearby tombs, as well as the Diktaian Cave, Psychro and Minoan houses at Zakros on the east coast. His successors also concentrated in the far east of the island, at Palaikastro and Praisos. Evans' Italian friend, Federico Halbherr, who had encouraged him to investigate Crete in the first place, began work on another palace, on a par with that of Knossos, at Phaistos in the south of the island; and on Late Minoan houses at nearby Ayia Triadha, on the north side of the Mesara Plain. Here Xanthoudides opened up a series of communal circular tombs of the pre-palatial period. Xanthoudides' colleague, Hatzidakhis, investigated some pretentious houses at Tylissos and discovered the palace at Mallia, on the north-east coast (later excavated by the French). One of the first professional women archaeologists, Harriet Boyd of the United States, began

work at a rather unorthodox palace at Gournia, halfway between Mallia and Zakros, while another American, Richard Seager, discovered a cache of exquisite early Minoan jewellery at Mochlos and a pre-palatial site at Vasiliki, just south-east of Gournia.

This flurry of activity in the early years of the 20th century dramatically changed the perspectives of Greek archaeology in a way that affected the study of later historical periods as well as prehistoric ones. Prehistoric sites would henceforth appear alongside historic ones in the programmes of all the international schools and institutes. The first well-preserved Neolithic sites of Greece, at Sesklo and Dhimini near Volos in Thessaly were discovered in 1901. At the same time, Dörpfeld, searching for Odysseus' palace (in Schliemann's footsteps), conducted a series of campaigns not on Ithaka but Levkas (1902-11), and found instead some important Bronze-Age cemeteries. In the early 1930s Winifred Lamb discovered another type site (cultural model) of the Aegean Early Bronze Age at Thermi on the island of Lesbos.

Mainland Bronze-Age sites also multiplied. Two areas of pioneering work were Macedonia and the Peloponnese. Stanley Casson, had, like his French counterpart Leon Rey, investigated prehistoric and other mounds in the Salonika area during World War I. Casson returned in 1921 to excavate the Bronze-Age cemetery and *tell* at Chauchitsa and a handful of other sites in Macedonia.

Carl Blegen, Secretary of the American School at Athens, in a model excavation at Korakou, south-west of Korinth from 1915 onwards, discovered a Bronze-Age complex built

around a *megaron* structure. In 1920 he was diverted to a hill at Zygouries, on the road between Mycenae and Korinth, which turned out to be another significant Middle and Late Bronze-Age site.

In the same year, Evans began a new investigation at Mycenae, together with Alan Wace of the British School. Blegen also cooperated. The summit was re-examined, as were the Shaft Graves and the nine beehive tombs. Wace and Blegen's experience of mainland sites brought them into conflict with Evans over the interpretation of Minoan-Mycenaean relations. Evans firmly believed in a Minoan dominance of the mainland, while Wace was inclined to see a blending of Minoan influences with a native culture quite distinct from the Minoan. The Wace-Blegen view gained scholarly weight as time went on. At Prosymna, on the hills northwest of the temple of Hera (situated between Argos and Mycenae) Blegen found a complete sequence from the Neolithic to the Bronze Age.

The "House of the Tiles" at Lerna, Argolid, *c*2200 BC. A veritable Early Bronze Age mansion 12 × 25m (40 × 82 ft), built of stone and mudbrick, with corridors and staircases to an upper floor, as well as having numerous rooms. The roof had stone and terracotta tiles. Although this was the largest house found at Lerna, others were quite substantial.

MAINLAND GREECE

As the 19th century drew to a close, archaeologists began to broaden the

scope of their investigations. This new work would greatly expand scholars'

comprehension of the overall development of Greek culture.

Profile female head in deep relief on a column drum from the temple of Artemis at Ephesos (h 0.30 m/11⅘ in). Traces of the original paint on the hair and elaborate earring are still visible. This figure was one of a group including men (one wearing a panther skin) processing around the base. King Croesus of Lydia (who died in 546 BC) is said to have paid for some of them.

The range of sites chosen by archaeologists in mainland Greece was already beginning to change around the turn of the century. While work continued at major Classical centres, many of the new projects reflect a growing interest in and emphasis on the pre-Classical or "Archaic" period of Greek history, on the emergence of *poleis*, early trade and institutions in the 8th-6th centuries BC. Athens too continued to draw much attention. Work continued on the Athenian Akropolis, where Gorham Phillips Stevens began the laborious task of drawing up the Erechtheion and William Bell Dinsmoor (who was to become a great architectural historian) followed with the Propylaia. The American School, after clearing the early 3rd-century theatre at Sikyon in the north-east Peloponnese (1889-91), began excavating the nearby city of Korinth in 1896. The city had been razed to the ground by the Romans in 146 BC and rebuilt only after Julius Caesar founded a colony of veterans there in 44 BC. What the American School discovered therefore was one of the finest Roman cities in the Greek peninsula.

Charles Waldstein had started clearing the site of the Heraion (temple of Hera) at Argos in 1892-5, one of the greatest civic sanctuaries of the Archaic and Classical period, and this was followed up by Blegen in 1925-8. In 1930 two major studies of archaic Korinthian society were begun, the Americans at the northern cemetery of Korinth and Humfry Payne of the British School at Perachora, a narrow peninsula on the western side of the Isthmus. Here a very early Archaic sanctuary (for Hera Limenia) was discovered, built on the shores of a small harbour together with a wealth of exotic as well as home-produced votive offerings.

At Delphi, the Sacred Way and its numerous treasuries and dedications were gradually emerging from the annual work of the French School, which was also continuing its work on Delos and in north-west Greece. New excavations at Olympia began in 1936 and continued even into 1941 under Emil Kunze and Hans Schleif. The German School had meanwhile resumed work at Tiryns in 1930, in parallel to Evans at Mycenae, at the temple of Apollo on Aigina and at Amyklai outside Sparta. Systematic excavation of the Kerameikos, a most important cemetery area on the north-west of Athens was begun by Alfred Bruckner in 1913, later taken over by Karl Kübler. Initial studies had been conducted by the Greek Archaeological Service, but shortages

The mid-6th century BC temple of Apollo at Korinth LEFT, one of the earliest surviving stone temples in Greece, stands on a low hill in the centre of what used to be the Greek city, but is now superimposed by the Roman Agora.

of resources prevented their making as thoroughgoing an excavation as scholars might have wished. A survey of the activities of the Greek Service lists over 400 sites investigated during its first century (1837-1937). Much of this work was unglamorous but fundamental for the future of the discipline. Here were the foundations of area surveys and urban studies in all the major cities and regions of Greece.

The British School conducted a wide range of excavations which complemented the work of other schools. The most glaring gap in the study of the Peloponnese at this time was Sparta. The British School began studying the ancient city site in 1906-9, but soon found a much more interesting feature – an Archaic sanctuary dedicated to Artemis Orthia with a remarkable series of dedications in ivory, bronze and lead, as well as terracottas and pots. Other key sites of the period between the two world wars were Phana on Chios, Siphnos in the Cyclades, and a number of Archaic sites in the Ionian Sea – Aitos (touched on by Schliemann) on Ithaka and Zakynthos.

Outside Greece proper, an ephemeral American expedition to Cyrene recovered the remains of Hellenistic buildings (1910-11). Italian political expansion in the eastern Mediterra-

nean, though oppressive to the Greek as well as Turkish inhabitants, enabled Italian archaeologists to initiate a series of major projects. In Alexandria Evaristo Breccia excavated an early Hellenistic cemetery belonging to the city in the suburb of Shiatby. Achille Adriani, Curator of the Graeco-Roman Museum, expanded the study of Ptolemaic material culture. A topographical plan of Alexander's city had been attempted by members of the Napoleonic expedition to Egypt but the depth of the Hellenistic levels and the modern superstructures imposed over them made excavation well nigh impossible. The Dodecannese, in Italian hands from 1912-45, was also explored. On the island of Kos, home of the Hippokratic school of physicians and, appropriately, seat of the most important Hellenistic shrine of the healer god, Asklepios, the sanctuary and sectors of the Hellenistic town were cleared following the preliminary work of Rudolph Herzog. On Rhodes, a number of sites belonging to the ancient city of Ialysos were investigated, as well as finds from the city of Rhodes. The sanctuary of Athena on the summit of a precipitous rock at Lindos on the eastern side of the island had already been excavated by a Danish expedition in 1902-14 under Kinch and Blinkenberg.

The theatre at Sikyon c300 BC ABOVE, first investigated by the American School in 1889-91, was cut out of the natural rock slope in a hollow between two well-defended terraces. The lower of these was the *akropolis* of the original city, which became the focus of a new city after 303 BC, when the upper terrace became the new *akropolis*.

WESTERN ASIA

Modern Greece encompasses the southern tip of the Balkan peninsula, but

the ancient Greek world extended all around the Aegean, including the coast

of modern Turkey.

Hellenistic theatre at Ephesos. The Archaic city, now on the western outskirts of modern Selcuk, was originally sited on a promontory. The modern shoreline is some 10 km (6 miles) away, but the continuing high level of the water-table in this area seriously impedes excavation. The Hellenistic and Roman centre of Ephesos lay a little further west, on a plateau that has been extensively investigated in the last 25 years by the Austrian School.

After the liberation of Greece following the War of Independence, the rediscovery of the East Greek communities was a different story from that of the mainland. Until the 1880s it was still possible to remove large pieces of sculpture and architectural fragments from Turkey. This made major excavation there more attractive to European museums, and the old antiquarian habit of concentrating on prestigious sites survived much longer.

In the early part of the 19th century, French and English travellers were still the most prominent in the area. Charles Texier (1802-71) was sent by the French government in 1833 and 1835 to describe and illustrate the major monuments, and in 1842 to remove the sculptured friezes from the temple of Artemis at Magnesia on the Maiander River, reputedly the work of a famous 2nd-century BC architect, Hermogenes. More important was Philippe Le Bas (1794-1860), who succeeded him in 1842 and produced a fundamental work on a whole succession of sites, which included the first proper ground plans and incorporated quite new sites (such as the sanctuary of the Karian Zeus at Labraunda). Georges Perrot, another emissary of the French government, this time an art historian, revisited the Hittite citadel of Boghaz köy (discovered by Texier) in 1861 and went on, with Charles Chipiez, to investigate built tombs and other standing structures in Lydia and Karia, including some of the most unusual funerary monuments of the Aegean world.

FELLOWS AND NEWTON

Charles Fellows (1799-1860) and (Sir) Charles Newton (1816-94) between them acquired a considerable amount of excellent sculpture for the British Museum. Newton acquired for it fragments of the Mausoleum (see box). Fellows began a lengthy journey in 1832 which took him from Italy to Greece and the Levant by way of Lykia. Lykia became the prime focus of his interest from 1839. This mountainous coastal region was a province of the Persian empire in the 5th and 4th centuries BC, but its rulers and nobility had employed Greek or Greek-trained architects and sculptors to design their tomb monuments. (Greeks designed their coins, too.) In 1842 and 1844 Fellows made detailed investigations at Xanthos, Pinara, Patara, Tlos, Myra and elsewhere, sending back the fruits of his missions to the British Museum in the form of monumental sculptured pillars with rafters and gables, imitating wooden constructions.

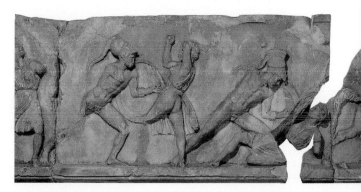

Charles Newton, who rediscovered the Mausoleum at Halikarnassos in the 1850s, LEFT. A frieze of Greeks fighting Amazons that decorated the top of the base RIGHT was among numerous sculptures acquired by the British Museum at this time. The most complete tomb of the mausoleum type BELOW, the "Nereid Monument", c400 BC, from Xanthos.

The Mausoleum of Halikarnassos, one of the Seven Wonders of the ancient world, was the grave monument of Maussolos, a 4th-century *satrap* (Persian provincial governor) of Karia. Newton, despite being an employee of the British Museum, managed to get himself appointed British Vice-Consul in Turkey, based at Mytilene on the island of Lesbos. Here and on Kalymnos, an island midway between the Halikarnassos peninsula and Kos, he conducted excavations in 1852-9.

Between 1856 and 1858 he explored the city of Halikarnassos itself, which had been turned into a fortress (Bodrum) in the 16th century. There was little trace of the Mausoleum.

He already had some idea of what he was looking for. The British Museum possessed some of the Mausoleum's (reused) sculptured slabs detached from the castle walls at Bodrum in 1846. Newton identified the site from a description of the Mausoleum and its setting in an ancient treatise. More sculptured fragments confirmed his suspicions. What Newton in fact came across were the foundations and basement of the building, including the looted burial chamber of Mausolos. His plans and detailed description of the site have since been the basis of all reconstructions of the original.

THE GREAT CITIES

Western Asia Minor included some of the wealthiest cities of the ancient

Greek world, such as Ephesos and Pergamon. Yet until the middle of the 19th

century it remained comparatively unexplored.

Carl Humann (1839-96), German engineer and amateur archaeologist, who in 1871 discovered some slabs of the Great Altar built into the Akropolis at Pergamon. Humann became interested in Pergamon while constructing roads and railways in the area. Later he draw plans of many ancient Anatolian cities, including Hierapolis, Tralles, Magnesia, Priene, Ephesos and Smyrna.

Apart from Halikarnassos, no detailed investigations had been carried out at any of the great historic cities of western Asia. Newton went on from Halikarnassos to investigate the Knidos peninsula. In 1858, he moved on to Didyma, where he began to remove some of the Archaic statues which formed a processional way to the sanctuary of Apollo. The oracular shrine at Didyma was left first for two French teams and then the great German archaeologist Theodar Wiegand. In the 1860s Pullan was working in the Troad and at Priene (a late 4th century planned city fully excavated by Wiegand and Hans Schrader from 1895 onwards), though he was primarily interested in the temple of Athena there, which was designed in the early Hellenistic period to inaugurate new architectural fashions.

PERGAMON

In the 1870s the Germans became more seriously interested in the sites of Asia Minor, beginning with Pergamon, where a self-taught ex fur-trader turned engineer, Carl Humann, had discovered marble reliefs with colossal figures built into the Mediaeval circuit wall. Humann was joined in 1879 by Conze, director since 1877 of the Berlin Gallery of ancient sculpture, with a team of excavators. Work began on the site of the Altar (now recognized as the Great Altar referred to by a Roman writer, Ampelius) which had already been located by Humann. They then moved to the lower slopes of the Akropolis just above it, the akropolis buildings, including an upper *agora*, the precinct or place of worship of Athena, a theatre set against a magnificent skyline, and the royal palaces of the Attalid kings (1879-93). From 1890 onwards the German Institute under Dörpfeld took over the organization of further operations on the lower slopes and in the lower *agora*.

MILETOS

The most ambitious programme undertaken by Wiegand was at Miletos, a city with origins in the Mycenaen age and a continuous history from the Archaic period. The site was far bigger than Priene, which was cleared in four years; by 1910 only the very centre of Miletos had been excavated, but great progress was made right up to World War I.

EPHESOS

At Ephesos the celebrated temple of Artemis had been located by another amateur, John Turtle Wood, between 1869 and 1874, and the first serious

Ionic capital from the temple of Artemis at the ancient Lydian capital, Sardis LEFT. The original cult was focused on the altar. A temple was not begun until *c*300 BC. The capitals reflect the best traditions of Classical Athens and at the same time herald Hellenistic trends. View from the Akropolis of Pergamon towards the Great Altar BELOW.

excavation of the Archaic levels was conducted by David Hogarth of the British School. But systematic excavation of the city area fell to the Austrian Institute. Preliminary investigations of the outlying cemeteries brought to light a remarkable vaulted stone tomb inside a huge mound near the village of Belevi, which combined native and Macedonian fashions.

SAMOS

Of the offshore islands, Samos, one of the most powerful island states of the Aegean during the Archaic and Classical periods, deserved special attention. Excavations here by the German Institute began in 1910. Samos town, lying below the modern one of Pithagorio (formerly Tigani) on the southern coast opposite the Mykale peninsula of the Asiatic mainland, has always taken second place to the sanctuary of Hera, 8km (5 miles) westwards. A tunnel on the outskirts of the town, which served as an aqueduct and potential escape route, was designed in the second half of the 6th century BC by a famous engineer, Eupalinos of Megara. It was found in 1885, lost, and relocated again in 1963. Early excavations focused on the temple of Hera, dating from the middle of the 6th century BC, which had been a milestone in Greek architectural practice.

OLYNTHOS AND ATHENS' AGORA

Two ambitious excavations on the Greek mainland, begun during the 1930s,

sought to re-create parts of an ancient city in a way that had not been

attempted since the discovery of Pompeii and Herculaneum.

Total excavation of the kind begun at Pompeii had been attempted at Priene, where the whole city was cleared together with its walls, sacred precincts and hillfort, though the finds were not related to the city plan. John Hopkins University launched a more ambitious project in 1928 at Olynthos, with the American School.

OLYNTHOS

Olynthos had been occupied in the 7th century BC by native tribes of the area (Bottiaians), then by Greek colonists originally from Chalkis in Euboia. It was refounded in 432 BC as the centre of a political league of Chalkidian cities by the Macedonian king Perdikkas, but was destroyed by his descendant, Philip II of Macedon in 348 BC. It was not reoccupied. This made it a first rate candidate for large-scale excavation. The city which emerged was a planned, well laid out grid of streets with comfortable houses arranged around courtyards each with a dining-room paved with a pebble mosaic, the earliest Greek mosaics known at the time. The material collected was published in detail and house locations were refer-

An ancient clay impression of the late 5th century BC ABOVE found in a dump in the Athenian Agora, with similar impressions taken from metalwork. The modern cast shows what the object from which the impression was made looked like. It was probably a bronze belt clasp.

Aerial view of the South Hill, Olynthos, from the south RIGHT. The narrow, winding streets and irregular house plans of the oldest phase are just visible skirting the contours. The new city lay on the lower, North Hill, whose regularly planned streets can be seen in the distance.

red to for each find. This is different from modern practice, where each stratum, irrespective of structures, is identified by a change in the character of the soil. The whole area to be excavated is then squared up and the finds from each square clearly identified for each stratum. Only in this way is it possible to relate changes in one structure to changes across the site.

THE ATHENIAN AGORA

The modern method of excavation is seen at its best in the recovery of the Athenian Agora. Sporadic digs had been conducted by the Greek Service and the Germans in the 19th century as opportunities arose. However, as at Delphi and the majority of ancient cities which had been built over in recent times, a systematic survey could only be carried out with large-scale expropriations, unthinkable without vast sums of money being expended in compensation. There was great pressure on the Greek government to make a formal decision about the future management of this site. Scholars judged it of the highest historical and archaeological importance. The American philanthropist John D. Rockefeller Jr (son of the well known millionaire) offered to make funds available if the work of exca-

vation and publication was handed over to the American School.

In 1931 the task of clearing some 300 buildings began. It was not a job to be left to the demolition gang, for old stone had frequently been reused in later structures. The level of the ancient city square was, in places, as much as 12m (40ft) down. By 1940 the outline of many ancient buildings was already emerging. Between 1946 and 1960 all the major buildings within the original concession had been explored. Publication of the finds was prompt and became a model for other publications of Classical sites.

NEW HORIZONS

Although it might seem that there could be nothing left to uncover today,

new approaches and methods make it possible to answer some fundamental

questions which had not even been posed 50 years ago.

Messene, a view along the north-west walls looking south. The Messenians, formerly subjected by the Spartans, reasserted themselves in 369 BC. According to the Sicilian historian, Diodoros, a new city arose in 85 days around the ancient mountain stronghold of Ithome with a 2.5 m (8 ft) thick circuit wall.

Following the inevitable disruptions caused by the two world wars, archaeology in the Greek world has expanded enormously, particularly from the 1960s onwards. In Greece, Italy, the Levantine ports and to a lesser extent elsewhere in the eastern Mediterranean, urban redevelopment has channelled the energies of archaeologists into rescue work in arbitrary and often tiny plots. Nevertheless, new techniques of exploration, such as air photography and geophysical surveys, have made it easier to pinpoint areas of potential major interest.

THE INTERNATIONAL SCHOOLS

It is only possible here to give a brief outline of the scope of post-war excavation, and progress at individual sites will form the background of the following sections. The international schools and institutes have continued research at those sites with which they have long been associated. The Germans completed the excavation of the stadium at Olympia, and resurrected the workshop of the great Athenian sculptor Pheidias where his colossal cult statue of Zeus was built.

From the Kerameikos area there is now a huge body of data on those communities which buried their dead in this part of Athens from the close of the Mycenaean age to 88 BC. In addition, the outline of the three main city gates on the north-west has been established together with adjacent buildings. New excavations at Aigina (from 1962) have revealed a much older temple under the Aphaia one (see p.51), as well as new statuary, both architectural and votive. On Samos much of the temple precinct has been cleared and many exotic votive offerings found.

The French have continued the work of restoration and publication at Delphi and Delos, and have opened up three major new areas of research, including the neglected city of Argos. At Xanthos in Lykia, present-day south-western Turkey, a native city incorporating Greek as well as Persian customs has gradually come to light. Symbolic of this fusion is an official decree, dating probably to 337 BC, written in Lykian, Greek and Aramaic.

A scatter of other Lykian sites and associated rock-cut tombs have been investigated by the Austrian Institute, in collaboration with the German Institute at Istanbul, including many of the cemeteries visited by Charles Fellows in the 1840s. The other major focus of the French School has been the island of Thasos. The Austrian Institute under Anton Bammer in 1968 started a new research pro-

Head of the life-size bronze Zeus (or Poseidon), *c*460-50 BC, found in a shipwreck off Cape Artemision, northern Euboea, in 1926 and 1928 (h 2.09 m/6 ft 7 in) LEFT.

gramme at the temple of Artemis at Ephesos which has, among other things, provided additional information for the appearance of coined money. A hoard of some 93 electrum coins discovered by Hogarth during his excavations in 1904-5 are perhaps the earliest coins yet discovered. Some appear to be Lydian (Herodotos, the 5th-century historian, claimed that the Lydians were the first to use money made from precious metals); others may have been produced for neighbouring Greek cities, such as Phokaia and Miletos.

The principal cities on the island of Euboia, Chalkis and Eretria, two of the greatest colonizing communities of Greece, have been studied by both the Greek Service and a Swiss mission.

Obverse ABOVE of a silver *tetra-drachm*, four-drachm piece, struck in the Macedonian region *c*490 BC showing two women raising a wine jar. The reverse BELOW has a simple impressed square.

Argos from the air LEFT: view across the ancient site from the north-west. On the right are the remains of the Roman Agora and theatre, whose original plan dates back to 300 BC. Dutch archaeologists have been active here since 1902, and the French School since 1952.

A rare unlooted tomb excavated from 1977 at Vergina, ancient Aigai, has yielded an extraordinary range of prestige armour, metalware and wall paintings. It was sealed hastily and some items, including a gilded Scythian bowcase and a pair of greaves, were left in the antechamber.

The theatre at Oropos ABOVE still retains its *proscenium*, a pillared hall which according to an inscription was built *c*200 BC. Paintings were hung between the half-columns. Above this there was a balcony and the *skene,* or scene building.

At Eretria a series of houses arranged in *insulae* inside the west gate, dating from the 4th to 2nd centuries BC, together with similar structures found at Korinth, Sikyon, Abdera, Rhodes, Athens and elsewhere, provide a range of house plans and confirm the regular use of figured pebble mosaics, a tech-nique hitherto known largely from Olynthos.

Town planning of the kind first documented at Olynthos has been detected at a wide number of sites, from Herakleia in the Crimean penin-sula to Paestum in Italy and Agde (Greek Agathe) along the Cote d'Azur.

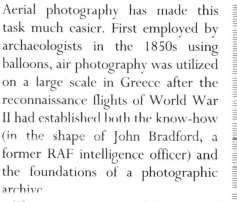

The river Strymon winding west-wards around the lower slopes of Amphipolis, an Athenian colony founded in 437 BC LEFT. Excavations conducted by D. Lazaridis since 1952 have revealed an extensive site with spectacular fortifications.

Aerial photography has made this task much easier. First employed by archaeologists in the 1850s using balloons, air photography was utilized on a large scale in Greece after the reconnaissance flights of World War II had established both the know-how (in the shape of John Bradford, a former RAF intelligence officer) and the foundations of a photographic archive.

The vast expansion of the city of Athens has brought with it scores of annual rescue operations in Attika, with the result that the relationship between Athens and the countryside is now much better understood. The Greek Service has also conducted planned excavations at the sanctuary of Artemis at Brauron, where young girls were sent to effect the transition to womanhood, and at Messene, the city built for the long-suppressed Messenians by the Thebans and their allies in 369 BC, and which the Spartans were unable to prevent.

EXCAVATIONS IN NORTHERN GREECE
Northern Greece has recently attracted especial interest. The string of colonies along the Aegean coast between Salonika and the Turkish border has received more if uneven attention, excavations being concentrated in larger cities such as Amphipolis and Abdera. But pride of place goes to Macedonia, where Professor Manolis Andronikos caused a world-wide sensation in 1977 with his discovery of a magnificent built tomb, containing a golden funerary casket (with a similar one in the antechamber) and an array of silver and bronze ware, weapons, armour and a gold diadem, matched by a magnificent gold wreath in the antechamber. Prof. Andronikos's identification of the principal burial with that of Philip II (doubt still remains about the second, female burial) has been given strong support by the forensic study of the bone material, especially the skull, found in the main casket. This shows damage to the right eye-socket of the sort inflicted by a missile. Philip was wounded in the right eye at the siege of Methone in 354 BC.

The tomb was one of three buried under a huge mound in what can be identified, on other grounds, as the royal cemetery of the Macedonian kings at Vergina ancient (Aigai). Further painted tombs of this period have continued to emerge, as well as the first wealthy Archaic burials, noble if not royal. Investigations at the ancient capital at Aigai form part of a wider research programme covering other Macedonian cities.

A painted marble throne (approx. 2 m/6 ft 6 in high) inside another tomb around Vergina ABOVE, close to the Hellenistic palace at the village of Palatitsa. The arms are supported by carved sphinxes and there is a marble footstool to match. Its significance in Macedonian funerary ritual is unclear.

THE GREEK SETTLEMENTS

The ancient Greeks sent colonists to all parts of the Mediterranean and Black

Sea coasts. Since 1945 sites in these regions have stimulated interest in the

relationship between Greeks and neighbouring peoples.

The most significant change in our understanding of the ancient Greek world since World War II has been the flood of information concerning Greek relations with non-Greeks. The names, dates and basic facts about Greek colonies were known from the literary sources, but, leaving aside Sicily and southern Italy, there was little exploration of these sites, despite the fact that the hellenization of southern France, for example, was a by-word even in Roman times.

WESTERN MEDITERRANEAN

In the western Mediterranean the chief focus has become the interrelationship between Greeks, Etruscans and Phoenicians. The Phoenicians had probably consolidated their hold on a number of key outposts in Spain and Sardinia by the 8th century BC at the latest, certainly before any Greeks became interested in the area. But the picture on Malta and in the Balearic islands is still unclear. The earliest indication of Greek settlement (as opposed to passing traffic) is on the island of Pithekoussai (Ischia) off the Gulf of Cumae, probably around 770 BC. It was unobtrusively if strategically located for trade with the Etruscan interior. Signs of iron working (the nearest iron source would be Elba) gives us the clue to the chief activity here.

SICILY AND SOUTHERN ITALY

There were Phoenicians as well as Greeks in Pithekoussai, and the same pattern is found in northern Sicily, where the former kept a strong toehold right up to the Second Punic War (218-201 BC). Sicily was extensively colonized by the Greeks and a vast wealth of new material, from planned cities (Megara Hyblaia, Kamarina, Selinus, Naxos and Syracuse itself) and temples (especially at Agrigento, Selinus, Himera) to cemeteries and offshore wrecks, is on display in a range of new and well-designed museums, notably at Syra-

Pezzino necropolis, Agrigento: almost 2000 closely-packed tombs, cut out of the rock or built of tufa slabs, have been exposed since 1980. The tombs range from the foundation of the colony in 580 BC to Hellenistic times. An analysis of the skeletal material is also expected.

Fresco from one of the short sides in the Tomb of the Diver, *c*480 BC, Paestum LEFT, discovered in 1968. The tomb was probably built for a native Lucanian, though the paintings are Greek in style. An underground shrine *c*520 BC found in the 1950s contained eight honey-filled bronze vases BELOW, LEFT.

cusc, Gela, Agrigento, Himera, Marsala and Enna. It is now possible to say something about the local Sicilian (Sikan and Sikel) population and what kinds of Greek traditions they found attractive.

Southern Italy has been explored as intensively as Sicily, with a similar range of new museums displaying the dense penetration of Greek articles and fashions among the native Italian peoples of the region, as well as the character of Greek settlement. Greek antiquities from Taranto and from Greek tombs in Apulia were of course collected in the 18th century and the well-preserved temples of Paestum and Sicily were long-running tourist attractions. As with Sicily, major

Elea or Velia, founded by Phokaians from the north-west coast of Asia Minor, about 535 BC. A fortified hill-site has recently been investigated between two small riverine harbours with a sanctuary, including several temples, altars and a *stoa* LEFT. The 4th-century BC Porta Rosa ABOVE is one of the earliest examples of the self-supporting arch anywhere in the Greek world.

archaeological investigations began in the late 19th century, but have boomed only in the last three decades.

THE BLACK SEA

The third-largest area of Greek settlement, around the shores of the Black Sea, has been studied since the 1950s by Soviet and Turkish archaeologists. Nineteenth-century excavation in the southern Ukraine and Crimea produced a galaxy of Skythian tombs dating from the early 6th century BC to the Hellenistic period, many of them containing luxury Greek imports – silverware, armour, weapons, and occasionally ivory and glass. Investigation of Greek colonies began in the early years of the 20th century in the Crimean peninsula and at Olbia near the mouth of the River Bug (from 1896). Later these were extended to include most of the documented colonies. Olbia has proved to be the earliest, the richest and the northernmost, probably because of its proximity to the Skythians of the western Ukraine. The latest and some of the most spectacular finds have come from Vani in Georgia, where a town identified with the mythical Kolchis (Medea's home and the origin of the golden fleece), dating mainly from the 4th and 3rd centuries BC has been excavated since the late 1960s. The most substantial finds in the Black Sea colonies, apart from the remains of both civic and domestic buildings, have been wine amphorae. The early ones came mainly from the island of Chios, but were later replaced by containers from Thasos, Rhodes, Kos and especially native versions manufactured at Herakleia, Sinope and Chersonesos.

CENTRAL AND EASTERN EUROPE

Romanian archaeologists have explored a network of settlements, both Greek and native, in the Danube estuary and its environs, the most important of which is Histria. In Bulgaria, evidence of contacts between Thrace and the Greek world has increased dramatically over the last decades. Finds demonstrate that

The underground shrine at Paestum, south of Naples, a small stone structure containing a bench that supports iron spits, with eight bronze and one painted-clay Attic vase under the walls ABOVE. Since there was no body within, perhaps this was a cenotaph or a nymph's shrine.

A bronze wine-mixing bowl (volute *krater*) (h 1.64 m/5 ft 4½ in) *c* 530 BC, RIGHT. It was discovered in a Celtic princess's tomb at Vix, Burgundy, in 1953. The bowl, which is in a Spartan-derived style, was probably transported by sea in sections, and thence up the Rhône valley, to be reassembled on the spot.

Greek coinage and architecture – as well as wine-drinking – were being imitated from the 5th century BC onwards by Thracian princes. In Albania, Greek finds have turned up not only at colonial sites, such as Apollonia, west of Fier, (with a planned street system, theatre and circuit wall of the 3rd century BC, and a cemetery from the 6th century BC onwards) and Epidamnos (Durrës), but also on native inland sites that acquired urban characteristics between the 4th and 2nd centuries. The earliest Greek imports there date from the 7th century BC. In southern Albania, the fortified citadel (later the city) of Butrint had a Greek type of theatre and circuit wall in the early Hellenistic period.

The Hellenistic north stoa at Apollonia LEFT, one of Korinth's major colonies on the Illyrian coast, half way between Bouthroton and Durres, (ancient Epidamnos). The site of the ancient city is now separated from the coast by a series of lagoons. Whereas Bouthroton lay in the still half-Greek region of Epiros, the hinterland of Apollonia was populated by non-Greek Illyrians.

Theatre at Bouthroton (Butrint), Albania, 3rd century BC ABOVE. The Greeks were unsure which of the tribes in north-west Greece should be considered Greek and which not. The sanctuary of Zeus at Dodona, not far from the Greek-Albanian border, was a nominal boundary. Bouthroton, on the coast, flourished in close proximity to the Korinthian colony of Kerkyra (Corfu).

FROM LENS TO LASER

Archaeologists' attempts to answer the questions arising from their

discoveries have been immensely assisted in recent years by modern scientific

techniques and technologies – microscopes, lasers and radiation.

Bronze horse's head found in the Aegean (National Archaeological Museum, Athens). Patinas have different colours, depending on the chemical conditions in which objects have survived.

The growing awareness during the 1970s and 1980s of the relationship between human society and its environment, particularly of land use, has strengthened the trend in Classical archaeology towards environmental and landscape studies. Archaeologists, geographers, geologists, meteorologists, anthropologists and historians have all benefitted from greater collaboration. After all, landscape history belongs just as much to geography as it does to history. Environmental observation is not, of course, anything new. However, the microscopic observation of plant and animal remains, together with more general studies of ancient climate and vegetation, have systematized the study of ancient diet and farming practices.

SCIENTIFIC ANALYSIS OF MATERIAL

A battery of modern scientific techniques is now available for analyzing the chemical components of metal tools, pots, glass and organic remains. Details about the methods of manufacture of a clay or metal object, as well as its chemical structure, can be studied in a petrographic microscope.

When an electric current is passed through a powdered sample from a given compound, and the light emis-

Mycenaean silver bowl inlaid with gold and niello, early 14th century BC, from Enkomi, Cyprus, with green accretions from a copper solder ABOVE LEFT and after conservation BELOW LEFT in the British Museum.

A microscope RIGHT specially designed for studying bone and plant material, after these have been retained from excavated soil by a method known as "wet sieving".

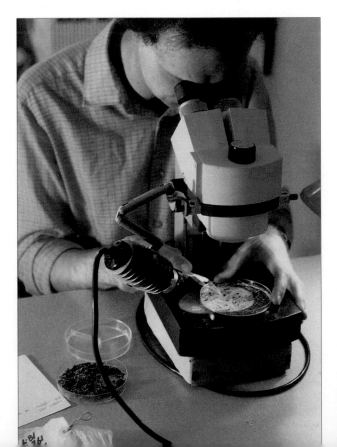

sions all focussed on a lens, these emissions will vary in length depending on the elements present and can be identified (this is known as optical emission spectroscopy).

The composition of clay, metal or glass objects can also be identified by X-ray diffraction. One technique is the artificial bombardment of a sample in a nuclear reactor, when the gamma rays emitted by the sample will vary depending on the decay rate of the elements present (neutron activation). Another technique is X-ray fluorescence, using the light rays emitted from the sample under X-ray bombardment to identify elements according to their known place in the spectrum, as in spectroscopy. Electron microprobes can be used for checking the overall distribution of a chemical within a larger sample, such as a coin.

These and attendant techniques can be used to answer questions such as "Was this glass cup made locally or imported?", or "To what sort of temperature would one have to heat this sword to achieve its demonstrated efficacy as a fighting tool?" They can also be applied to wider questions. The isotopic composition of lead – that is, the proportion of uranium and thorium present in lead ores – has recently been used to "fingerprint" silver objects, since these constituents are not altered by the processes of extraction and refining. Bronzes are notoriously difficult to analyze, because any chemical profile of the copper ores is confused by the common addition of scrap metal of various origins. In principal the same argument applies to silver, but the fingerprinting of the lead isotopes in silver is sufficiently distinctive to enable correlations to be made between silver

products and known ore sources. Preliminary studies show that Attika's Laurion field, the island of Siphnos and a third major source, perhaps in western Anatolia or Macedonia, were the most important sources of silver.

DATING TECHNIQUES

Several dating techniques are currently in use. There is the better known radio-carbon (measuring the rate of decay of the C^{14} isotope in organic material) which must be carefully correlated against tree-ring calibration (the measurement of tree-rings based on 100-year-old oaks and 1000-year-old bristlecone pines). Recorded changes in the earth's residual magnetism and a variety of isotopic charts are used. "Thermoluminescence" is a method of counting the electrons which accumulate in the crystal lattice of pottery. The measurement of argon gas, produced as a result of radioactive decay in potassium-bearing objects, and the decay of thorium and uranium-234 from natural uranium, are two methods particularly suited to the study of bone and shell samples. Oxygen isotopes have been applied in the identification of marbles.

The identification of oxygen isotopes has also been adopted to date the eruption at Akrotiri, Thera, when large amounts of dust and sulphur compounds were emitted. The traditional date, c.1500 BC, is based on correlations with Egypt. Ice cores in Greenland, however, show increased acidity around 1644 +/− 20 BC, and a climatic deterioration has been noted on compacted tree-rings in northern Europe around 1624 BC. This need not mean the traditional dates are wrong. More correlations are required to interpret the ice core samples.

Dendrochronology is a method of scientific dating based on tree-ring counting. Very long-lived trees, such as North American bristle-cone pines, have been used to build up a historical tree profile from early prehistory. Tree-ring dating has also been used to verify radiocarbon dates.

THE WORLD
OF THE
ANCIENT GREEKS

Greek culture flourished in the
last 2000 years BC. What made
the Greeks different from their
Mediterranean neighbours was
their compulsion to write down
everything. This has made it
easier to reconstruct details
of everyday life, giving us
glimpses into private lives as
well as public attitudes.

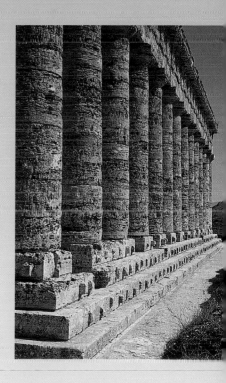

PRE-MINOANS

The foundations of the better-known Minoan and Mycenaean civilizations of Crete, the Aegean and mainland Greece built on the heritage of Early Bronze Age society which flourished during the third millennium BC.

The Palace societies of the Minoan (Middle Bronze Age) and Mycenaean (Late Bronze Age) periods developed from well-established agricultural communities on the Aegean islands and mainland. The propagation of vines and olives, as well as cereal cultivation and stock-breeding (mainly sheep and goats but increasingly cattle also), greatly enhanced the economic potential of the whole Aegean world. The range of available foodstuffs can be glimpsed from carbonized remains found in a mansion at Lerna in the Argolid; apart from cereals (two standard varieties of wheat, emmer and einkorn, barley and oats), there were almonds, broad beans, peas, vetches and a kind of tree strawberry. Olive and vine growing are less labour intensive than cereal cultivation and in combination provided enough food to make a small community virtually self-sufficient.

Among the most intriguing problems concerning the Aegean Bronze Age are the origins of the Palace societies on Crete and the later Mycenaean kingdoms on the mainland. Another major question concerns the interaction of cultures on the Greek islands, clearly of fundamental significance in the Early Bronze Age, with those of the mainland and Crete. Recent work in central Greece and the Peloponnese has revealed a great deal about society before the appearance of a distinct Mycenaean culture, while on Crete the pre-palatial stage is emerging.

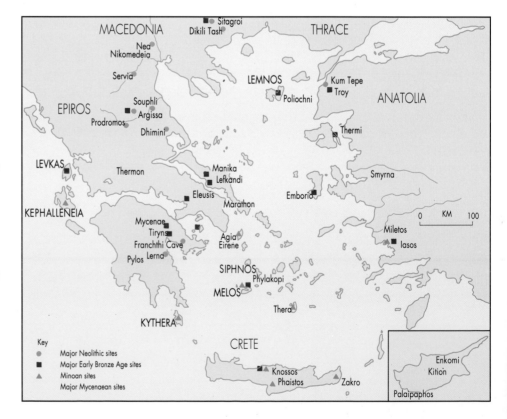

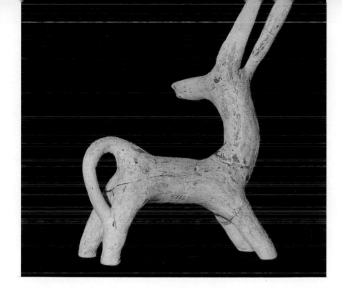

Terracotta statuette of a deer from a tomb in the Mesara Plain of southern Crete, pre-palatial period (2500-2000 BC). Animals and simple geometric shapes were the main decorative forms used in metal as well as clay.

The more efficient use of labour throughout the year and the higher yields obtained from mixed farming enabled some individuals to concentrate much more fully on specialized handicrafts.

Field walking (see pp.52-3) in Lakonia and other parts of the Peloponnese has revealed that Bronze Age settlement was far more extensive than had previously been supposed. In the Early Bronze Age (c. 2900-2000 BC) the population lived mainly in dispersed farmsteads. However, some larger villages have also been revealed. The recently discovered building complex at Myrtos in southern Crete and its counterpart at Vasilike on the opposite side of the hills have separate rooms designated for different functions – kitchens, storerooms with large jars, living and workrooms and a household shrine, all built around a central court. These, with their early Middle Bronze Age successors at Aghia Photia and Khamaizi were the precursors of the Middle Minoan palaces.

MARITIME TRADE

Early Bronze Age society was wealthy, innovative and restless. Clay models and drawings of boats on sealstones reflect the maritime interests of the Cretans in this period. The distribu-

tion of certain kinds of object, from gold vessels and jewellery to marble figurines and clay two-handled mugs or animal-shaped vases shows that there was a good deal of contact between Troy (levels I-V) and the Cycladic islands, Crete and western Asia Minor. Regular communications between Crete and Egypt were established, providing imports of gold, ivory, faience (glazed clay) ornaments and stone vessels. Some contacts, albeit occasional, were also maintained with communities on the Ionian Sea, including present-day Albania, and of southern Italy. At the same time, distinctive regional cultures began to emerge in Troy, the Cyclades and Crete which were to crystallize in the following period.

Reconstruction of an Early Bronze Age house from Kolonna, Aigina, BELOW. Most of the houses found on the Greek mainland (and at Troy) were long, freestanding structures with mudbrick walls. They were often built on stone footings, with a porch at one end and a storage room, sometimes of apsidal form, at the back. The hearth is usually in the main room.

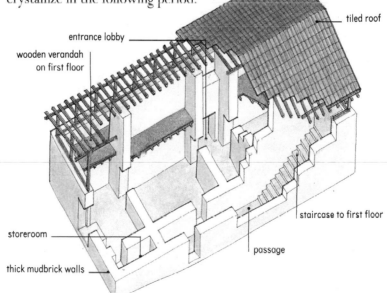

entrance lobby
wooden verandah on first floor
tiled roof
staircase to first floor
storeroom
passage
thick mudbrick walls

THE MINOANS

The ancient Greeks had memories of a glorious past in the shrine of Minos,

the Labyrinth and the Minotaur. Archaeologists have uncovered a powerful

Bronze Age civilization which is even more impressive than the legends.

A unique terracotta disc (*c*1600 BC) from Phaistos ABOVE is inscribed on both sides with stamped signs running in a spiral from the edges to the centre. Some of the signs have been recognized on other Minoan objects so it is possible that the script may be Minoan. However, it has not yet been deciphered.

Settlements on Crete in the Minoan period RIGHT were widely dispersed throughout the island although the more sheltered northern coastline has the greatest concentration. Recent work has revealed more sites in the hitherto sparsely represented western parts of the island.

Crete does not seem to have been affected by the changes which occurred around 2000 BC in mainland Greece. Arthur Evans called the society he had discovered at Knossos "Minoan" after the legendary king Minos, whose technical achievements (the labyrinth) and sea power became part of a powerful oral tradition which continued to be respected by later writers, including Thukydides, Aristotle and the Roman geographer Strabo. Minoan culture developed directly out of the Cretan Early Bronze Age. The craft specialization already referred to (pp.88), coupled with wide overseas contacts and the construction of planned multi-functional architectural schemes are symptoms of a more differentiated society. An emerging social hierarchy, whose wealth was made manifest in Early Bronze Age jewellery and other articles in precious metals, evolved into the administrative order of the first palaces.

THE PALACES

Little is known about the earliest palaces, at Knossos and Phaistos (constructed *c.*1900 BC), because they were rebuilt 200 years later to form the main complexes which survive today. These, like their predecessors, seem to have been more ambitious and elaborate versions of the functional cellular units arranged around a courtyard which were beginning to appear in the third millennium BC. What distinguishes the palaces is the quality

of the workmanship and the sophistication of the designs (based on a "Minoan foot" of 30.36cm), incorporating well thought-out sequences of rooms, wide staircases and upper storeys, vistas and variegated façades. Although the dressed masonry blocks are of gypsum (hydrated calcium sulphate), a softer building stone than those used in later periods, they were very carefully finished. Painted wooden columns were used to support ceilings and upper floors, while most available interior walls were plastered and painted with scenes of everyday life ("the Cupbearer", "la Parisienne", "the Prince of the lilies" at Knossos; "two boys boxing" and the "panorama" from Thera), or simpler decorative schemes (the griffins and

Our knowledge of Minoan life and art has been immensely enriched by the discovery of remarkably well preserved Minoan town houses on the edges of the volcanic crater which split the island of Thera (Santorini). A boy returning with his haul of fish LEFT is among the numerous scenes of daily life dating from the Late Minoan period unearthed at Akrotiri in the south west of the island.

A spouted vase decorated with floral patterns in white, orange and red over a dark slip ABOVE. This style is called "Kamares" after the finds first made in the Kamares cave sanctuary on Mount Ida, and was the prevailing pottery type of the period c2000–1700 BC.

The celebrated pendant from Mallia RIGHT, c1700 BC, with two wasps sucking a drop of honey, shows that the fundamental goldsmithing techniques of filigree and granulation (using a fish glue) were being used with great skill.

Gold ring from Knossos of the Neo-Palatial period (1700-1450 BC) depicting a cult scene ABOVE. A priestess stands in front of a goddess. Deities are usually represented on a larger scale than human beings.

A gold, votive double axe from Archalokori, Crete RIGHT. Double axes are one of the commonest ritual symbols both in Minoan and Mycenaean culture. Most were of bronze, set up in shrines on poles or carved in stone.

Kamares-type cup of eggshell-thin clay painted with dark slip, picked out in white and red c1800 BC BELOW.

lilies of the Throne Room, the dolphins in the Queen's bathroom at Knossos; a landscape in springtime in House Delta or the antelopes in House Beta on Thera). Among the best indications that in Minoan society aesthetic and practical considerations went hand in hand are the drainage channels and primitive flush toilets.

CRAFT AND NATURE

A zest for nature is apparent in all Minoan crafts. Clay vases were often decorated with plant and marine motifs (including lilies and palm trees, fishes and octopusses), utilizing colour contrasts to great effect. Pottery was made on the slow (hand-turned) wheel but the shapes are magnificent and the walls extremely thin. The pottery of the second palace period was painted a lustrous black, decorated in red, white and orange ("Kamares ware"). Late Minoan (15th century BC) pots had darker shapes painted on a buff ground.

The same appreciation for the natural world is apparent in the exquisite gold jewellery pendant from Mallia (now in Heraklion) showing two wasps sucking a drop of honey, or the subjects chosen to decorate figurines and sealstones in ivory and bone, soft and hard stones. The harder marbles, limestones and steatites (a type of soapstone) were carved in elaborate forms, including boxes and vases of various shapes. Some of the most attractive vessels were carved or hammered in high relief with rural scenes, such as the procession of men carrying scythes on the steatite "Harvester vase" in Heraklion and the two gold cups from Vapheio in Lakonia, showing the taming of a wild bull and a group of bulls.

Metalwork reached a very high standard of craftsmanship. A wide variety of specialist bronze tools and weapons, including elegant inlaid daggers and elaborately engraved ritual axes have been found in tombs and sacrificial deposits.

Direct Minoan influence in the form of architectural features, tomb types or substantial quantities of pottery can be seen on the islands to the north of Kythera, Rhodes, the Cyclades and also on parts of the Anatolian coast. In the second palace period (c. 1700-1450 BC) Cretan luxury objects were exported north to the Peloponnese and the Dodecanese, and east to Cyprus, while Minoan pottery found its way to Delphi, the Lipari islands, Troy, Samos, Chios and the Levant. Minoan influence has also been discerned in the architecture, metalwork and some of the more exotic items found in the Shaft Graves at Mycenae, and in Late Bronze Age (c. 1550-1450 BC) pottery of the Greek mainland.

PEOPLE OF THE LINEAR B TABLETS

In 1900 Arthur Evans unearthed some brick-like clay tablets with characters written on one face in close rows. The characters suggested a script. Two separate scripts were subsequently distinguished, Linear A (still undeciphered) and Linear B. Linear B was recognized by Michael Ventris as an archaic form of Greek in the 1950s. Thousands of clay tablets inscribed with this syllabary have been found at Knossos, Mycenae, Tiryns, Pylos, and graffiti are even more wide spread. The social structure they reveal is a strongly hierarchical one.

The references to land ownership are complex. There are lists of personnel engaged in various tasks, including naval and military assignments. Most of the texts are inventories of livestock and agricultural produce (sheep, goats and pigs are prominent, cattle and especially horses, less so), various metal objects are described in some detail. Many entries refer to something like "tribute" or "contribution"; from such evidence a theory is derived that the palaces were redistributive centres (there are no references to buying and selling, though some lists might equate to rations).

Clay tablets scored with symbols in the Linear B script, an archaic form of ancient Greek TOP AND BOTTOM RIGHT. Most of the texts are inventories of livestock and agricultural produce (especially sheep, goats and pigs) as well as manufactured articles (textiles and metalware). Various officials are referred to, revealing a complex chain of command. Sir Arthur Evans CENTRE.

THE MYCENAEANS

A mainland counterpart to Minoan Crete, the palace culture of the

Mycenaeans, emerged in the 16th century BC. Many of the earlier

civilization's achievements were used and developed by their successors.

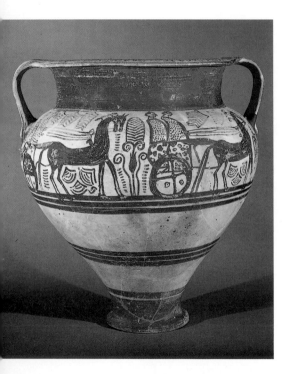

A Mycenaean stemmed bowl *c* 1400 – 1300 BC from Maroni, Cyprus, decorated with a procession of chariot riders. The light, two-wheeled chariot drawn by a pair of horses appears for the first time in Europe around the middle of the second millennium BC. In the Mycenaean world it seems to have been used both for military and parade purposes, as it was in the Near East.

A perceptible change occurred in the cultural pattern of the Greek mainland towards the end of the Early Bronze Age (*c.* 2000 BC). A number of sites were burned and the fundamental features of mainland society after this phase were entirely different. There may have been a population movement from the eastern side of the Aegean into the mainland. However, it was probably unconnected with the new pottery style which evolved at a slightly later date. This new style was dubbed "Minyan" after the examples found by Schliemann in the chamber tomb at Orchomenos, Boiotia (see p.62). At Troy itself there was a sharp break in culture between levels V and VI. Here, as in mainland Greece, the horse made its appearance after *c.* 2000 BC.

THE DORIANS

What used to be called the Dorian invasion (colonization of mainland Greece by Dorian Greeks) is much too simplistic a description. Nevertheless, the distribution of matt-painted pottery in the eastern parts of central Greece and the Peloponnese contrasts with an equally distinctive grouping in the corresponding western regions. This has been compared with the known historical distribution of the Doric and north-west Greek and Arkadian dialects. However, certain identification of archaeological groupings with ethnic or linguistic ones is notoriously difficult and tends to be hypothetical.

CULTURE BEFORE THE SHAFT GRAVES

Mycenaean culture before the period of the Shaft Graves was unpretentious. Many sites were strongly fortified, as Troy was throughout its history and the Early Bronze Age Cycladic settlements, but unlike Cretan ones. Houses were built on the *megaron* plan, consisting of a mud brick hall with an apsidal end and porch, all on stone footings, roofed probably with wooden beams and thatch. The location of the hearth in the centre of the main room, rather than in an open yard, betrays the northern origins of this house plan. The Mycenaeans were herders and hunters as well as farmers. Cereals, pulses and olives were their mainstay; vines are not so well represented. Burials were made in slab-lined cists or pots, sometimes covered by an earthen mound.

THE SHAFT GRAVES

A rapid increase in material wealth is reflected in burials before *c.* 1600 BC, around the time of the first Shaft Graves (Circle B). These graves contained clay and gold drinking cups, a profusion of bronze weapons, an electrum death mask and a carved rock crystal jug, probably of Minoan workmanship. The finds from Circle A, excavated by Schliemann, were richer still (see p.63). Not only did these contain items of intrinsic value, but stone vases and ostrich egg shells which were probably imported through Crete. The militaristic preoccupations of the Mycenaeans, quite at variance with their more easy-going Minoan neighbours, are apparent from the start. Stone reliefs, metallic vessels, gold rings and other ornaments are adorned with scenes of pursuit or combat. Some of the skeletons recovered from Circle B were almost 2m (6ft) high, which suggests that it was not just their battle gear that made these warriors formidable.

CRETE

Mycenaean culture during the subsequent period is best represented on Crete. Fire destroyed Knossos and every other significant site on the island around 1450 BC (almost certainly the work of a natural disaster). The palace at Knossos remained deserted for a generation, but was then reoccupied by Greek-speaking mainlanders (Mycenaeans) till c.1380 BC, when a further disaster brought an end to the island's cultural dominance in the Aegean. The Mycenaeans did not penetrate the whole island, but there was a revival at most of the major palace and country sites. Their presence can be detected from intrusive warrior burials in vaulted stone tombs entered via long passages, as well as by the appearance of Linear B texts. Cretan pottery in this period shows a fusion of local and mainland features (the "Palace style").

CONTACTS ABROAD

In the period 1400-1200 BC, the great age of the palaces at Mycenae, Tiryns, Pylos and central Greece, Mycenaean contacts abroad can be traced by the distribution of Late Bronze Age pottery: from eastern Thessaly and the north Aegean to Epiros, the Ionian islands and beyond to southern Italy,

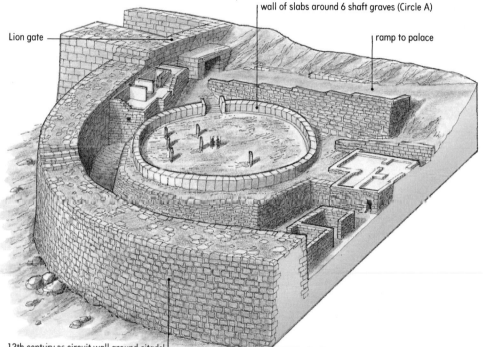

Lion gate

wall of slabs around 6 shaft graves (Circle A)

ramp to palace

13th century BC circuit wall around citadel

Sicily and Sardinia; Troy, Miletos and southern Turkey to Cyprus and the Syro-Phoenician coast. In Egypt Mycenaean pottery has been found at more than 20 sites. While the producs of Mycenaean potters did not have the pretensions of the more flamboyant Minoan styles; it was cheap, simple and easy to reproduce. The Mycenaeans learned a great deal from the Minoans about the beauties of stone architecture, wall painting and carved stone and metalwork. They also learned to sail and outdid their predecessors in that art too.

The Shaft Graves inside Circle A at Mycenae (reconstruction). Originally, these deep pits belonged to the large cemetery that covers the western slopes of the citadel, although their position indicated burials of special status. The Mycenaeans continued to inhume their dead, but usually placed them in rock-cut chamber tombs or corbel-vaulted, built chambers (beehive tombs).

95

DESTRUCTION AND DISPERSAL

In the 13th century BC the whole Late Bronze Age world of the eastern

Mediterranean experienced a severe crisis. Wars, natural disasters, migrations

and invasions toppled previously powerful states.

One of a series of clay temple models found among votive offerings in the temple of Hera at Perachora, *c*800 BC BELOW. It gives a good idea of what the temple itself looked like – a mudbrick hall with a steep, thatched roof and broad eaves, with a porch held up on two double columns and tiny windows high up.

Map of the Aegean in the 8th century BC RIGHT. Far more is known about burials in the Dark Ages (*c*11–800 BC) than about settlements. The earliest phases of the Greek *poleis*, the majority of which were well established by 700 BC, are often scanty. Domestic building was obviously flimsy and has left few traces. Even the most ambitious structures of the time, all temples, had light brick and pole frames.

The Mycenaean world ended violently, but not (as has been suggested) at the hands of northern invaders. Despite the destruction of many major sites, some *c*.1250 BC (Zygouries, Mycenae), many more *c*.1200 (Mycenae again, Tiryns, Gla and Thebes in Boiotia), others continued into the 12th century (Argos, Asine, Athens and Perati in Attika, Iolkos, Korakou, Lefkandki and Nikhoria in Messenia, Naxos and the Ionian islands). Earthquake damage seems responsible for weakening a significant number of sites (Tiryns, Dendra, Mycenae, Sparta). The rebuilding of Mycenae, and extensive new evidence from Tiryns, shows that we are still dealing with the same people. Feuding between the Mycenaean sites is the message we get from many myths which probably date back to this period, not only the Trojan war, but the Seven Against

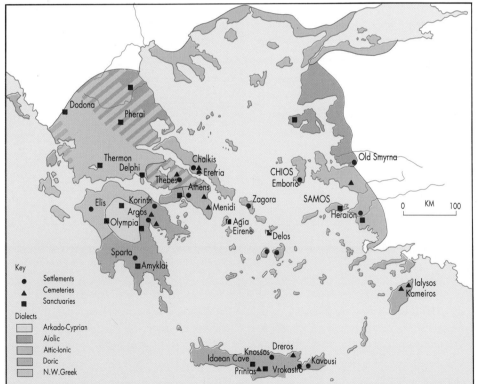

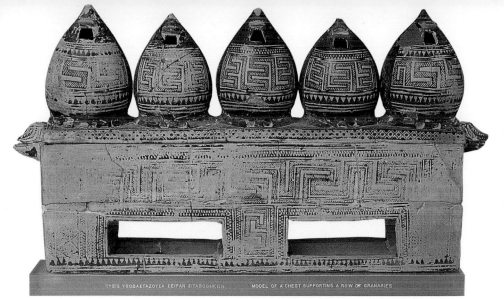

Painted clay model of a linen chest, surmounted with five beehive-shaped granaries with trap doors. Found in a woman's cremation, c850 BC, near the Areiopagos hill in Athens, with a fine Geometric amphora for holding ashes, some smaller vases, clay and glass necklaces and two massive gold earrings.

Thebes (from Argos), the stories of Theseus, Jason and the Argonauts, and similar tales.

A SHIFTING POPULATION

There was a substantial change in settlement patterns during the post-Mycenaean period. Completely new pottery forms appeared at Troy, traceable to the Danube. Cyprus received an influx of Mycenaeans which is attested both archaeologically and linguistically (the Cypriot dialect is closest to the Greek of the Linear B tablets). Many of those sites still occupied around 1200 BC were abandoned during the century and the immigration of Ionians and Aeolic speakers to the west coast of Asia Minor followed.

THE DARK AGES

The Mycenaean world went out with a groan rather than a bang in the 12th century BC. The 11th century BC marked a transition between two very different worlds. The Dark Ages (c.1050-750 BC) began a new era, symbolized by a new style of pottery, the "Geometric". A new set of bronze and iron objects appeared. Individual burial in stone cists (boxes) and, increasingly, cremation, replaced the old communal inhumations. The introduction of iron technology trans-

formed the lives of the impoverished Mycenaean survivors. Some of these trends are also found in north-west Greece and Macedonia, themselves regions of profound change at this time. The most interesting new evidence here comes from a *tell*, Assiros Toumba, in central Macedonia, where a sequence of levels from the Late Bronze Age to the 8th century BC shows a very well developed system of agriculture and the communal storage of foodstuffs (not unlike the southern palaces in the early phase).

LEFKANDI

The breakdown of the sophisticated Bronze Age social and economic network affected all aspects of life. Although most of the evidence for the period up to 750 BC comes from burials, these give some idea of the gradual increase in population and prosperity in what were to become the major centres of political life. The most spectacular finds have emerged from the cemeteries of Lefkandi in Euboia. Around 900 BC there was a bronze foundry, perhaps using Cypriot copper. Cypriot, Egyptian and Levantine imports – beads, rings, vases – soon followed. Even more surprising was the discovery in 1981 of a huge aisled building c.950 BC, of mudbrick on stone foundations.

Limestone head of a goddess from the spring of Kyane at Laganello, Syracuse c600 BC (0.558 m/22 in). The goddess wears a tall headdress (polos). The head is executed in the "Dedalic" style typical of the 7th century BC. This was characterized by a frontal emphasis, oval faces and thick wig-like tresses. The style was of Egyptian origin, but became a stylized motif for combed locks.

THE RISE OF THE POLIS

The characteristic self-ruling community of the ancient Greek world was the

polis. *It emerged in the 8th century, as a sense of the community of place*

began to override other traditional social loyalties and networks.

Athenian *didrachm* (two-drachm) silver coin *c*545–515 BC ABOVE, weighing about 8.6 g (133 grains), the commonest denomination struck at Athens in the earliest civic issues. The reverses have a simple square punch mark with a tiny lion's head. Coined money was a relative late-comer. It now seems that the earliest eastern models were not produced before *c*600 BC. A 9th-century BC bronze bowl from Lefkandi RIGHT is a Syrian import.

The *poleis* were not cities in our sense of the term; at least, not until the Hellenistic age after the death of Alexander the Great in 323 BC, and even then they retained an intimate relationship with the surrounding land. When Aristotle said, at the beginning of the *Politics*, that man was a political animal, he did not mean that men and women were city-dwellers. He meant that it was natural for them to form autonomous communities, that civilization was about organization, because it was only in community life – within a legal and judicial framework – that people could aspire to their real virtues and capacities.

THE EMERGENCE OF THE *POLIS*

The "heroic" culture of the Dark Ages was abruptly challenged in the mid-8th century BC by the emergence of autonomous political communities, known as *poleis*. In the *polis*, loyalty was based on common cults and legends while membership was open to in-dependent farmers as well as to the upper classes. The increasing pros-perity of small landowners thanks to more intensive farming is usually con-nected with this development. Aris-tocrats asserted their status within the *polis* by monopolizing magistracies and priesthoods.

THE EARLY *POLIS*

What we find in the earliest days of the Greek *poleis* fits in rather well with Aristotle's much later analysis of the importance of social organization. Those items which had previously been buried with individuals (and especially rich aristocrats) – armour and weapons, bronze cauldrons, ela-borate dress pins and ornaments – were now more usually dedicated at civic sanctuaries, along with huge numbers of small bronze, and some-times lead, figurines, at first only of animals, but later also of warriors and women. These sanctuary sites, often at a distance from the settlement itself, became the primary object of public expenditure and artistic endeavour.

The *polis* was intended to provide those things which had to be done collectively, and villages continued to

Argos from the air LEFT: the "Aspis" (shield) hill, one of two forts overlooking the ancient city. The 6th-century BC walls on the Aspis were built directly over older fortifications belonging to a Bronze Age settlement c2000 BC.

form part of the wider *polis* network. This can be seen most clearly in Attika, where villages or wards (*demes*) were in fact genuine constituents of the *polis*. It was the deme that decided who was or was not a citizen, and the *deme* members who elected Councillors to the city. The chairman and local council had real political power, and the villages themselves were sometimes little short of towns judging by the local sanctuaries (such as Sounion, Rhamnous) and the provision of amenities (such as a theatre at Thorikos).

The religious dimension of political change should not be underestimated. The earliest evidence that we generally have on the new *poleis* is almost entirely religious, expressed in the foundation of sacred precincts (*temenoi*) and temples. These temples were an assertion of secular authority over territory, as well as focuses of ritual. Their purpose was to unify disparate social (and in the colonies ethnic) groups.

THE HEROIC AGE

Lefkandi (p.164) shows that the great preoccupations of 8th century BC Greek society, the sense of social pride and the nostalgia for a past heroic world, were already there two cen-

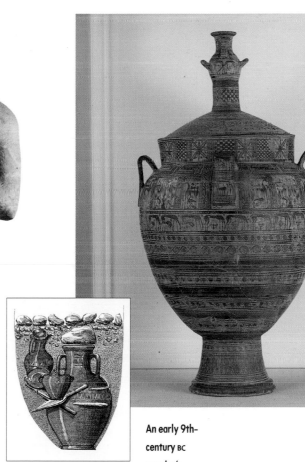

An early 9th-century BC warrior's cremation from the Areopagos, Athens, CENTRE also contained iron weapons, a horse bit and a whetstone. An 8th-century Cycladic vase found in Cyprus ABOVE, (h 1.2 m/3 ft 8 in) shows the sophistication of Late Geometric vase painting. The Ram-bearer from Thasos, a typical votive statue LEFT.

The ancient city of Chios underlies the modern one. We know more about ancient Chiot culture from two sites in the south of the island, both excavated by the British School in 1951-4. At Katofana, a small promontory in the south-west, are the ruins of a temple to Apollo.

turies earlier. The continuity between Late Bronze Age culture and the historic period beginning in the 8th century BC has long been sought in the epic poems of Homer, which were put into writing some time in the second half of the 8th century (see box).

Hesiod (see p.102) in his agricultural precepts, the *Works and Days,* describes the myth of the races: first there was an age of gold, in which people were close to the gods; then followed ages of silver and bronze, an age of heroes and finally the last, contemporary age, of iron.

Stories from the heroic age, which we can take to mean the Mycenaean, were retold by one generation to another. Then, around the middle of the 8th century BC, figured scenes appear on Late Geometric pots. They

are of two main types, funerary processions and heroic scenes. The latter may in some cases represent known stories, but the heroic flavour is what impresses most. In the same period offerings were being made in the entrance of old Mycenaean beehive tombs, and mainland cults to obscure local heroes begin to flourish.

The funerary processions seen on vases are symptomatic of a new social hierarchy. The recently dead are treated on a semi-heroic level, but this very notion implies exclusivity. Burial practices would indicate that, after a social levelling in the Sub-Mycenaean, elite groups emerged during the 10th to 8th centuries BC, which reasserted themselves in different ways during the 7th and 6th centuries BC. This is consistent with written sources.

At Emborio in the south-east of Chios there was an Early Bronze Age and Mycenaean settlement on the coastal peninsula. In the 8th century BC a new site was fortified on a steep inland hill. The town itself straggled down the hillside RIGHT from the west, but was abandoned for the valley before the end of the 7th century.

HOMER'S HEROIC WORLD

Nothing is known about the life and background of Homer, widely acknowledged in antiquity to have been the author of the two epic poems, the *Iliad* and the *Odyssey*. It is difficult even to be precise about when and where he composed the poems or whether they were written down in his lifetime, since they belong to a tradition of oral composition. They were well known in many parts of Greece by the mid-7th century BC and certain linguistic features, as well as many references to locations in western Asia Minor indicate their probable area of origin.

The *Iliad* does not describe the origins or course of the Trojan War (stories dealt with by a slightly later group of poems, the "epic Cycle"), but one incident only, the dispute between the hero Achilles and the leader of the Greek forces, Agamemnon, king of Argos. The *Odyssey* (sometimes attributed to a different author), does not follow on directly, but relates the adventures of Odysseus on his way back home from Troy.

Homer deliberately attempted to recreate a lost Bronze Age world, not only by evoking ancient tales but also by suppressing, though not always consistently, certain contemporary features of society. For example, the use of iron is everywhere substituted by bronze. Some features in the epics are genuinely old, such as the geography of the Peloponnese and Troad; Homer's kingdoms are the palace kingdoms of the Linear B texts in geographical though not in economic terms. However, Homer had no notion of their social complexity, which he replaced by a patriarchal social structure based on the extended household but run as a self-sufficient unit. The heroes are clan leaders who reluctantly acknowledge the overall authority of Agamemnon.

Odysseus tied to the mast of his ship so that he could hear the sirens' song ABOVE. An early 5th-century BC *stamnos* (round-shouldered wine jar) by the Siren Painter (h 0.35 m/13⅘ in). A detail BELOW from the east frieze of the Siphnian Treasury at Delphi, c 525 BC, showing the battle between the Olympian gods and the Giants, an earlier race of deities.

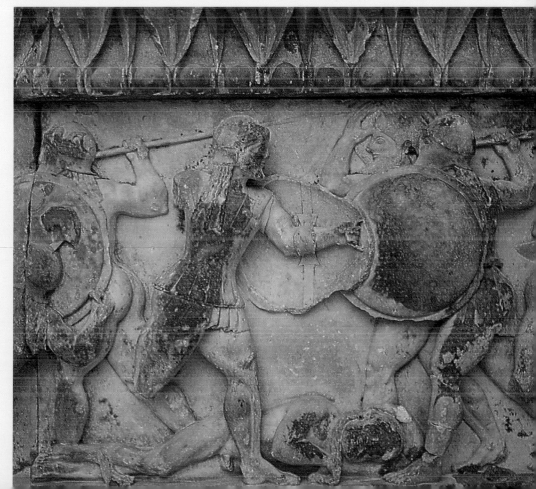

THE GREEK FARMER

At the core of the polis *was the humble peasant farmer. His ideal was to*

avoid drought and famine by growing a variety of crops and to have enough

leisure to take part in the political and cultural life of the city.

An olive press base found inside a private house at Halieis, north-east Peloponnese ABOVE. A collecting bowl for the oil stands in front of the spout.

Contrary to the impression given by the ubiquity of Greek objects around the Mediterranean agriculture, not trade, was the basis of the economy. From the earliest days of the *polis*, the provision of adequate arable land was the over-riding preoccupation of each community. At first, attempts were made to increase arable land at the expense of neighbours; then colonization provided a back-up. Hesiod, the 7th-century gentleman farmer, addressing his greedy and lazy brother Perses in the *Works and Days*, takes us through the seasons with practical advice on how to farm, when to sow and plant, and what farmers' priorities are.

The emphasis on timing is most important. Aristotle's pupil, Theophrastos, repeating an old proverb, "the year brings the crop, not the soil", was reflecting on the huge annual fluctuations in harvests which are still the main challenge for Greek farmers today. Productivity depends on a balance between the soil type, climate and water supply. In the Aegean most of the rain falls between September and May. Excessive drought in the summer months will reduce the harvest, while an excessive downpour can ruin it altogether. A good farmer by Hesiod's book does everything he can to ensure a good harvest. But in the eventuality of a disaster, he must rely on his neighbours (hence the need for good neighbourliness) and, failing that, on outside help from the state. In Classical Athens the food supply had top priority on the city Council's agenda, and in the 4th century laws were passed to prevent speculators trying to profit from fluctuations in corn prices and to oblige merchants to bring their corn to Piraeus.

THE FARMING COMMUNITY

Hesiod's father had been an unsuccessful trader, and the poet's distaste for trading was probably coloured by this experience. However, it also reflected the more general view that trading did not contribute to the common good and might even undermine local produce. Although the aim of each citizen farmer (and of each community) was to be self-sufficient, this was a theoretical ideal rarely achieved in practice. The mutual self-help of villages was seen by Aristotle as the seed from which the *polis* idea grew.

Field survey (see p.52–3) suggests that around each village there was intensive exploitation in the form of gardens and byres. Agricultural writers reflect the wider appreciation of digging to aerate and lighten the soil, turning over grass as green

An Attic Black Figure drinking cup with band ornament on the exterior LEFT, showing a man raising his goad to an ox yoked to a plough. Walking in the opposite direction is a sower.

manure and leaving the ground fallow in alternate years. Land leases on the other hand show no evidence of a desire to intensify productivity, although the prices of leases in different areas show that there was a clear idea of a property's average yield and that some soils were much more productive than others.

We know a little more about Hesiod than we do about Homer because Hesiod was prepared to introduce personal details into his poems. He was evidently the son of an immigrant from Kyme in western Asia Minor who had moved to Askra in Boiotia. Hesiod won a tripod for his recital of a hymn at the funeral games of the aristocratic Amphidamas of Chalkis, Euboia. His preoccupation with the origins of the gods in the short poem, *Theogony,* is reminiscent of Homer and contemporary Near Eastern "wisdom literature", including the Bible. The *Works and Days* is a didactic treatise in verse on farming and seafaring, addressed to his brother Perses, though this may be a literary device.

White-ground cup with a hunting scene RIGHT; along the inner row a deer is pursued by a huntsman and dogs; in the outer row there is a variety of agricultural pests – birds, snakes, foxes and a scorpion.

Interior of an Attic cup with a *tondo* design LEFT, showing a huntsman with his stick and a dog, *c* 550 BC. Hunting was a popular sport, and the huntsman is often seen with a dead fox and hare. The Athenian Xenophon wrote a treatise on the virtues of hunting, dealing with hares, wild boar and deer.

ARISTOCRATIC SOCIETY

The wealthy and well-born men imbued with heroic ideals who had

dominated Greek society in the Mycenaean Age remained the most

influential social group in the poleis, *whatever the form of constitution.*

An Attic Red Figure plate from Chiusi, Etruria, *c*515 BC, showing a Scythian horseman. The plate is inscribed "Miltiades is beautiful" *(Miltiades kalos)*. These so-called "kalos" names appear on Attic pottery in the late 6th and early 5th centuries, and the names are often from distinguished Athenian familes. The Miltiades referred to is unlikely to be the victor of Marathon (too old), but might be a younger kinsman.

Democracy is the best-known of Greek political institutions, but in practice it was rare and short-lived. Most Greek states, for most of their history, were ruled by hereditary elites with, from the 5th century onwards, brief interruptions of democratic government. The hereditary elites were usually composed of a number of clans which claimed an ancient and illustrious ancestry back to the time of the Trojan War or a little later. Some of these heroes had been elevated to royal status. In Chios and its opposite number on the mainland of Asia Minor, Erythrai, there were clans calling themselves "sons of kings" (*Basilidai*) and kings were common elsewhere in the cities of Asia Minor. Monarchy was strong in the Peloponnese before the 7th century BC, and was built into Sparta's constitution. Theseus was the most famous of the nine legendary kings of Athens. The Macedonian kings claimed descent from Herakles; their peers in Epiros from Achilles' son Neoptolemos.

Elsewhere, the ruling elite was made up of the heads of households of the traditional landholders. Where the terrain was better suited to horsebreeding there was a ruling cavalry class, such as the "horsebreeders" at Chalkis on Euboia, close to the Lelantine Plain, and their counterparts at Kolophon and Magnesia in Asia Minor, both situated in broad river valleys. In the latter two, the term was not restricted to aristocrats, but horsebreeding was probably a major source of their elites' wealth.

Thessaly was the great horsebreeding ground in the Greek mainland. It never seems to have formed a coherent political entity in Archaic and Classical times. Powerful families concentrated around four cities, and they monopolized the post of general, known as the *tageia*. Larissa, the

northernmost city, seat of the Aleuad clan, was the most important, together with its southern counterpart, Pharsalos. The dynasty at Krannon was short-lived by comparison. Pherai, just inland of the huge, almost land-locked Gulf of Pagasai, the largest natural harbour in northern Greece, was not significant until the 4th century BC.

TYRANTS AND ARISTOCRATS

In the 8th century, aristocratic families still led the community in secular and religious affairs, but their monopoly of authority was increasingly being challenged. Aristotle tells us that tyrants (see box) were usually drawn from the people to serve as their protectors against injustice. However, he goes on to say that in

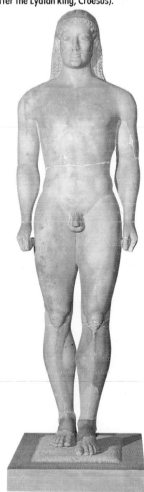

Marble *kore* from the akropolis LEFT, *c*520–510 BC. It was dedicated by a wealthy lady, but possibly made by a Chian sculptor. Much original colour is preserved. Her male equivalent BELOW from Anavysos, Attica, *c*530 BC commemorates Kroisos (named after the Lydian king, Croesus).

Bronze Apollo from Piraeus harbour, c530-20 BC (h 1.92 m/6 ft 2 in), one of the earliest surviving hollow-cast bronze statues and still at an experimental phase of the technique. He originally held a bow in the left hand and a *phiale,* or libation bowl, in the right.

An Attic Black Figure amphora c500 BC. From 566/5 BC onwards, such jars, filled with oil from the sacred olives of Athena, were awarded as prizes for athletic events in the quadrennial Great Panathenaic Games. They have been found at some unlikely places for competitors to have come from – North Africa, Etruria and South Russia.

earlier days tyrants were aristocratic outsiders who exploited the contemporary tendency to elect magistrates for long tenures and then extended or abused these official positions to establish personal rule contrary to law.

ARISTOCRATIC CLANS AND THE *POLIS*

Although the aristocratic clans continued to prosper, the very concept of the *poleis* was at odds with their lifestyle and priorities. Where the *polis* expected community loyalty, the elite preferred personal contacts with their peers in other cities and abroad.

The most detailed evidence for individual noble families comes from Athens. The defence of Hellas against Persia (490-479 BC) united noble cavalryman, hoplite farmer and later, working-class power through the experience of war. Miltiades of the Philaid clan, who had ruled over the native Thracians and Greek colonists of the Chersonese peninsula as despot for some 28 years, was recalled to Athens and became one of the victorious generals at the battle of Marathon in 490. His son Kimon was one of the last *grands seigneurs*, who dispensed cash and opened his estates to the public but vigorously opposed democratic reforms. He was later prosecuted by Xanthippos the Alkmaionid, father of the celebrated democratic politician, Perikles.

ARISTOCRATIC FAMILIES

Two famous Athenian families were particularly prominent in the 6th and 5th centuries BC.

The Philaids traced their ancestry back to Philaios, a son of the hero Ajax. The elder Miltiades was invited by a Thracian tribe to rule the Chersonese peninsula in the 540s. He was succeeded by his half-brother's sons, Stesagoras and Miltiades.

The Alkmaionids were named after Alkmaion, an Olympic victor of 592 BC. It was one of the most famous in Athens and included the great political reformer of the late 6th century BC Kleisthenes, as well as Perikles. The family was proud of its opposition to the Athenian tyrant, Peisistratos; others were less convinced.

The evidence from Athens during the 5th century BC also shows the gradual erosion of aristocratic power. The holding of the high office of archon, initially restricted to aristocrats, was opened to all citizens in 487 BC. Ostracism, a vote to send a leading citizen – most likely to be well born – into exile, was introduced to curb ambitious politicians.

After the death of Perikles in 429 BC, the frequency of prominent politicians from a non-aristocratic background increased. After the *coup d'état* in 403 by the Thirty tyrants, who hated the radical democracy and felt excluded from their birthright, the old nobles fell under suspicion. In the 4th century, the increasingly professional character of political life made it less attractive, though wealthy men and women continued to play an active role as benefactors of public works.

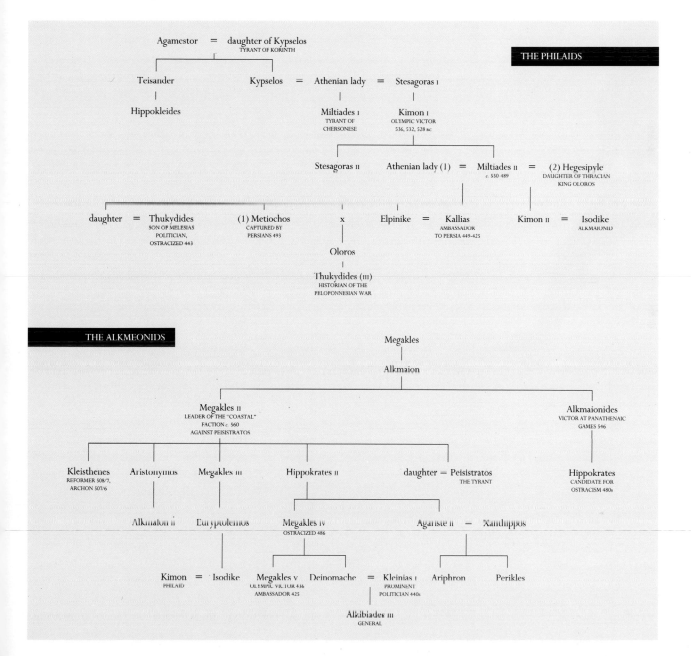

THE CULT OF THE BODY

The lifestyle of the Greek aristocrat has been vividly preserved in the art and literature of the Archaic Age. The preoccupations of these leaders of society shaped the civilization of the Classical world.

Bronze statuette in Spartan style of a running girl, *c* 540 BC. Figures like this were often used to decorate large bronze wine-mixing bowls and jars. On the whole, there is a clear distinction in Greek art between athletic men and soft-skinned women. However, some bronze statuettes, not just from the Spartan sphere but from Samos and elsewhere, show that athletic women were not excluded.

The word "Aristocracy" means the rule of the best. A variety of Greek terms were used to denote this perceived social group – *gennaioi, esthloi, kaloi k'agathoi, eupatridai* – all of which have connotations of excellence and good birth. Even Aristotle, coolly analyzing the requirements for high office, was unable to get away from the assumption that birth, wealth and virtue are all linked. This provides a clue to the revival of monarchic rule in the 4th century BC, and of the continuing magnetism of the ethos of excellence. The greatest exponent of this ethos was the 5th-century poet, Pindar, and when Alexander the Great burned down the city of Thebes in 335 BC, Pindar's house was the only building spared.

In practice there were many aristocrats who did not live up to this reputation, and for whom the competing ambitions of social distinction, meritorious achievements and riches were often contradictory. The 6th-century poet Xenophanes berated his fellow Kolophonian stud farmers for their vapidity.

While they yet stood free from the hated yoke of the tyrant, off to the council they went, proud in their purple attire. They were tricked out in useless finery picked up from their Lydian neighbours, number-ing, all in all, just one thousand men, pleased with themselves and peacock proud of elaborate hair styles, every inch of their skin wet with the costliest scent.

ATHLETIC CONTESTS

The same poet was equally critical about the wider social values of athletic competitions:

Nor does (the city) have much joy out of a man of this sort. Though he may win great fame in many Olympian contests, never a penny does he bring into the coffers of state.

Xenophanes was not criticizing competition so much as kudos. Athletics and particularly horsemanship, feasting and drinking remained the preoccupations of the nobility. Athletic contests, originally held at the funeral games of the nobility, were especially popular in the Peloponnese. The Spartans treated athletics as a standard element of their military training. The great panhellenic festival at Olympia, traditionally founded in 776 BC, was followed 200 years later by the introduction of three more, at Delphi (586), and two near the Isthmus of Korinth, at Isthmia (580) and Nemea (573). Whereas the athletic contests were open to all, horse-racing excluded all but the very rich. The four-horse chariot race was the most pre-

Banqueting scene from the Tomb of the Diver, Paestum, *c*480 BC LEFT. Two men share the same couch on the right and one of them holds a lyre. Those on the left-hand couches are holding up drinking cups for a game called *kottabos*.

stigious of all. Awards at the main festivals were symbolic crowns of olive, laurel, celery or pine, but victors usually received due recognition in their home towns, at public expense.

THE NOBILITY AND FASHION

Many of the surviving memorials set up by private individuals, whether dedications or grave monuments, belong to nobles (although there are interesting exceptions). Where the nobility led, others followed. What was the top fashion for society ladies immortalized in marble reappears as the excessively long train of a nymph on a Red Figure cup. Poetry, whether informal, such as might be sung at private drinking parties, or formal, for public festivals, was couched in the terms of contemporary upper class lifestyles. The atmosphere of aristocratic drinking parties (*symposia*), so aptly conveyed in the painted cups of the late 6th and early 5th century, soon percolated down to ordinary Athenians, who built specially-designed dining-rooms for this purpose.

Marble slab (*stele*) from Athens LEFT, carved in low relief, showing an athlete holding a *strigil* (a bronze scraper). Beside him stands a boy ready with a bottle of oil for the young man to rub on, and a towel.

Attic Black Figure band cup ABOVE, *c*540 BC, from Corinth with a two-horse racing chariot. Horse-racing, then as now, had a mystique of its own and conferred tremendous prestige on the winner (the owner, that is, not the charioteer).

THE TYRANTS

Rule by a single individual was an anomaly in the ancient Greek world, even if many poleis *experienced it occasionally. But in the Greek colonies of Italy and Sicily, this was a common form of government.*

Bronze charioteer from Delphi dedicated by Polyzalos, the younger brother of the tyrants Gelon and Hieron, in honour of a chariot victory either in 478 or 474 BC. Fragments of the chariot, the horses' legs and the inscribed base have been recovered (h 1.8 m/5 ft 9 in).

Around the turn of the 6th century BC a tyrant, Hippokrates, with a large mercenary force, brought a host of cities along the east coast of Sicily under one ruler for the first time, and made Syracuse his base. This was the kingdom later appropriated and extended by Gelon, an aristocrat from Gela, and his brother, Hieron. Gelon allied himself with another despotic ruler, Theron of Akragas (Agrigento), cemented by marriage. It was Theron's territorial expansion towards Himera which brought down a Carthaginian invasion. The petty ruler of Himera, Terillos, united with his son-in-law Anaxilas of Rhegion, and together they invited in the Carthaginians.

The subsequent victories of Gelon at Himera (480 BC) and Hieron in the Bay of Naples (474 BC) gave them enormous prestige in the Greek world, while their ambitious building programmes and fine silver coinage were the envied models of other Greek states. More temples were built at Akragas during the 5th century than in any other Mediterranean city apart from Athens. The Sicilian historian of the 1st century BC, Diodoros, explains that the wealth of Akragas was derived from Carthaginian tribute paid after the battle of Himera. Pindar celebrated the equestrian victories of

Anaxilas, Gelon and Hieron in some of his finest poems. In his first Olympian Ode he honoured Hieron:

> Water is the best thing of all, and gold/shines like a flaming fire at night./More than all a great man's wealth. But if, my heart, you would speak/Of prizes won in the Games,/Look no more for another bright star/By day in the empty sky....In Sicily's rich sheep-pasture/He gathers the buds of all perfections./And his splendour shines in the festal music,/Like our own merry songs/When we gather often around that table of friends.

TYRANTS

The Greek word "tyrannos" originally meant "ruler". However, for many writers of the 5th and 4th centuries BC, the word had already acquired negative connotations, although Aristotle, in the *Politics*, writes seriously about the methods which a would-be tyrant might use to maintain power. Among the most notorious tyrants of the Greek world was a string of Sicilian despots from Phalaris, in the 6th century, who roasted victims in a brazen ox, to Dionysios I (430-367 BC) and Agathokles (361 289 BC), of Syracuse, both ruthless towards all parties in the pursuit of power.

The social and economic problems which beset many Greek *poleis* between c.650 and c.550 BC provided the opportunity for individuals to establish personal rule by acting as mediators between well-to-do citizens and the disgruntled, disenfranchised masses. Some mediators refrained from exploiting their unusual situation, such as Pittakos of Mytilene, Lesbos (c.650-570 BC) and Solon of Athens (c.640-560+ BC), two of the "Seven Sages" of archaic tradition, all of whom were associated with the drafting or interpretation of law codes. Some tyrants who overrode the rule of law, such as Kypselos of Korinth (c.600 BC) and Peisistratos of Athens (c.600-528/7 BC), nevertheless enjoyed a fairly positive reputation. Tyrants continued to emerge in various *poleis* up to the Roman occupation of Greece and their rule is often difficult to distinguish from a hereditary kingship.

Tyrants were expansionist; colonization abroad masked social tensions at home. Flamboyant diplomacy and public works were more to their taste than social practice, whatever sympathy they are reputed to have had for the masses. They did not attempt to root out the causes of injustice the division between landowners who were now citizens and the landless who were not.

GREEK SOLDIERS

Another characteristic feature of the **polis** *was the phalanx of heavily-armed hoplites. On the battlefield their body armour and concerted tactics proved superior to the lighter-clad and often less disciplined infantrymen.*

Bronze statuette of a hoplite soldier from the sanctuary of Zeus at Dodona, north-west Greece, 6th century BC. He wears a Korinthian helmet, a breastplate shaped to conform more or less to anatomical forms over a short tunic, plus leg guards (greaves).

During the 7th century BC the Greeks developed a suit of armour and a specialized mode of fighting. This combination made Greek soldiers some of the finest troops in the Mediterranean world for the next 400 years. Many soldiers were prepared to travel long distances in search of employment.

On the left leg of one of the colossal statues of Rameses II at Abu Simbel in Nubia (southern Egypt) is a Greek inscription:

> When king Psammetichos came to Elephantine (the First Nile Cataract), those who sailed with Psammetichos son of Theokles wrote this; and they ventured above Kerkis as far as the river allowed; Potasimto commanded those of foreign speech and Amasis the Egyptians; and Archon the son of Amoibichos wrote this and Peleqos the son of Eudamos.

We have here not merely testimony of Greek mercenaries in Upper Egypt in 593/2 BC, but evidence of second-generation Greco-Egyptians. Greek mercenaries were fighting in the Near East in the 7th century. A Greek bronze shield and greave (leg guard) dating from this period were found at Carchemish. Around the turn of the 7th century Antimenidas, the brother of the Lesbian poet Alkaios, was fighting for the Babylonians. These were the forerunners of the mercenary armies used by the Persian kings in the 4th century BC (perhaps 30,000 of whom confronted Alexander the Great at the battle of Issos in 333 BC).

HOPLITES

A combination of features made the Greek hoplites (heavy-armed infantrymen drawn from the ranks of citizen farmers) formidable. The standard equipment included a light shield with off-set rim held by an elbow-band and handgrip, a thick bronze breastplate, a bronze helmet, thrusting spear and sword. This equipment was hot, unwieldy and vulnerable against light troops or surprise attack. Hoplite tactics could only be applied on flat terrain, which is hard to come by in Greece. Battle was formal, with mutually accepted rules of engagement. Success lay in discipline – the whole battle line (phalanx) moved ideally as one man, sweeping all before it. The aim was to force the enemy off the battlefield.

BODYGUARDS

A connection has sometimes been made between the advent of hoplite warfare during the 7th century BC and the rise of tyrannies more or less in the same period. In reality the two were

probably connected, but not directly. Aristotle talks about the necessity of bodyguards in a tyranny, but he also emphasizes that these were usually outsiders whose sentiments would not be subverted by the community; for example, the Athenian tyrant Peisistratos had a Thracian bodyguard.

CITIZEN SOLDIERS

The known facts, however, do not support subversions backed by new armies of disgruntled middle-class farmers. Social changes were more complex. Much more probably the development of hoplite armies was the result of a compromise between the wealthier aristocratic clans, heirs to the tradition of cavalry or single combat backed by personal retainers, and a growing class of well-to-do farmers who could afford the expense of full armour.

The division which arose was between these wealthier groups in society who were in a position to protect their rights, and its poorer, dispossessed members. Here perhaps lie the origins of the social tension so characteristic of the 7th century BC and the fierce debate over land rights. This same division continued into the better documented Classical period, when we know that the hoplite was considered to epitomize the citizen soldier. Those who could not afford hoplite gear became the most vulnerable, and only the radical Athenian democracy of the mid-5th century finally eliminated the distinction.

Red Figure Attic *lekythos* (oil flask) *c*470 BC, by the Oinokles Painter (h 0.43 m/17 in) ABOVE. A warrior, in a closer fitting cuirass than the sort worn 100 years earlier, holds his sword ready to cut off a lock of hair, perhaps in honour of a dead comrade. Beside him stand his shield and a helmet with decorated cheekpieces. A band cup *c*550 BC signed by the potter and painter Archikles and Glauketes gives an idea of the massed fighting characteristic of hoplite warfare LEFT.

TRADERS AND TRAVELLERS

The ancient Greeks were eager to report their experiences in far-flung places.

In this way, exploration led to the development of history and geography as

systematic subjects.

A diving balloon used to take artefacts from the sea-bed to a decompression chamber. A camera suspended from a balloon can photograph marine remains in shallow water which may not be visible to the diver.

Whereas Homer's *Iliad* is pre-occupied with heroic morality, the Odyssey revels in the fantasy of exploration – the 8th century BC's equivalent of science fiction. The Greeks were interested in new land; the unpredictable results of farming in Greece meant that flexibility was always an advantage. Good relations with native communities like the Skythians, the Thracians, and the kings of Egypt and Cyprus, were therefore a prerequisite. But adventure, both for its own sake and as a source of new resources, was extremely attractive to seafarers.

Ironstone, silver, copper and gold were the major attractions for Greeks in the south-eastern Black Sea region. Ivory tusks from Al Mina probably found their way to Samos, Ephesos, Athens and other parts of the Greek mainland, where finely carved figurines were made, often influenced by Syro-Phoenician fashions. Phoenician and Cypriot metalware has been found at the major Greek sanctuaries, Crete and the Athenian Akropolis. The abstract Geometric patterns on pottery, jewellery and sheet metal were replaced, from the late 8th century BC onwards, by winged monsters, shaggy lions, grazing deer and that peculiar mish-mash of Greek and Oriental, the gorgon. Naked god-desses with wig-like hair also entered the repertory and became a major formative influence on Greek art.

The earliest named adventurers are mentioned by the historian Herodotos, writing in the 5th century. He refers to Kolaios, a Samian merchant, blown off course on his way to Egypt (*c.*638 BC) who, having first baled out the initial colonists of Cyrene with extra food supplies, then got even further off course and passed through the Pillars of Herakles (Straits of Gibraltar), where he found Tartessos, the Phoenician colony and base for the Atlantic tin trade, in the bay of Cadiz. One-tenth of the proceeds was used to make a bronze bowl dedicated at the temple of Hera. It had griffins on the rim, and was supported by three kneeling figures, the whole said to be about 4m (13ft) high.

KNOWLEDGE FROM WRECKS

Concrete evidence of seafaring is now provided in a spectacular series of excavated shipwrecks. Studies of this kind require a considerable amount of technological input, not least because many wrecks are buried 45m (150ft) under water. Modern apparatus, for both the documentation and retrieval of data, includes cables and lifting balloons, air hoses for cleaning and lifting debris, underwater and low-level balloon photography. The oldest known wreck in Greek waters (*c.* 1350 BC), which sank off Ulu Burun, southern Turkey, was carrying an exotic variety of goods from Africa and the Near East. The standard sailing route from the Levant hugged the coast of Turkey between Cyprus and Rhodes.

Many more wrecks are now known from the period between the 6th and 1st centuries BC. One excavated in 1982-6 off Giglio, Tuscany, was of pinewood and provisionally reconstructed as a fore-and-aft rigger (this design has not previously been documented before the 2nd century BC). It was carrying copper and lead ingots, a large store of *amphorae* (2-handled jugs, Korinthian, Lakonian, east Greek, Punic and Etruscan) but also fine pottery, both Greek and Etruscan. Also on board there were the sorts of things you would expect the crew to have – clay lamps, fishing weights, a wooden plate, coins, a writing tablet, and wooden shipbuilding tools including, uniquely, calipers. Others might be speculative sale items – pieces of amber, fragments of inlaid furniture, a fine bronze Korinthian helmet (also found on the new 6th-century ship

from Fosso di Kamarina). A set of musicians' pipes probably belonged to one of the crew members.

The excavators think that this was an Etruscan ship. It can be compared with two Greek vessels, one of which sank off Kyrenia, Cyprus, probably in the early 3rd century BC, the other off Porticello, north-east of Reggio di Calabria around the turn of the 5th or early 4th century BC. Both were constructed in a similar way, the timbers fixed with mortise and tenon joints, the frames with copper nails. The outer side of the hull was sheathed with lead strips. The Kyrenia ship carried a large cargo of *amphorae* (Rhodian, Samian and others), millstones from the Dodecanese together with 10,000 almonds, hazelnuts, pistachios, olives, figs, grapes, garlic and sprigs of dried herbs. The Porticello vessel was probably very small 16-17m (52-56 ft) in length, with a capacity of about 30 tons. It too contained a cargo of *amphorae* (at least 100 were raised illicitly) from Carthage, western Greece, Mende and Byzantion, fishing weights, lead and silver ingots, and some fine Attic pottery, together with fragments of three life-size bronze statues.

Limestone statuette of a god holding a lion, from Naukratis, Egypt, *c* 550 BC. The Greek craftsman was influenced by Egyptian and other Near Eastern prototypes, both in the style of the carving and in the peculiar pose of the lion.

Attic plate by Lydos, *c* 560/50 BC, decorated with a Gorgon's head RIGHT. The Gorgon was originally an Oriental monster; early versions have horns and lion-like features. In the 6th century the Gorgon was made to look more like a woman.

THE GREEK COLONIES

It is difficult to understand the reason behind the extraordinary expansion of

Greek settlements from c. 700 onwards. The periodic discrepancies between

population size and resources can only have been one factor among many.

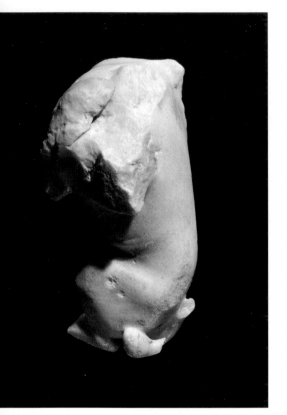

Marble sphinx from Al Mina, Syria, *c*470 BC (h 0.175 m/7 in). The head, the sickle-shaped wings and feet are missing. Crouching sphinxes were often used to crown funerary and other monuments in the 6th and early 5th centuries BC. This tiny sculpture must have had some decorative use.

From the middle of the 8th century to the close of the 6th BC, Greek cities sent out formal colonies, that is, a selected group of individuals led by a delegated founder, accompanied by magistrates responsible for the allocation of land, and priests for the organization of cults derived from the *metropolis*. Foundations like this were known as *apoikiai*, literally homes from home. One of the best known cases is Cyrene, founded from the island of Thera soon after 650 BC by an aristocrat, Battos (later king), following an instruction from the Delphic Oracle.

Two points are striking. One is the compulsion under which the allotted candidates were sent – never to return. The second is the nature of the reception they were given. For example, a temporary settlement was made on an offshore island, Plateia. The colonists then moved to the mainland but after six years were persuaded by the native Libyans to move to a less vulnerable location further inland. The cooperation of the Libyans with the people of Cyrene is an important reminder that not all colonies were met with hostility.

Hunger was one obvious motive for emigration, but the process as a whole was far from simple. The distribution of colonies in the west corresponds with the scope of Mycenaean exploration (not considered a colonizing phenomenon). Actual migration slowed down to a trickle in the 5th and 4th centuries BC, before the new rush following Alexander the Great's eastern conquests. The distant inland provinces of Asia were not popular, however, and a very serious revolt occurred among the first colonists there after Alexander's death. Most Greeks wanted a landscape and climate that was familiar – preferably a coastal site with a good harbour.

WHEN IS A COLONY NOT A COLONY?

At sites where Greek pottery has been found, it is not always possible to tell whether it was a Greek settlement, or whether Greek pottery was used by the local people. The hinterland of southern Italy, Sicily and the Black Sea shores have a penumbra of native sites which, from the 7th and 6th centuries, readily acquired Greek painted pottery and copied it in a local idiom. Some of these sites contain material from the 5th century BC which is almost wholly Greek. Had Greeks taken over? Had the local culture simply become more homogeneous?

At Mina, at the mouth of the river Orontes, was probably the most important trading centre in Syria before it was outfaced by Seleukeia, the

Late 8th-century BC cup *(skyphos)* LEFT, found at Al Mina (h 0.8 m/ 31½ in). In shape and use of the multiple brush it resembles mainland products. The clay and interior circles are of local or Cypriot origin. A jug from Aigina BELOW *c*700-650 BC shows the reverse movement of Oriental motifs (the griffin head, "Tree of Life").

harbour of Antioch. The excavated sector includes warehouses, which from their earliest stages (9th-late-8th century BC) contained Greek pottery, mainly Euboian, on a noticeable scale. Were these imported by native merchants or are we dealing here with resident Greeks along with Cypriots? After a major break some time before 700 BC, the pattern changes. During the 7th century some Euboian wares continued to appear, but most of the fine pottery was from eastern Greece. (There was also a scatter of Greek pottery at some inland sites). After the Persian take over in the 530s BC Greek trade livens up again. Are we dealing with a Greek enclave in a Syrian town, or just a very popular line of tableware?

An Athenian enclave has been postulated at Pichvnari, a substantial, though as yet unexcavated native site on the south-west coast of Georgia, USSR. Archaeologists searching for the colony of Phasis, in the legendary land of the golden fleece, Kolchis, have found a network of native sites. Some of these have elite native burials full of rich, imported plate and jewellery. At Pichvnari about half the excavated burials do not differ from Greek ones, the other half are dubbed "hellenized", that is, they contain both Greek and native material.

PIONEERS IN EXPLORATION

The same men who speculated about the origins of the Earth were interested

in its geography and climate. Among the earliest Greek scientists were the

first map-makers and professional travellers.

This is how we might imagine the geographer Hekataios' map of the known world *c* 500 BC, ABOVE. Note the surrounding ocean, the central position of the Mediterranean and the symmetrical location of rivers. The polarities reappear on Herodotos' map BELOW, with many new factual details.

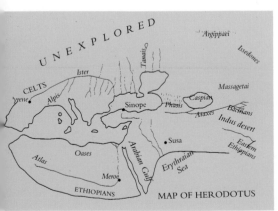

MAP OF HERODOTUS

The Phoenician syllabary of the 9th century BC was adopted by Greeks as the basis of a script which first came into wider use during the 8th century. The first Greek philosophers of the 7th century had a lot of catching up to do in the spheres of astronomy and astrology, which had been highly developed by the Chaldeans (Babylonians), and in geometry and arithmetic, at which the Egyptians excelled. The Egyptians knew Pythagoras' theorem before Pythagoras.

ASTRONOMERS AND MATHEMATICIANS

The first Greek thinkers were likewise practical men and were learning fast. Thales of Miletos predicted to within a year a total eclipse of the sun in 585 BC. He made contributions to navigation and adjusted the local calendar. Annoyed at being thought too academic, he bought up an option on all the olive presses on Lesbos at a time when observations told him there would be a bumper harvest.

For Thales and his successors there was no distinction between theory and practice. Empedokles used a wineskin to demonstrate that air has substance, and a water clock to show atmospheric pressure. The greatest mathematician of antiquity, Archimedes of Syracuse (*c.* 287-212 BC), not only wrote a series of treatises on mechanical and geometrical problems but he was also the inventor of a screw for raising water, and many other spectacular machines which were used to defend Syracuse against the Romans. For these men, however, science was not just a matter of observation.

SPECULATIVE THOUGHT

Greek speculative thought took two major directions; the first was towards cosmology. Thales was the first to move away from a mythological basis for the origin of the world. He thought that everything must ultimately derive from water. Anaximander (611-546 BC) moved beyond this and preferring a balance of opposites to a single original substance, envisaged a genesis of humans from fish. The logical outcome of this trend was the atomic principle formulated by Parmenides and Demokritos.

MAP-MAKING AND GEOGRAPHY

Map-making was another Milesian speciality. Anaximander made the first map of the known world, probably on a bronze tablet (like that used by the tyrant Aristagoras of Miletos in 499/8 BC when lobbying for support against the Persians). The geographer Hekataios (another Milesian) was the first man to attempt a descriptive geography of Europe and Asia, but it was nothing like the *Histories* of his successor, Herodotos.

THE FATHER OF HISTORY

The historian Herodotos, son of Lyxes, was born in the cosmopolitan city of Halikarnassos in south-western Asia Minor. He left the city for Samos some time before the mid-5th century, when a relative of his was assassinated.

Halikarnassos soon afterwards became a member of the Delian Confederacy led by Athens, but Herodotos spent most of the following decades travelling around the eastern Mediterranean. He watched and listened, asked and wondered, about the source of the Nile, the shape of continents and the customs of different peoples.

Herodotos was much preoccupied with the events immediately preceding his birth, with who did what in the Great War against the Persians (490-479 BC). In the process he uncovered a great deal about the differences between Europe and Asia, Greeks and non-Greeks.

In the *Histories*, he set out to show the achievements of other nations as well as his own, as he felt this would elucidate the origins of the conflict between Greeks and Persians. Although he discerned a moral divide between on one side the overweening ambition of the Persian kings (and Xerxes in particular), and Greek valour and virtue on the other, his enquiries into customs and history are uncoloured by any of the partisanship of many of his successors. The first great narrative historian was a worthy model.

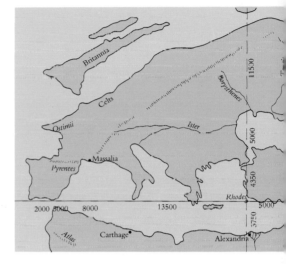

The first map with any pretensions to accuracy (using triangulation and measurements in stades) was that of Eratosthenes (c275-194 BC). The measurements were based on two lines, a north-south one running through Meroe, Alexandria and intersecting the west-east line at Rhodes. The eastern side of the map extended as far as the River Ganges.

An archer in Scythian dress LEFT. Early Attic Red Figure plate by Epiktetos, c520-510 BC. The Scythians represent the northernmost peoples with whom the Greeks had any contact and were thought to express the reserve and agility appropriate for a northern climate.

THE PERSIAN WARS

The armed struggle between the Greek poleis *and the Persian Empire made a deep impact on Greek society. The unexpected Greek success was immortalized in art and literature, gaining legendary status.*

Apollo in the centre of the west pediment of the temple of Zeus at Olympia as the spirit of reason laying his authority over the unreason of drunken centaurs ABOVE. In the decades after the Persian Wars reason became closely associated with the Greek way of life in the minds of intellectual Greeks. A Greek hoplite RIGHT overcoming a Persian infantryman on a Red Figure plate, *c*475 BC.

The confrontation between the mainland Greeks and the Persians between 490 and 479 BC left an indelible mark on Greek consciousness. It came to represent the ultimate conflict between Greeks and barbarians, freedom against slavery, discipline over lassitude, frugality over excess. It crystallized a sense of moral superiority over non-Greeks in general based on intelligence, rationalism and the virtues of *polis* citizenship. Simply stated, the equipment, discipline and tactics of Greek armies at Marathon in 490 BC and Plataia in 479 BC defeated the seasoned and hitherto extremely successful troops of the "King of Kings", who was backed by the enormous resources of a vast empire stretching from the Indus to the Black Sea. In the Bay of Salamis in 480 BC, 380 Greek ships, 200 of which

were Athenian with significant contingents from Aigina and Korinth, defeated some 1200 Persian vessels – faster, larger and higher Phoenician ships backed up by Ionian Greeks. This was the first significant Greek international naval victory.

THE PERSIAN TAKEOVER IN ASIA MINOR

In the 8th and 7th centuries, the distinction between Greeks and barbarians was vague. From the 7th century onwards Greek *poleis* in Asia Minor came under Lydian and then Persian control. First they were besieged, then made to pay tribute money. This was the background of Xenophanes' bitter remarks about the Kolophonians. But Greeks, natives and immigrant administrators had managed to co-exist. The art and poetry of Ionia and the offshore islands Lesbos and Samos reflect the conflicting emotions of life on the fringes of a wealthier, more sophisticated society. The Greek cult of Artemis at Ephesos was fused with a local one in which natives were also important.

GREEK "MORAL SUPERIORITY"

Herodotos, who attempted to chart the relationship between Greeks and Orientals for well over 100 years before the main conflict, was himself a

native of Halikarnassos, and went to a good deal of trouble to find out the customs and history of other nations. Though generally appreciative of the cultural heritage of the Near Eastern civilizations, he eventually felt obliged, in the light of events to see the Persian assault as arrogance and the Greek victory as the reward of virtue. The exiled Spartan king Demaratos is made to say to the Persian King Xerxes, during the advance along the north Aegean coast in 480:

> So it is with the Spartans; fighting singly, they are as good as any, but fighting together they are the best soldiers in the world. They are free – yes – but not entirely free; for they have a master, and that master is Law, which they fear much more than your subjects fear you.

Similar sentiments were expressed in Aischylos' tragedy, *The Persians*, staged in 472 BC, and he and his fellow dramatists continued to explore the theme of Greek virtue and foreign barbarity (and, during the Peloponnesian War, Greeks copying alien barbarity). At a time when the Sophists (professional teachers and knowledge experts) were making their mark in Athens, intelligence was also becoming synonymous with intelligibility, articulate (Greek) speech with articulate thought. The supreme expression of Greek superiority is Aristotle's verdict in the *Politics* that:

> Hunting ought to be practised – not only against wild animals, but also against human beings who are intended by nature to be ruled by others and refuse to obey that intention – because war of this order is naturally just.

SPARTA

Discipline, self-denial and loyalty were the qualities associated in the Greek imagination with the militaristic polis *of Sparta. These were epitomized by their glorious self-sacrifice at Thermopylae.*

"Leonidas", a fragmentary marble sculpture from the Akropolis of Sparta. It was perhaps part of a commemorative group in honour of the 300 Spartans (out of a total of 4,000 dead on the Greek side, many of them Helots) who, together with their king, Leonidas, fell in defence of the Pass at Thermopylae in 480 BC (h 0.78 m/30¾ in without crest).

The Spartans enjoyed an outstanding reputation in antiquity for personal morality, frugality, hardihood and courage. This has been dubbed the "Spartan mirage" because the idea of Sparta was such a powerful one among contemporary Greeks, while evidence of it is hard to come by. They produced no historians; they were neurotically secretive; they were so frightened of rebellion that they allowed youths or magistrates to kill Helots indiscriminately. But what outsiders admired was their professionalism, direct speech and matchless discipline.

EARLY SPARTA

The earliest material evidence of Spartan power comes from two sanctuaries close to the city itself. The first is that of Artemis Orthia, where rich and extremely varied dedications were made from the late 8th century onwards, some undoubtedly booty from the First Messenian war. This lengthy affair was fought some time in the last quarter of the century. The second is the Menelaion, or sanctuary of Menelaos and Helen, founded at about the same time as the dedications begin at Orthia. Aristocratic Spartan competitors had also been active from the earliest days of the festival at Olympia.

The only contemporary written sources for early Sparta are the 7th-century poems of Tyrtaios (uplifting exhortations to war) and Alkman (hymns and festival pieces). Tyrtaios fought in the Second Messenian War in the mid-7th century, which confirmed Spartan control over the whole of the southern Peloponnese for somewhat less than 300 years.

THE SPARTAN WAY OF LIFE

Both Plutarch and one of his chief sources, the Athenian Xenophon, attributed almost everything that made up the Spartan way of life to a legendary figure, Lykourgos, despite the fact that different stages in its development are detectable (though not necessarily dateable). The ancient constitution regularized a council of 30, known as the *Gerousia* (council of men over 60), which included the two kings (one from each of the royal dynasties) and was responsible for the preparation of business, and an assembly of Spartan citizens who were entitled to support or reject a proposal. However, room was left for the Gerousia to override what was deemed a "crooked" decision. Later, five "Ephors" were introduced, magistrates with executive, judicial and disciplinary powers who effectively ran the state.

The ancient city of Sparta consisted of four central villages around a low akropolis on the southern bank of the River Eurotas, in the centre of a small plain, 5 km (3 miles) wide. At its western edge is Mt Taygetos LEFT.

An attractive white-ground cup made in Lakonia (by non-Spartans) c 575–525 BC ABOVE). A base in blue-grey marble BELOW, perhaps a votive relief from the shrine of Menelaos south-east of Sparta, showing a man and woman on either side (Menelaos and Helen?) c 575–50 BC.

The assembly of Spartan citizens or "Equals" constituted a professional military elite. At Sparta the family was completely subordinated to the *agoge*, the system of military training. Numerous "rites of passage", which became obliterated elsewhere, survived in this regime. At the age of seven a Spartan boy was put into the first-year group of the *agoge*, which he would follow until retirement age. Each year-group went through various stages of training, which involved tests of ingenuity and endurance as well as athletics and singing. By the age of 20 a youth became a full citizen but had to go through all kinds of subterfuges in order to marry, and even then did not live with his wife and family before the age of 30. Each citizen owned a piece of land farmed by the state slaves, the Helots, and was obliged to pay contributions to the communal messes. If he failed to do so he could be demoted to sub-citizenship. The seriousness of such demotions is reflected in a major conspiracy c. 397 BC, planned by ex-citizens in league with Helots and *Perioikoi* (inhabitants of Lakonia who were non-Spartans).

Between c. 650 BC and the end of the 6th century the Spartans became masters of the entire Peloponnese. Argos, Arkadia, Sikyon, Pisa and some other states within and without the Peloponnese had supported the Messenians against Sparta. At first, Spartans behaved aggressively towards them, but gradually they evolved a more conciliatory approach to their neighbours which eventually turned into a bilateral alliance. The last tyrant at Korinth was eliminated c. 582 BC. They supported the Elians in their dispute with Pisa over control of the sanctuary at Olympia c. 570 BC. Tegea was won over to an alliance by a mixture of brinkmanship and war around 550 BC. Argos, hitherto the most formidable opponent, was defeated in the famous "Battle of the Champions" c. 545 BC. On these foundations emerged the Peloponnesian alliance led by Sparta.

INTERNATIONAL APPEAL

Sparta's international reputation at this time was unequalled. The Lydian king Croesus appealed to her for help against the Persians. Subsequent appeals came from the Samians (c. 525 BC and 518 BC), from some Scythian tribes, and from Ionian leaders preparing an uprising against Persia in 499 BC. But the Spartans refused to be drawn into overseas commitments — rightly as it turned out, for Sparta's victory in the Peloponnesian War exposed the inherent weaknesses of her repressive regime.

ATHENS

The bright beacon of high Athenian culture continues to shed its light. The virtues of intellectual curiosity, tolerance and political liberty prized so much by ancient Athenians still remain the touchstones of Western civilization.

The temple of Athena Nike (of Victory) on the south-western corner of the Akropolis. An altar to the goddess in this role was dedicated on this spot in 566 BC, on top of a Mycenaean bastion. A small sanctuary was built during the Persian Wars and a marble temple was commissioned *c*447 BC. A surviving inscription from the Akropolis tells us that the architect was Kallikrates, who collaborated with Iktinos on the Parthenon. We know from Aristophanes' play *Lysistrata* (411 BC) that the priestess was called Myrrhine; her epitaph and a marble vase have been preserved in her name.

The Athenians are better known than any other Greek *polis*, not only because they were among the most powerful and successful cities, nor even because of their undoubted artistic achievements, but because we have far more information about them. The Greeks were great scribblers; the Ionian philosophers had explored the structure of the world and the Aiolic poets the nature of emotional experience. The Athenians were also pioneers in drama, history and the language of law and administration. In the middle of the 5th century Athens became the intellectual centre of the Greek world.

At the beginning of the 5th century Herakleitos, the Ephesian philosopher, and the Eleans, Parmenides and Zeno, had been the first to consider what kinds of discourse were most helpful for finding out about the world. Their argumentative approach was taken up by the Sophists, men like Protagoras of Abdera (who drew up a code of civil law), Hippias of Elis, Prodikos of Keos and Gorgias of Leontinoi who taught at Athens and were highly influential. Athenians like Antiphon (architect of the narrower constitution of 411 BC) and Thrasymachos built on these revolutionary ideas in their own ways, as did Sokrates and his most famous pupil,

Plato. Herodotos made Athens his home and recited extracts from his *Histories* before moving to the new colony of Thourioi. Hippodamos of Miletos, the town planner, redesigned the Piraeus area. The "atheist" Anaxagoras and the artist Pheidias were some of the more famous names in the circle of Perikles, an outstanding speaker and politician.

ATHENIAN LIFESTYLE

At the end of the first year's fighting in the Peloponnesian War (430 BC) Perikles gave the funeral speech for the victims, in which he sketched out the characteristics of an Athenian lifestyle. The Spartans were his chief foil as the principal enemy, but the contrast between the Spartan and the Athenian way of life was also the most marked. Whereas the Spartans relied on compulsion to maintain their power, repressed individuality for the good of the state, and were constantly in training and armed to the teeth, Perikles praised the Athenian preference for persuasion, their refusal to give up their relaxations and aesthetic pursuits, and their reliance on hard calculation and daring rather than conventional military tactics to win battles.

The contrast is of course exaggerated. Those states which suffered at the hands of Athenian officials, policemen and tribute collectors while they were members of the Athenian-led Delian Confederacy (479-403 BC), not to mention those that suffered actual military assault, would probably have given a different assessment. Perikles himself admitted that the empire which the Athenians built up (ostensibly to continue the war against Persia) and which was undoubtedly the chief cause of Spartan aggression, was maintained by force. But his claims about Athenian freedom of speech, of the openness of his city to other Greeks and foreigners, and of the willingness of the Athenians to share the benefits of their institutions with others, entirely justified the view that Athens was the "school for Hellas".

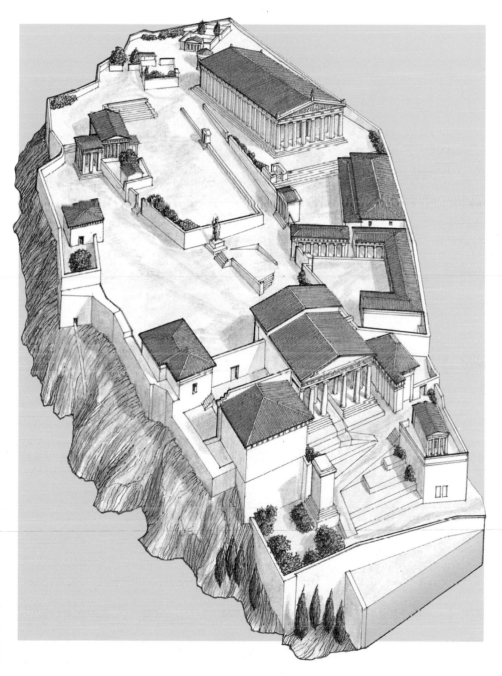

Under the Peisistratid tyrants the Akropolis became a private citadel. A 30 m (100 ft) long temple to Athena already existed on the site of the later Parthenon c 570-60 BC, and another to Athena and Erechtheus was built in the 520s south of the later Erechtheion ABOVE. Most of the buildings that gave the Akropolis its characteristic appearance in antiquity arose under the new democracy, in the period c 47-406 BC LEFT.

ATHENIAN DEMOCRACY

The democracy of ancient Athens, with its sovereign assembly of the citizen

body, was far more radical than any democracy of today. But well known

families continued to be influential in 5th century politics.

Marble head of the Athenian orator
Demosthenes (384-22 BC) ABOVE;
copy of a bronze full-length portrait
by the artist Polyeuktos *c*280 BC, set
up in the Agora of Athens. Bronze
ballot discs inscribed *psephos
demosion* (official ballot) used to
condemn a defendant BELOW; hollow
ones were used for acquittal.

In the early 6th century the Athenian law-giver, Solon, gave legal definition to the existing class structure at Athens. The wealthiest group had a minimum property qualification of 500 *medimnoi* (measures) of wet or dry produce; Knights were those men who could provide a minimum annual income of 300 measures; next were the *Zeugitai*, those who could afford a yoke of oxen and equivalent to 200 measures. The landless (*thetes*) were not eligible for political office of any sort though they might sit in the Assembly and, more importantly, now had the right of appeal to the lawcourts. In the 5th century, however, it was this last class which acquired real power under the radical democracy, since the people's Assembly and the popular courts became the main decision-making organs.

Solon cancelled the oppressive debts with which the landless population of Athens was then encumbered. In one of his poems he describes how he tore down the boundary stones (*horoi*) on which debts were inscribed. But he failed to root out the causes of oppression, because landowners could still charge the rents they liked. However, the right of appeal opened the way to a new relationship between the orders. The tyrant Peisistratos (561/0-527/6 BC) went some way towards relieving the problem of debts in his deliberately populist approach and by introducing rural judges.

DEVELOPMENT OF TRUE DEMOCRACY

The foundations for true democracy were laid by the Alkmaionid Kleisthenes. Despite the fact that he did not start off as a pro-democrat, he ended up as a populist leader because his immediate opponent was a supporter of the Peisistratid family. Kleisthenes destroyed the traditional power bases of the aristocratic clans by dividing up the whole of Attika into a new administrative framework which was also the basis for democratic government.

This fragment from a list of eponymous magistrates (men after whom each Athenian year was named) inscribed on a marble slab *c*425 BC LEFT includes those who fulfilled the post between 527/6 and 522/1 BC. A ballot box found in one of the law courts on the north-east side of the Agora BELOW.

In 508 BC all the citizens of Attika were divided into 10 new tribes, each of which was to be allotted three pieces of land, one on the coast, one on the plain and one in the hills. Each of these plots of land consisted of the villages (demes) which voted for the 50 councillors per tribe who made up the new deliberative body of government. The deme thus became the smallest organ of government and the overwhelming majority of Athenians belonged to wards outside the city itself. The tribes also voted for the 10 generals responsible for all military activity, and under the radical democracy this was really the only senior office in which a man could make a successful long-term career (councillors could serve for up to two years only).

But as yet the highest offices of state were still appointed, not elected by lot. In 487/6 BC membership of the Areiopagos, still the senior administrative body made up of ex-magistrates appointed for life, was changed to selection by lot. In 462 BC Ephialtes, the leader of a radical group of which Perikles was a member, prosecuted members of the Areiopagos for maladministration and secured the removal of virtually all its executive powers (except certain judicial cases including homicide).

The Council, the Assembly and the people's courts were immeasurably strengthened as a result.

This in essence was the "radical democracy", which was briefly interrupted by reactionary coups in 411 and 403 BC, but thereafter reintroduced. It survived fundamentally unchanged until the Roman period, when the Areiopagos was revived. In the 4th century BC, the democracy was arguably even more radical than it had been in the 5th, when the litigiousness of the Athenians made the people's courts supreme.

FREEDOM OF INFORMATION

As the architects of the first democracy, the Athenians thought it necessary to keep a record of their official transactions and a surprising number were committed to stone and preserved on the Akropolis. Inscriptions on metal plates or stone *stelai*, recording law codes or inter-state alliances, were not new (though the surviving examples date with a few exceptions from the 6th and 5th centuries). But in 454 BC the Delian League, set up to maintain the freedom of the Greeks against Persia, agreed to move its treasury from Delos to Athens. The Athenians had dominated this forum from the start; they had the largest ship contingent and, as other states increasingly preferred to pay money into the war-chest in place of ships, the Athenians could justify their political ascendancy with their nautical dominance.

From 454 BC the allies were required to send fixed contributions to Athens, where the Alliance Treasurers took 1/60 of each city's contributions as "first fruits" (as in a ritual sacrifice) to Athena. Before the move these monies were probably paid to Delian Apollo. An annual record of the "first fruits" was taken and inscribed on a marble *stele*, listing the amount dedicated by each allied state. Late payers appear to have been added on afterwards. These payments represent one of the most important sources of economic data of the ancient world, though interpretation is difficult. Every four years tributes were reassessed, and the changes made over time, taken together with other inscriptions of the period, provide valuable independent evidence for Athenian foreign policy and allied reactions.

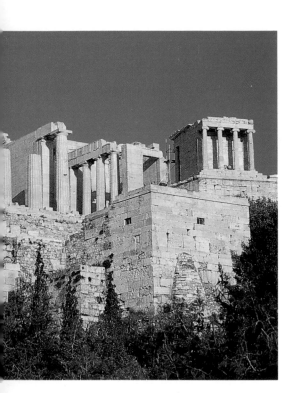

The Propylaia, gateway to the Akropolis (437-2 BC) and temple of Athena Nike (427-4 BC), as seen from the Areiopagos hill. The Persian sack of the Akropolis in 480 interrupted work on the first Parthenon. Work on its successor (RIGHT, at sunrise) was delayed until 447/6 by the Greek vow in 479 BC that ruins would not be rebuilt until this sacrilege had been avenged. A rapproachement with Persia was achieved in 449.

PERIKLES –
SOLDIER AND POLITICIAN

General view of the Akropolis of Athens ABOVE. Roman copy of a portrait bust of Perikles as general RIGHT. It was Perikles who urged the Athenians to use tribute money from the allies for public works at Athens. The Tholos, or meeting house, of the councillors in session, built c465 BC BOTTOM.

Perikles was the most influential politician in the years when the Athenians were at the peak of their power in the 440s and 430s. His father Xanthippos, who probably came from a respectable family, married Agariste of the Alkmaionid clan (see p.107). Xanthippos was one of the more radical aristocrats. He was a prominent general in the campaign of 479 BC against the Persians, having prosecuted one of the heroes of the battle of Marathon and former "tyrant" of the Chersonese peninsula, Miltiades, in 489 BC. Perikles followed his father's political line of using the legal process to gain political influence by prosecuting Miltiades' son and the last of the *grands seigneurs*, Kimon, in 463 BC.

As a military leader Perikles was one of many well qualified and distinguished generals in the middle decades of the 5th century. He was re-elected general year after year more for his rhetorical and managerial than his military skills, and had engineered a rapprochement with Persia around 449 BC. This enabled the Athenians to concentrate on extending their influence over the Greek *poleis* of the Aegean. It was he who crushed the uprisings in Euboia (446 BC) and Samos (440 BC); and he who maintained a tough, if not openly belligerent stance towards the Spartans and their allies. Perikles actively encouraged the extension of Athenian overseas ties, both in the Black Sea region and in Sicily. His policy in the early years of the Peloponnesian War (431-404 BC) was to avoid open battle and attack the Spartans' home ground, the Peloponnese.

Perikles is the politician most closely associated with artistic and intellectual developments in Athens and personally promoted the architectural reconstruction of the Akropolis.

129

TOWN PLANNING

While most Greek towns developed piecemeal, an element of planning was

always present in the foundation of the colonial settlements, and frequently

imposed on the civic areas of older cities when they were rebuilt.

View along the fortification walls of Aigosthena, on the Korinthian Gulf. Mount Kithairon, the traditional boundary between Attika and Boiotia, hemmed it in to the north. The walls and towers of this Megarian fort are among the finest examples of 4th-century BC military construction.

Since land was such a vital commodity, and political rights so closely tied to land ownership, it comes as no surprise to learn that the Greeks of the historical era were careful about the way that territory was allotted. The division of land was the first pragmatic step in the foundation of a colony. What was happening at the same time in the older mother-cities of mainland and east Greece is still being revealed. For obvious reasons, plans of any size are only available for cities which were abandoned or destroyed, although aerial photography can be extremely useful for pinpointing ancient streets belonging to a grid plan, as at Rhodes. At Halieis (near modern Porto Cheli) in the Argolid, building outlines of a submerged 4th-century city and its 6th-century, carefully planned predecessor show that the later grid system was refining a pre-existing scheme. There was a similar process at Megara Hyblaia in Sicily, where two different phases are discernible from the slight change of orientation in the street plan.

CIVIC ATHENS

At Athens, as must have been the case in many older *poleis*, systematic planning arrived late and was adopted in a more piecemeal fashion. Civic develop-ment is best seen on the Akropolis itself and in the Agora. The Akropolis had been the seat of a Bronze Age fort and palace, but only in the 6th century did any substantial shrines appear. There is a series of carved and painted limestone figures which decorated some small buildings, then the foundations of the first Hundred Foot Hall (*Hekatompedon*) and the Old Parthenon on the same site as the Periklean one. This older temple, together with a monumental gateway, was symbolic of the new democracy after the overthrow of the Peisistratid tyrants, who had used the Akropolis as a fortress for their own security. But the original Parthenon and gateway were damaged during the Persian sack in 480 BC and were replaced within a more closely-knit design and two more temples, the tiny Athena Nike and the Erechtheion, whose odd shape was intended to accommodate a number of cults connected with early Athenian history.

The Agora ceased to be used as a burial ground around 700 BC, and may already have served as a meeting-place, although the earliest architectural evidence begins in the 6th century. The tyrants were more interested in general amenities, such as fountain houses and huge temple projects (like Olympian Zeus), than in the organization of civic business. The

A tower from the Aigosthena fort (recently damaged in an earthquake) LEFT. The restored *stoa* of Attalos II of Pergamon (159-38 BC) in the Athenian Agora BELOW. This is a good example of a two-storeyed, two-aisled Hellenistic colonnade backed by rooms that were mainly used as shops.

burst of activity following the introduction of Kleisthenes' reforms produced a Council chamber, the first lawcourt building and the Royal *stoa*, where the chief magistrate (archon) officiated. After the Persian sack, these buildings were recommissioned and new ones added – the circular *tholos*, where the standing committee of councillors dined and slept, and the Painted *stoa*, so called because of the paintings by the famous artist Polygnotos of Thasos displayed there. The Painted *stoa* was the repository of Solon's laws and a popular meeting-place for lawyers and philosophers (notably Zeno, whose Stoic followers took their name from it).

PUBLIC BUILDINGS

Public buildings had modest requirements in ancient Greece – a roof and some shelter against strong seasonal winds but plenty of circulating air in the heat. This explains the popularity of the *stoa*, an aisled hall with a back and two short side walls. Most of the buildings which sprang up on the remaining sides of the Agora were *stoas*. By the 2nd century these malls were being used to redesign or tidy up older civic areas, to create regular squares and terraced platforms.

Alongside the aisled hall, banks of seats, originally cut into a hillside

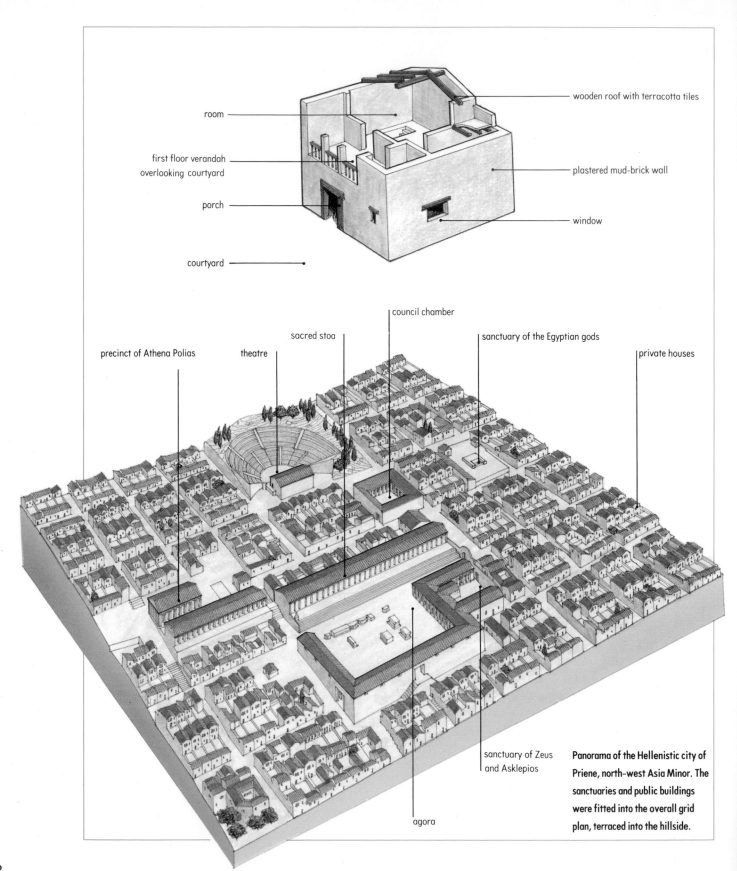

room

first floor verandah overlooking courtyard

porch

courtyard

wooden roof with terracotta tiles

plastered mud-brick wall

window

precinct of Athena Polias

theatre

sacred stoa

council chamber

sanctuary of the Egyptian gods

private houses

sanctuary of Zeus and Asklepios

agora

Panorama of the Hellenistic city of Priene, north-west Asia Minor. The sanctuaries and public buildings were fitted into the overall grid plan, terraced into the hillside.

COLUMNS

to enable viewers to see a theatrical performance, or initiates a ritual one, were incorporated first into stone theatres large and small, and then, in the 2nd century, into Council chambers, as at Athens, Priene and Miletos. The old gymnasia of Athens (the Lyceum, Academy and Kynosarges) were outside the city and consisted of parkland around a shrine. In the 4th century a regular series of structures begins to be found in gymnasia, including the exercise yard (*palaistra*), while in the Hellenistic period libraries and other facilities would also be grouped around it.

PRIVATE HOUSES

Houses grew more luxurious but the plan remained essentially the same, a series of rooms built around a square or rectangular courtyard. There was usually a roofed portico along one side where most of the domestic work would be carried out. Rooms with particular functions can rarely be identified, except for the *andron* (men's dining-room) which was the best decorated, usually with a mosaic floor. Hip-baths are usually found in a small bathroom near the kitchen. Most houses were too small to allow for separate women's quarters, unless they were located upstairs. Masters and servants must have shared rooms.

The Greeks may have been influenced by Egyptian and Near Eastern traditions, both in the Bronze Age, and from the second half of the 6th century BC. The older of the two principal architectural orders, known as Doric, retained a notional connection with the rationale of woodwork, with straight-sided flutes, a simple cushion and block capital and triglyphs representing beam ends. The Ionic order was always more varied and elaborate. The characteristic volute capitals were but the commonest of a range of foliate forms, later including the Korinthian (volute and akanthos leaf). Ionic columns were supported on an elaborately profiled base.

Capital of a Doric column from the Parthenon *c*440 BC TOP RIGHT, with the slab-like *abacus* separating it from the architrave blocks. A prepared Doric column drum from the Akropolis CENTRE; the underside was roughly picked and only a narrow margin left smooth. Ionic capital from the Propylaia, Athens, *c*437-2 BC, BELOW LEFT; Korinthian capital from the *Tholos* (rotunda) at Epidauros, *c*350 BC BELOW RIGHT.

MASTERS AND SLAVES

Free or slave, citizen or metic, landowner or landless, man or woman — these

categories defined the structure of ancient Greek society. A person's category

was vital to their status and the possession of legal rights.

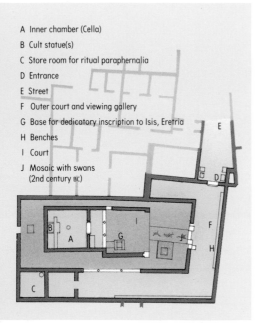

A Inner chamber (Cella)

B Cult statue(s)

C Store room for ritual paraphernalia

D Entrance

E Street

F Outer court and viewing gallery

G Base for dedicatory inscription to Isis, Eretria

H Benches

I Court

J Mosaic with swans
(2nd century BC)

Plan of the shrine of Isis and other Egyptian gods at Eretria ABOVE. A simple room with a porch and open court was built in the late 4th century BC, in the domestic quarter on the south-eastern outskirts of the city. Various additions were made during the next 200 years. Votive relief in honour of the Thracian goddess Bendis RIGHT, introduced as an official Athenian cult in 430/29 BC. The ceremonies, including torch races, form the background of Plato's opening scene of the *Republic*.

The individual unit in society was the household, the *oikos*, a term which included all dependants, both the immediate family and slaves. The partition of land to all heirs kept families small. It is a commonplace that Greek society relied on slaves to supplement its labour force, yet we have very little reliable information about how slavery came into being and virtually no statistics. From the 8th century onwards, we know that citizenship was linked to landownership and in later centuries non-citizens were banned by law from owning land. Grants of citizenship were rare in the Greek world and were often connected with diplomatic manoeuvres or political idealism (as at Athens after the Peloponnesian War).

Between the citizen farmer and the slave, who was completely in the power of his owner and unable to own property, had no independent legal rights and thus no right to contract marriage (no legal family in fact), there was a large ill-defined class of landless individuals, many of whom would have come under what historians call modes of unfree labour.

UNFREE LABOUR

"Unfree labour" included subject peoples who had lost their status completely through conquest. These included the *Helots* of the Spartan state

and other probably pre-Dorian groups in the Peloponnese, the *Klarotai* on Crete, the *Penestai* in Thessaly, the *Killyrioi* at Syracuse, all of whom were technically serfs (people tied to the land). But we also hear of other categories, such as *pelatai* (clients), who were in one way or another indebted to landowners. The difference between these groups and slaves was legal rather than economic, although this was often a matter of degree rather than substance. The law code of Gortyn in Crete gives various sums for redress in assault cases to slaves as well as free men and women. The economic dividing line was between those who worked for themselves, whether farmers, labourers or tradesmen, and those who worked for others, which usually meant as slaves. Where we have detailed inventories of craftsmen, it seems that citizens and "metics" (see below) carried out the managerial and specialist jobs and slaves the less specialized ones. On the other hand workshops of any kind other than the purely domestic type were run and supervised by slaves. The Athenians also had a police force made up of 300 Scythian archers, all of them slaves belonging to the *polis*.

ACCREDITED FOREIGNERS

At Athens, Perikles' citizenship law of 451 BC reduced anyone whose parents were not both citizens to "metic" status. A metic was an accredited foreigner, usually a merchant, who took up long-term residence in the city. He would be sponsored by a citizen and registered as such in his deme of residence, would pay an annual poll tax and was eligible for occasional property taxes, and might have to undertake and fund various public works, just as wealthier citizens did, though not the costly task of fitting out ships. Metics could not participate in politics and law because they were non-citizens, and were disbarred from marrying citizens. Not only that, they were enrolled separately in the army. But they did have protection under the law and in the 4th century special legal conventions as well as the introduction of maritime courts for the settling of merchants' disputes facilitated transactions, while the granting of land rights and tax exemption became increasingly common.

The squire of Memnon, a legendary king of the Ethiopians, who fought for his uncle Priam at Troy, was killed by Achilles and immortalized. Detail of a neck amphora by the artist Exekias, *c*540 BC. In Homer's day the location of the Ethiopians was vague, but in the 7th century Greek mercenaries were getting to know the Sudan and Ethiopia. In art, Ethiopians ("Burnt-faced men") are distinct from Egyptians. Negro heads were a popular exotic motif and made an ideal subject in Attic black glaze.

BIRTH, MARRIAGE, DEATH

The ancient Greeks achieved their own understanding of the cycle of life.

Despite a rudimentary grasp of biology, dissections and medical observations

directed Greek thinking away from magic towards a scientific approach.

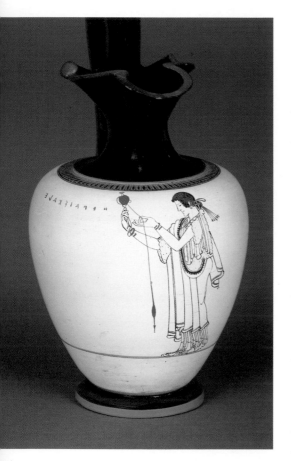

Attic white-ground jug with trefoil mouth. Spinning and weaving cloth were the most time-consuming domestic activities for women. Every kind of fabric object, from pillows and blankets to winter cloaks, was made in the home. Imported embroidered cloth and silk were rare luxuries before the Hellenistic period.

The Greeks derived their ideas about conception entirely from analogies with animal anatomy and from frank discussions with prostitutes. In Aischylos' *Eumenides* Apollo is made to say that the mother does not beget a child but is merely a nurse for the male seed. This view seems to have been widespread and was legitimized by Aristotle, although others, including some authors of the Hippokratic works (and the 3rd-century doctor of Chalkedon, Herophilos, who is said to have discovered the ovaries) gave women a joint responsibility for the embryo.

PREGNANCY AND CHILDBIRTH

Greek knowledge of genetic transmission was understandably uncertain. Some features were easily recognizable, but Aristotle assumed that all deformities were genetically transmitted. Sterility is such a major preoccupation of the Hippokratic writings that it would be easy to assume that this was a major problem. It could become a serious problem for women, whose principal function in marriage was to conceive. A different problem was the unwanted child. There is some evidence that exposure of newborn babies was common, but the secrecy in which it was done makes it impossible to say more.

Abortion was in theory disapproved of (the Hippokratic oath mentions this unequivocally) but in practice the suggestions made by doctors to women who got themselves into trouble show that this was not necessarily the case. But even in the Christian era, those who supported abortions on medical grounds were opposed to it on social or personal ones. Plato approved of abortion for eugenic purposes and Aristotle for limiting population growth beyond an acceptable level. A distinction was made between the unformed (without sensory perception) and formed foetus, though the dates of a pregnancy could only be guessed at. A foetus could apparently come to term any time between the seventh and eleventh month, though the eighth month was unlucky (because even) and the baby non-viable. Aristotle's analysis of embryonic development is much more accurate (based on experiments with hen's eggs). He correctly identified respiration as the first biological function to develop and the heart to be the principal life-giving organ.

Gymnastics were recommended by Plato for the pregnant mother, while Aristotle thought a daily walk, not too much salt and no alcohol was the way to ensure a healthy baby – no different in fact from today's advice. It is interesting to speculate whether the low Spartan birthrate, which was one of her undoings in the 4th century BC, might be attributed to temporary amenorrhoea due to excessive exercise on the part of women.

Childbirth was accepted as being a woman's affair but we do not know enough about who took the decisions that mattered. (Doctors always write authoritatively about problem cases but did not attend births routinely). Midwives were certainly the chief helpers. The 2nd century AD handbook of gynaecology by Soranos is the earliest treatise on obstetrics to have survived; he recommends as midwives women who are qualified dieticians, surgeons and pharmacists, and free from superstitions – few midwives can

A woman passing a baby to another woman on a Red Figure *stamnos*. We know remarkably little about the life of children in antiquity. Before the 5th century BC, children are virtually invisible in art, or appear as miniature adults. Thereafter artists began to take an interest in the differences between adults and children. The growing fashion for scenes of daily life at this time provides more evidence of early childhood – learning to crawl, walk and take lessons in writing, music and athletics. Babies did not lack special provision, whether it be feeding bottles, pedestal potties or toys.

for natural milk. Phaedra's relationship with her nurse in Euripides' *Hippolytos* is reminiscent of Juliet's in Shakespeare.

GROWING UP

The acceptance of the infant by society took place at the autumn festival of the *Apatouria* ("feast of common fatherhood"), which was organized by the ancient *phratriai*, or brotherhoods. These were pseudo clan organizations based on spurious hereditary ties, perhaps the democratic equivalents of genuine hereditary aristocratic clans known as *gene*. The infant was inscribed into the *phratria* and at the age of 18 into the tribe. Most of the evidence comes from Athens but there were similar ceremonies elsewhere. It is not clear whether girls went through the same or some analogous process, since after 451 BC a woman's legitimacy with respect to citizenship became much more important.

For girls the change from childhood to womanhood was associated with marriage and the physical movement from the father's to another man's home. Whereas the coming-of-age of boys was a clear-cut event, marked especially by a two-year military apprenticeship known as the *ephebeia*, there is no direct equivalent for girls.

MARRIAGE

Marriage was not, it seems, a very formal affair, though it was an opportunity for a good celebration. All that was required was the exchange of a dowry from the father or guardian (*kyrios*) to the husband, and a verbal consent. It is usually assumed that women did not actually make use of the dowry in their own right. But it sounds most unlikely that a new wife

Aphrodite and Eros encouraging a young bride ABOVE, on the interior of an Attic Red Figure cup, *c*410 BC. The *pyxis* (toilet box) BELOW, *c*420, omits the ritual bath, for which a special water jar was used. Assistants dress the bride while others wait for the bridegroom's procession.

have been quite so well qualified. In earlier times experience was probably the basic requirement.

The arrival of a new baby was symbolized by an olive wreath on the door for a boy, a tuft of wool for a girl. A ceremony of acceptance (*Amphidromia*, or running around) took place around the family hearth five days after birth, then came presents from kin and friends, and on the tenth day the child received a name. The high incidence of infant mortality encouraged cults to various deities who took care of children. Despite an apparent lack of interest in child development (except by philosophers interested in methods of socializing the child), the importance of nurturing affection through breast-feeding was recognized by some writers. Wet nurses were not unusual, however, in the absence of appropriate substitutes would come into an alien household without some equipment to make her feel at home. Solon wanted to abolish dowries except in the case of heiresses (whose rights to marry or remarry were subjected to close supervision). His aim was to stop marriage from being treated primarily as a means of acquiring wealth, but he took it for granted that a woman had some possessions of her own. What evidence we have suggests that there was a tendency (in Athens, at least) for women to be married to more distant relatives, and certainly in a way which would enhance the overall interests of both families.

DEATH

A good deal of what we know of the Greeks is derived from burials, but Greek attitudes to death seem to have

been a bit vague. The geography of Hades is confused and the ordinary deceased had no effective powers in the world of the living. There was no articulate notion of retributive justice after death, except among Pythagoreans, though some select "heroized" individuals were translated to heaven. Unmarried girls and the war dead were the only groups given special prominence.

A woman standing on a ladder drops incense and spices into a dish to be dedicated to Aphrodite and Adonis; others, accompanied by Pan and Eros, dance and play castanets. The festival of Adonis on a Red Figure water jar, mid-4th century BC LEFT. BELOW Six terracotta objects from a girl's tomb, c420 BC: a doll on a chair, miniature vase and boots.

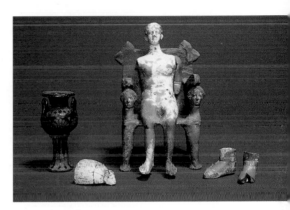

Three white-ground vases with polychrome decoration LEFT, used as tomb markers. From the left: two mourners beside the deceased; Charon, ferryman to the Underworld; two mourners tie fillets around a funerary stele. A stone stele from Geraki, near Sparta (c480 BC) BELOW, showing a distraught youth.

GREEK RELIGION

For the Greeks there was no distinction between sacred and secular. Gods and goddesses inhabited all layers of the natural world and could intervene in human affairs at any time.

Attic *stamnos* (storage vase) by the Villa Giulia Painter, *c*450 BC, ABOVE. A woman uses a ladle to measure out a wine offering while a flute-player stands by. Perhaps a scene from the winter festival of Dionysos, the *Lenaia*.

Theatron means a place for viewing religious spectacles. Greek theatres were always closely associated with cult and some, like that in the sanctuary of the Kabeiroi outside Thebes RIGHT, were used exclusively for religious purposes. A temple formed the "scene" building, and an altar stood in the centre of the *orchestra*.

What we see in Greek sanctuaries in the form of altars and offerings – the visible evidence of the most basic features of religious behaviour – seems at first to have little to do with the gods of Homer, the 12 Olympians who were not just more powerful but more perfect images of man. The earliest feature of the Greek sanctuary was usually the sacrificial pyre. Later it was a stone-built enclosure rather than a block altar. The sanctuary itself was an area of sanctified ground, which was sometimes given a formal processional entrance. The temple was a later addition, the house of the deity in which the cult statue was located, but a building essentially unconnected with ritual activity.

Temples had a greater social than ritual significance. Even at Athens, where secular buildings on a generous scale appeared earlier than elsewhere, temples were the most expensive and most durable structures. They were the repositories of sacred treasure and the most obvious symbols of civic, rather than strictly religious identity. There was no boundary between the sacred and the secular since in a sense the divine inhabited the whole natural world. What changed gradually was the human emphasis in the relationship between nature and man.

RELIGION AND THE STATE

In the early days of the *polis*, the principal sanctuaries on which a city's resources were lavished and with which various special civic legends were associated are less often found at the centre of town and more often some way from it, whether in a suburban context or on the very boundaries of *polis* territory. The suburban sanctuaries at Thebes, Argos, Halieis, Delos, Naxos and Paros were dedicated to Apollo, those at Sparta and Ephesos to Artemis. At Korinth

and particularly at Eleusis, north-west of Athens, there were sanctuaries to Demeter.

Elsewhere a community might spread its influence, whether by military or other means, much further afield, and these territorial gains would be marked by a temple on a suitably lavish scale. This is the case with the great temples dedicated to Hera – on the outskirts of Argos, on Samos, at Perachora, Olympia, Epidauros; or others to Apollo – at Amyklai by the Spartans, at Phanai by the Chiots, at Klaros by Kolophon and at Didyma by Miletos.

There were, of course, important early sanctuaries within communities too, and those on akropolis sites were frequently dedicated to Athena – Athens, Sparta, Miletos, Lindos. What is striking is the tendency to associate major cult sites with such a limited number of tutelary deities.

DEDICATIONS

In many of these early sanctuaries deposits of exotic objects or materials have been discovered. In the Idaian Cave on Crete there were Phoenician silver bowls and bronze tambourines, and similar ones come from Olympia, Perachora and Dodona. Other bronze "shields" of eastern character have been found as far away as Delphi. Ivory tablets, figurines and other ob-jects have come to light at Ephesos, Samos and Chios, the Orthia sanctuary near Sparta, Perachora and further afield, at Delphi, Thasos and Corfu. According to Herodotos foreigners did make dedications at Greek sanctuaries, but many of these mementoes were made by Greeks.

Animals form the most important single category of personal dedications between the 9th and the end of the 6th century. The kinds of animals chosen differed slightly from one sanctuary to another. At Olympia 99 per cent were horses and cattle; at Delphi these were joined by deer and birds. Birds and horses predominated at Orthia near Sparta and at Pherai in Thessaly. The animals reflect a general interest in nature, though cattle suggest a deliberate reference to agriculture. There is no reason to believe that the statuettes are inanimate representations of sacrificial victims.

During the 6th century human statuettes began to take the place of the animal ones, together with various kinds of vessels. This change of practice might indicate a new view of man's place in nature, a more assured sense of control and a greater preoccupation with human affairs. In the Peloponnese and at Dodona one of the most popular figures for dedication became the hoplite, in Arkadia, shepherds. More elaborate and expen-

Man sacrificing at an altar in front of a herm BELOW. "Doubleen" neck amphora by the Edinburgh Painter, early 5th century BC. He holds a branch in one hand and a libation bowl in the other.

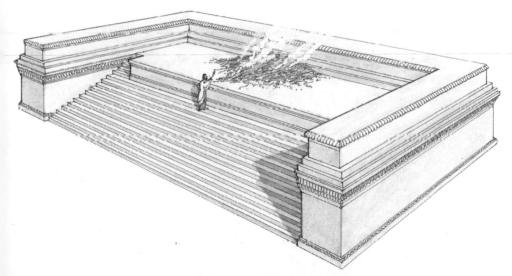

Altars, always the principal focus of Greek cult practice, were usually little more than a heap of ashes. They took a more elaborate form in east Greece, where marble pi-shaped enclosures, often preceded by steps, were introduced in the 6th century BC. Reconstruction of the altar Temple of Hera at Samos LEFT.

sive were marble and bronze statues and reliefs, often representing the dedicant him or herself.

ANIMAL SACRIFICE

The sacrifice of a domestic animal was considered part of the natural order. If the animal were not sacrificed, something could go wrong with this order. One "explanation" of sacrifice is contained in a treatise on vegetarianism by the 3rd century AD writer, Porphyry, which he might have learned from Aristotle's pupil, Theophrastos. He describes how an ox felled in a fit of anger eventually became the correct sacrifice of the Athenians in the festival known as the *Bouphonia* (Ox-slaying), which took place at harvest time. At Athens the axe was

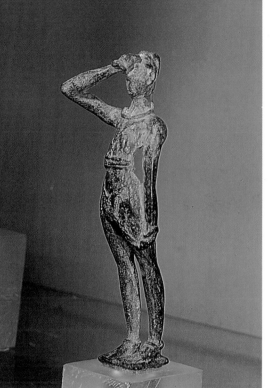

Minoan bronze statuette of a worshipper ABOVE from the villa at Tylissos, Crete, *c*1700-1450 BC. Attic Black Figure amphora *c*540 BC RIGHT, showing a cult statue (Apollo?) standing inside a shrine on Ionic columns, flanked by cauldrons. The lion on the roof may be a shorthand way of indicating a decorated pediment.

literally made a scapegoat and tried by law. Elsewhere such ceremonies reflect a degree of guilt and it was customary to offer the animal barley grains, at which it would lower its head, as though in assent.

Different deities required different animals on specific days of the month. The calendar of festivals was an extension of this monthly scheme, with sacrifices, feasts and games or other displays celebrating a specific deity. The Attic calendar is far better known than any other and the names of the months and of the festivals correspond with those of other Ionian cities. Animal sacrifice was a communal affair because no family could eat a whole carcase. A communal meal, for most perhaps the only meat meal until the next festival, was the most efficient method of consumption, as well as being more enjoyable. Xenophon describes how he annually organized a harvest festival in honour of Artemis on a piece of land bought from his mercenary pay in Asia. He would invite all his friends and neighbours and sacrifice a tithe of the produce, then share out the meat, together with wild boar and venison from the woods, barley, bread, fruit and nuts all washed down with wine.

The festival calendar followed the agricultural year. The beginning of the Attic year was in July, towards the end of the grain harvest, and culminated in the procession, games and literary contests of the Panathenaia. The new year began with festivals of ploughing and sowing. Fertility festivals for women and young men were followed by those for the soil. The highlights of winter and spring were the dramatic festivals of Dionysos, before the serious work of harvesting began.

GODS

The Olympian pantheon of the classical period came from a variety of sources. Zeus the Thunderer is clearly identified in legend as a younger sky god who overcame older "earth" gods, the Titans. His brother Poseidon, the sea god and patron of bulls, was already worshipped in the Bronze Age, along with Apollo and Artemis (solar and lunar gods), Dionysos, god of ecstacy, and Hermes, the messenger and mediator, together with a dove goddess (later Aphrodite). Athena inherited some of the attributes of the old snake goddess. Athena and Hephaistos became patrons of human wisdom, intelligence and craftsmanship. The origins of Zeus' consort, Hera, the fertility goddess Demeter and the war god, Ares, may be no less ancient.

Large-scale cult statues (such as Apollo, CENTRE, from the temple of Zeus at Olympia) often conform to an idealized image of the Olympians. Popular images reflect more immediate concerns, especially fertility. A limestone statuette from Megara Hyblaia, Sicily TOP RIGHT shows a goddess suckling twins. A marble votive relief from the sanctuary of Pan and the nymphs on the Akropolis slopes BELOW shows a group of Olympians with Pan, three nymphs and the horned river god Acheloos in a rustic setting.

GREEK TRAGEDY

The great tragedians of ancient Athens — Aischylos, Euripides, Sophokles,

whose powerful plays still entrance theatregoers — are the medium through

which many first become acquainted with the living world of the Greeks.

Marble portrait bust of the dramatist Aischylos (525/4-456 BC); a Roman copy of a Greek original of the 5th century BC, in the Capitoline Museum, Rome. Portrait sculpture was still at a very unpractised stage at the time of the poet's death and any likeness of him is bound to owe much to the artist's imagination.

Impersonation, the use of masks, paint and costume, sacred stories and mythical combats are the stuff of ancient ritual in all cultures. What made Greek drama, particularly tragedy, which was the first of the three dramatic genres to acquire true individuality, different was its epic dimension. Most of the themes in tragedy come from Homer or the post-Homeric Epic Cycle; the measured pace and preoccupation with heroic behaviour are also Homeric.

The earliest tragic performances were staged at the spring festival of Dionysos (the Great Dionysia) probably at the instigation of Peisistratos who also had a hand in the editing of a definitive copy of the Homeric epics. Three poets presented three tragedies, each with a pendant "satyr" play, a less serious look at the relations of gods and men through the activities of Dionysos' anarchic non-human followers. From 432 BC onwards tragedies were also performed at the winter festival of Dionysos, the Lenaia. The plays of Aischylos were repeated after his death by popular approval and in the 4th century the masterpieces of other major dramatists were revived and thereafter performed all over the Greek world by travelling players.

What we know of tragedy is almost entirely confined to the surviving plays of the three great tragedians, Aischylos (525/4-456 BC), Sophokles (c.496-406 BC) and Euripides (c.485-406 BC), although the titles, and sometimes the plots and fragments of these and other authors are referred to in other sources. Perhaps 90 titles can be attributed to Aischylos, but only 7 survive together with 7 out of an alleged 123 by Sophokles and 19 out of 92 by Euripides.

THE STATELY OLD MASTER

Aischylos was often considered the greatest of the three as well as being the earliest. In Aristophanes' comedy *The Frogs* (405 BC), Aischylos wins a competition between himself and Euripides for the prize of greatest dramatic poet. The competition brilliantly satyrizes the more obvious characteristics of both men's work, which in turn reflect the primitive and mature stages of Classical tragedy. The older man puts on muffled, enigmatic figures who make equally enigmatic utterances; the latter overly realistic anti-heroes in rags speaking in disjointed modernistic lyrics. True, Aischylos' style is stately, but it is also intense, concentrated and colourful.

In the *Agamemnon* (458 BC), the first play of the only surviving trilogy, Queen Klytaimnestra murders her husband in the bath. It is not the

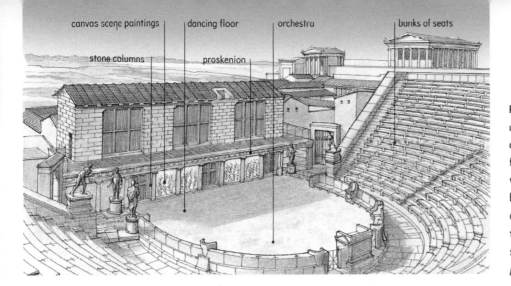

canvas scene paintings   dancing floor   orchestra   banks of seats

stone columns   proskenion

Reconstruction of a Greek theatre LEFT. In the 5th century the stage consisted only of the circular dancing floor (orchestra) and sets made of wood and canvas. Permanent stage buildings appeared during the 4th century. There is little evidence of the raised wooden stage, supported on the columned proskenion, before the 3rd century.

bloody murder that rivets the viewer but the strange forces which ensure that one fatal step follows another. In the sequel, the *Choephoroi (Libation Bearers)*, their son Orestes murders the Queen. This vicious cycle of revenge has to be broken by the intervention of law. Thus, in the final play, the trial of Orestes takes place on the Areiopagos hill, while the Furies are changed by Athena's intervention into the *Eumenides* (kindly ones).

THE HUMANIST

Euripides' surviving plays show experimentation with a variety of styles. The structure of the genre had changed – Sophokles brought in the third actor and knit the chorus more firmly into the plot. Euripides began to move in a different direction, reducing the role of the chorus and loosening the structure. His characters are real human beings under the masks of traditional heroes, many of them quite outside the heroic mould. Theseus in the *Medea* (431 BC) is spineless and irresponsible beside his passionately wronged and jealous wife; Phaedra is a sensitively drawn woman who cannot repress her unspeakable love for her stepson. *Hippolytos* (428 BC), a man seemingly without emotion.

Both Euripides and Sophokles wrote plays which retold the story of the *Libation Bearers*. Aischylos had not dwelt on the morality of Klytaimnestra's murder and his Elektra disappears halfway through the play. In Euripides' *Elektra* (c.415 BC), the princess is married off to a peasant and moans disconsolately about her ignominious fate, although her husband is a pleasant type. Orestes, on the other hand, is presented in a much more amoral light.

THE INNOVATOR

Sophokles' play of the same name is more or less contemporary with Euripides'. Its power lies in the character of Elektra herself. The anguish and confused emotion of the relationship with her mother are at the core. Elektra is one of the colossal characters in Sophoklean drama, whose single-minded determination brings both positive and negative results. All three dramatists were preoccupied with the obscure motives of divine action. Whereas Aischylos interpreted this as a seamless web of action and reaction, Sophokles and Euripides were more inclined to point out the arbitrary character of divine intervention. However, these were interpretations of Homer's Olympian gods, rather different from the figures of Greek popular belief.

A sherd of late Red Figure pottery from Taranto ABOVE, c 340 BC, showing an actor in costume and elaborate buskins holding a sword in one hand and a tragic mask in the other. Scene from a satyr play by Aischylos, *The Interior Decorators* BELOW, with a line of satyrs, bringing on pieces from a throne. Red Figure water jar, c470–60 BC.

145

GREEK COMEDY

The comic plays of Aristophanes show another side of the ancient Athenians

— their willingness to have fun at the expense of leading citizens, the gods,

and even sacred ceremonies.

The heyday of classic ("Old") comedy is known almost exclusively from the work of one man — Aristophanes (*c.*450-*c.*385 BC). As a genre it was by no means confined to Athens; comic plays were being staged by Epicharmos in Sicily from the early 5th century, and official Athenian performances at the City Dionysia did not begin until 488/7 BC, spreading to the winter Lenaia by 440 BC. Early comedy is difficult to reconstruct.

THE CHORUS

By Aristophanes' day the chorus of 24 held pride of place, from both a dramatic and thematic viewpoint. The plays are named after the chorus, which often takes on the role of a particular group in society, for example, the Athenian horse breeding class in the *Knights* (424 BC) and the miners of Acharnai in the *Acharnians* (425 BC). But there is usually a strong injection of fantasy, too. The *Wasps* (422 BC) are a chorus of stern working-class jurymen; the *Birds* (414 BC) citizens of an ethereal never-never land; the *Frogs* hop about the marshes of the river Styx, poking fun at Dionysos as he tries to get into the Underworld.

The chorus is always outspoken, so that individuals, real in the case of politicians, or imaginary, get equal, often savage treatment. In theory nothing is sacred; gods appear rarely but are as fallible as mortals (Dionysos and Herakles in the *Frogs*, Apollo and Hermes, the Triballian god in *Birds*). The nearest thing to blasphemy is the parody of a chorus of initiates of the Eleusinian Mysteries in *Frogs*, but Aristophanes mimics the style for ef-

Terracotta statuette of a comic actor playing a runaway slave, seated on an altar, *c*350-325 BC ABOVE. Scene from a south Italian comedy, *c*375 BC, painted on a Paestan wine-mixing bowl RIGHT. The actors are shown climbing a ladder to a raised stage. They wear typical padded costumes and comic masks. Comedy developed earlier and had an independent tradition in south Italy.

fect; he quite pointedly avoids criticizing the content of the ritual. Serious issues are addressed, and, in view of the fact that the majority of his surviving plays date from the war period, peace is by far the greatest preoccupation.

However, serious ends are sought through non-serious, often hilarious means. In the *Acharnians* (425 BC) the protagonist Dikaiopolis makes a private peace treaty and enjoys its benefits, to the chagrin of his famished fellow-citizens and the equal anger of armourers. In the *Peace* (421 BC), following a genuine if ephemeral treaty between Athenians and Spartans, Trygaios flies to heaven on a carefully fattened dung-beetle to free Peace and bring her back to earth. In the later years of the war, more drastic measures are contemplated, such as a Greece-wide sex-strike in *Lysistrata*, 411 BC), while *Women at the Thesmophoria* of the same year is much more escapist. The women of Athens have taken exception to the way Euripides represents them all as harlots and murderesses and plan to get rid of him.

THE 4TH CENTURY

The early years of the 4th century were almost as grim as the war years themselves. In *Women in the Assembly* (c. 392 BC) the voteless female Athenians try to subvert the constitution by dressing up as men with the aim of holding all property in common. The protagonist in *Wealth* (388 BC) is a blind man who bestows his favours on all the wrong people. But when his sight is restored at the sanctuary of the healer-god Asklepios, and he begins to rearrange his blessings, chaos ensues.

It is not easy to see the social realities through this inverted telescope. Comedy needs stereotypes and easily recognizable targets. Aristophanes did succeed in touching raw nerves, but many of his plays failed to win first prize. The *Clouds*, a highly inflated satire on Sokrates' teaching, is known to us in a version which was never staged; the original one flopped.

Pandora standing in the midst of the gods after her creation ABOVE, on the upper register of a kalyx *krater* by the Niobid Painter, c460 BC. On the lower register is a chorus of Pans or satyrs dancing to the flute.
Terracotta of a comic actor dressed as a young woman, c350 BC, LEFT. All women's parts were played by men in Greek drama.

SECTION

3

THE
GAZETTEER
OF SITES

The surviving remains of ancient Greek culture form only a tiny fraction of what we might have seen 2,000 years ago. Clay houses and wooden roofs with their interior furnishings have disappeared. What brings the fragments of pottery and the stone pillars to life is their setting and atmosphere.

culture from the 8th century BC to the Roman Empire. On Thasos, in southern Italy and Sicily, the traditions of Greek colonists can be seen interacting with native customs and developing different idioms of expression. The wealth and success of the Macedonian kings is now revealed in their ancient capitals at Vergina and Pella. The panoramic landscapes of Rhodes and Halikarnassos were the forerunners of Hellenistic urban plans, foremost among which were Alexandria and Pergamon, while Delos became one of the greatest

INTRODUCTION

A visit to Greece can be overwhelming and confusing unless you make an advance plan of places to see. The following sites represent a selection from among the most interesting, the best presented or best preserved. It is not intended to be comprehensive. A different selection might include the fascinating culture of Cyprus with its local, Greek and Levantine traditions; Thebes, in Boiotia, which has an impressive Mycenaean as well as Classical past; the Greek and Roman city of Korinth, with its harbours and akropolis, among the finest fortified sites in Greece; or the islands of Chios and Melos. For more ambitious travellers, there are Greek antiquities in Afghanistan, Albania, Bulgaria, Georgia and the southern Ukraine, Libya and Syria.

No selection can omit Athens. In addition to the monuments of the Akropolis, Agora and Kerameikos, Athens has a large, comprehensive display of Greek antiquities in the National Archaeological Museum, and a host of smaller unique collections. Athens can serve as a convenient base from which to tour Attika, central Greece and the Peloponnese. Knossos and Mycenae are unrivalled as representative centres of the Minoan and Mycenaean periods. The island of Euboia offers a miniature panorama of Greek culture from the Bronze Age to the Roman conquest of Greece. The great sanctuaries of Delphi, Olympia, Samos, Ephesos and Epidauros show different aspects of Greek worship, architecture, politics and

commercial and cosmopolitan centres of the same age.

The gazetteer sites are arranged in geographical order, taking Athens as the starting point, then covering the Greek sites, followed by those in Turkey and ending with sites in Alexandria, southern Italy and Sicily.

BLACK SEA

BULGARIA

THRACE

Nestos

Strimon

Amphipolis

Limenas THASOS

CHALKIDIKE

SEA OF MARMARA

Skamander

AEGEAN

SEA

Pergamon (Bergama)

Kuikos

TURKEY

AIOLIS

Hermos

EUBOIA

Eretria

Chalkis

Lefkandi

BOIOTIA

ATTIKA

N-TH

Kithairon

Kephisos

Eleusis

Athens

Brauron

Mycenae

Thorikos

iryns

Epidauros

Sounion

Nauplia

Smyrna (Izmir)

Sardis

IONIA

Kaister

SAMOS

Belevi

Ephesos (Selçuk)

Priene

Miletos

Maiander

KARIA

DELOS

Harlikarnassos (Bodrum)

KOS

CYCLADES

Kameiros

DODECANESE

Lindos

RHODES

SEA OF CRETE

Tylissos

Knossos

Mallia

Arkhanes

Zakros

Phaistos

Gortyn

151

The Acropolis from south side looking up at the Parthenon

ATHENS

Athens was already an important site in Mycenaean times, with a walled palace on the Akropolis. Athenian topography and monuments are better documented than those of any other ancient city except Rome, so we know a great deal about its architectural history. During the 7th century BC, the area of the later Classical city began to be reorganized into designated public spaces. In the early 6th century BC the Agora north-west of the Akropolis became the chief meeting-place, and public buildings began to accumulate around it. The most intensive period of building occurred during the 5th and 4th centuries BC.

Virtually all the city's public buildings were seriously damaged in an attack by the Germanic Herulians in AD 267. The recovery was slow, but although the new fortifications surrounded a much smaller area, the number and quality of buildings in the 4th and early 5th centuries AD suggest that a true revival had taken place.

What did reduce Athens to subsidiary status was the closure of her philosophical schools by order of the Emperor Justinian in AD 529.

The ancient city occupied an area of about 2.25 sq km (¾ sq mile) which still forms the core of the modern city of Athens. The Akropolis, Areiopagos and Pnyx, together with the area of the ancient Agora, a large piece of land adjoining the Sacred and Dipylon Gates which includes the Potters' Quarter (Kerameikos), and an area of parkland around the Arch of Hadrian and temple of Zeus Olympeios, are designated archaeological zones. The irregular outline of the street system around this core reflects the pattern of the Classical city walls.

AKROPOLIS
The Akropolis is an outcrop of semi-crystalline limestone that rises on average 91.5m (300 ft) above the city with precipitous slopes. In modern

times it has been restored to its appearance at the end of the 5th century BC, when an elaborate building programme initiated in c447 BC by the statesman Perikles was completed.

TEMPLE OF ATHENA (PARTHENON)
A team of exceptional architects – Pheidias, Iktinos and Kallikrates – began work in 447/6 BC on the temple of Athena. This was later known as the Parthenon (virgin's shrine), a name originally applied to the back room alone.

Unlike the majority of Greek temples, it was built entirely of marble.

PROPYLAIA
The entrance to the Akropolis was redesigned (437-2 BC) by the architect Mnesikles to create a dramatic impression on the approaching visitor and to enhance the appearance of the monuments behind it. A ramp on a substantial retaining wall in the polygonal style had already been built in the middle of the 6th century

BC. Mnesikles broadened the existing ramp and created a unified building complex. A columned hall became the central feature, flanked by projecting wings, with a new art gallery on the north soon balanced by Kallikrates' temple of Athena Nike (427-5 BC) on the south.

ERECHTHEION
Athena had been honoured on the Akropolis in two separate temples from the middle of the 6th century onwards. The Erechtheion also had links with more shadowy figures of Athens' mythical past, including the legendary kings Erechtheus and Kekrops. The

last structure (421-05 BC) belonging to the Periklean programme.

THE AGORA
The first significant architectural developments in this area date from around the end of the 6th century BC, when the sons of the tyrant

The Parthenon, Acropolis

Temple of Poseidon, Cape Sounion

CHRONOLOGY

*c*3000 BC
Late Neolithic habitation.

1100–600 BC
Age of Geometric art.

*c*600 BC
Solon's political reforms.

560–527 BC
Personal rule of Peisistratos.

508 BC
Political transformation of Attika.

462 BC
Radical democracy instituted.

431–405 BC
Peloponnesian War with Sparta.

405–03 BC
Rule of the 30 Tyrants.

403 BC
Reintroduction of democracy.

4th CENTURY BC
Athens revives Aegean empire.

86 BC
Athens sacked by Romans.

396
Invasion of Visigoths.

529
Philosophical schools closed.

582–3
Athens suffers destruction.

153

Tower of the Winds, behind the Roman agora

Karyatid from the south portico of the Erechtheion

Peisistratos built a fountain house in the south-east corner and a grandson laid the altar of the Twelve (Olympian) Gods. A number of important civic buildings date from the decades immediately succeeding the years of tyranny (510 BC onwards), including a law court on the south side and a bank of structures on the west including the Old Council Chamber.

The buildings of the Agora reflect the evolution of Athenian political life. In the early years of the 5th century the provision of special facilities for magistrates and councillors is consistent with the introduction of a truly representative procedure in government.

A remarkable little building, the Royal Stoa, had many functions. It was the office of the King Archon, one of the three principal magistrates at the time who continued to adjudicate in religious and certain legal matters; the Council of the Areiopagos, whose later brief was rather similar, sometimes met there. Copies of the law codes of Drakon and Solon were available for inspection either within or just outside it.

In the 470s and 460s BC further specialized buildings began to appear in the Agora – the rotunda (tholos) providing sleeping and eating accommodation for councillors in session. In the 440s the generals' headquarters and a plethora of sanctuaries and stoas began to appear on the south and west sides.

PNYX

Athenian citizens who assembled on the Pnyx to debate laws and proposals could be more easily accommodated on the grassy hill slope facing the city from the west than in the Agora. In the late 5th century a new retaining wall was built on the opposite, city side; the Assembly now faced south.

THEATRE OF DIONYSOS

A theatre area connected with the sanctuary of Dionysos on the south side of the Akropolis was probably in use from the later 6th century onwards. The structure of the present theatre incorporates the first complete stone-built auditorium and stage of the 330s and 320s BC, although the stage area and paving were subsequently rebuilt in the 1st and 2nd centuries AD.

Under the Peisistratid tyrants a huge temple to Olympian Zeus was begun in the south-eastern quarter and was completed 700 years later by the Emperor Hadrian. The Akropolis was filled with a variety of larger and smaller shrines, predominantly of poros limestone. The old temple of Athena, later replaced by the Erechtheion, was of limestone with gutters and roof tiles as well as pedimental sculpture of island rather than Attic marble.

The city walls, one of the most characteristic features of Athens, are less in evidence today.

Piraeus was almost another city again. The fortification of the harbour began in the late 490s, when Themistokles (c528-462 BC) began the task of creating an Athenian navy. A regular street plan was designed during Perikles' administration. Ship-sheds and dry docks (excavated in 1885 and recently rediscovered) were built in the same period.

Eleusis (Elevsis): 22km (14 miles) sanctuary of Demeter and Kore.
Brauron (Vraona): 35.5km (22

miles) off the Sounion road via Markopoulo; sanctuary of Artemis Brauronia and Museum in one of the oldest communities of Attika.
Thorikos; about 48km (30 miles), nearest villages Keratea and Plaka; akropolis with theatre, sanctuary and mine shafts.
Sounion: 64km (40 miles), sanctuary of Poseidon and temple of Athena.

Temple of Asklepios on south slope of Acropolis

MUSEUMS

Athens National Archaeologial Museum: an unrivalled collection of antiquities from the whole of Attika, including sculpture, pottery and bronzes, and specialist collections from different regions.
Akropolis Museum: architectural and votive sculpture from the Akropolis.
Benaki Museum: includes jewellery from prehistoric to Byzantine periods.

South portico of the Erechtheion

Temple of Athena Nike, Acropolis

HOW TO GET THERE

By air to Elliniko airport, 6km (4 miles) south-east of the capital (internal and international flights); by sea to Piraeus harbour, half an hour from the city centre by electric railway (to Omonoia Square), bus or taxi. The railway terminus from northern Greece (and connecting with European routes via Belgrade and Gevgelija) is Larissa Station north-west of the city centre. Adjacent to it is Stathmos Peloponnesiou, the terminus for Korinth and the Peloponnese. Regular KTEL buses tour the city and suburbs of Attika, including Sounion, Marathon, Elevsis, Oropos.

155

Labyrinthian basement of Rotunda

EPIDAUROS
AND THE
NEW HEALING

The sanctuaries of Asklepios, the healer god, were as much sanatoria, health farms or spas, as places of worship. Epidauros in the north-eastern Peloponnese, administered by the polis of Epidauros on the coast (near Old Epidauros) and shielded by mountains from the territories of Argos, Korinth and Troizen, was the most prestigious centre of the cult in the Classical period and received a galaxy of splendid buildings spanning the whole of the 4th century BC. In Hellenistic times attention shifted to Kos (which denied any association with Epidauros) and Pergamon (which accepted it), whence Asklepios passed to Rome (293 BC).

At Epidauros tradition identified the site as Asklepios' birthplace, but there is no cult evidence before the 6th century BC. Instead, an ancient spring festival in honour of a local fertility god, Maleatas (later merged with Apollo), was celebrated on Mount Kynortion (modern Kharani), and as Apollo Maleatas this cult continued beside Asklepios at a smaller sanctuary on the slope.

In the 5th century Asklepios was more popularly thought of as son of Apollo. Epidauros came into prominence only in the later 5th century, when the cult was received at Athens in 420 BC and the tragedian Sophokles became its priest. There was a revival at the sanctuary in the 2nd century AD, and worship on the site continued in the form of a Christian basilica. The principal installations were damaged by Goths in 395.

THEATRE
At the far south-eastern end of the site, built into the slopes of Mount Kynortion, is the best preserved theatre of the 4th century BC in Greece (and location of a modern drama festival). The cavea (auditorium), which seats 14,000 spectators, was built of local white limestone and faces the sanctuary area. Fifty-five rows of seats divided into two wedges surround the circular orchestra, or dancing floor. The foundations of a stage building lie at the rear. The architect was Polykleitos the Younger, who also designed the Tholos.

KATAGOGION (HOSTEL)
On a plateau north-west of the theatre is a square hostel resembling the Leonidaion at Olympia, but in this case the original arrangement of rooms around four instead of one courtyard, with four entrances, was not altered in Roman times.

PALAISTRA
Between the hostel and the precinct there was a series of subsidiary buildings providing additional facilities for visitors. To the west was the stadium and close by was a square exercise yard with a Doric colonnade, surrounded by rooms of various sizes, some of which were dining rooms (support blocks for the couches are preserved).

TEMPLE OF ASKLEPIOS
The sanctuary and its religious buildings occupied less space than the "secular"

facilities. The original cult of Asklepios centred on a square enclosure with a courtyard, altar, shrine and rooms for sleeping in. In the later 370s BC, a Doric temple was built nearby in the middle of the precinct. It was one of the smallest in the Peloponnese but also one of the richest in terms of materials. An inscription found in 1885 records that the overall managment of the project was in the hands of an Athenian architect, Theodotos, and that the construction work took 4 years and 8½ months (quick for a Greek temple). It also provides a rare insight into the methods of masons, artists and sculptors. Peloponnesian limestone was used except for the pediments and other carvings, for which Pentelic marble was imported.

4th century theatre

ENKOIMETERION (SLEEPING OR INCUBATION AREA)
Immediately adjacent to the northern side of the temple was a long, columned hall divided into two sections, the later one having two storeys. In the south-east corner was a well for bathing water, beside which tablets were found recording miraculous cures.

THOLOS (ROTUNDA)
This is the most curious of all the buildings on the site. Originally there was a series of underground concentric circular passages closed off in one direction, forming a miniature labyrinth (diameter 13.36m/44ft). This was enlarged within a few decades of the temple's completion by the construction of a podium and a circular roofed building made of poros limestone.

The healing ministry of Asklepios involved a combination of techniques, including dietary recommendations, exercise, bathing, auto-suggestion and other kinds of psychological therapy, as well as prayer and sacrifice. It was assumed that there was a relationship between a person's health and his state of mind, his physical and his spiritual being. This is why visitors slept in close proximity to the god's shrine, so that he would inspire their dreams and bring about a change. A determined effort to change the state of one's physical system by practical means was seen as a parallel response.

Epidauros Museum houses reconstructions of the tholos, temple of Asklepios and Propylaia (monumental entrance) and architectural sculpture (mainly casts). The finest sculptures from the temple of Asklepios are in the *National Museum, Athens*.

30km/19 miles from Nauplia to the sanctuary, known as Ieron Ligouriou.

CHRONOLOGY

7th CENTURY BC
Apollo established at Mycenaean sanctuary on Mount Kynortion: cult administered from *polis* at Old Epidauros on coast.

5th CENTURY BC
Emergence of Asklepios, son of Apollo, as principal deity of lowland shrine.

EARLY 4th CENTURY BC
New building programme, including temple of Asklepios, rotunda, sanatorium *(abaton)* and subsidiary temples and secular accommodation.

293 BC
Cult of Asklepios established at Rome.

86 BC
Sanctuary sacked by soldiers of Roman general Sulla.

Lion Gate with Grave Circle behind

MYCENAE AND THE LATE BRONZE AGE

A new network of palace-citadels sprang up in the Greek mainland from the 15th century BC. "Well built" Mycenae, "of the broad streets" and "rich in gold" (in Homer's words), which had been occupied from the Early Bronze Age at least, was probably the first of these citadels. It was soon followed by Tiryns, and in the 14th and 13th centuries BC by other palace-citadels such as Sparta (?) and Pylos in the Peloponnese, Athens, Orchomenos and Gla in central Greece, and Iolkos further north. They were constructed by a warrior aristocracy whose wealth, wide contacts and martial lifestyle are best reflected in the burial goods from the Shaft Graves at Mycenae.

WHAT YOU WILL SEE TODAY

FORTIFICATIONS
The citadel at Mycenae (moden Mikinai) occupied the triangular summit of a low hill between two gorges. The rocky summit is enclosed by a thick curtain wall of large, closely fitting boulders, preserved on average to a height of 4.6-10.6m (15-35ft), reaching 17m (56ft) on the south-west. The Mycenaeans excelled in this style of building using large, unworked stones. These massive fortifications were begun in the 14th century, followed by Tiryns and Dendra, Argos and Athens, as well as a host of subsidiary forts and eventually, a huge wall across the Korinthian isthmus. The famous Lion Gate, and similar constructions at Gla and Tiryns, were built in the 13th century BC.

THE "MEGARON"
Only sectors of the rising ground inside the akropolis of Mycenae have been investigated so far. These include an area just inside the Lion Gate (Grave Circle A and adjacent buildings); the core of the palace on the summit itself, including a megaron, court and Throne Room; and a residence located on the south-east side.

The citadel is surrounded by a variety of related monuments, including many large private houses, nine tholos (beehive) tombs, Grave Circle B (with 14 Shaft Graves), and cist tombs belonging to the ordinary population. The nucleus of the Mycenaean palace was a large open court onto which faced the Megaron unit — a portico behind which was an anteroom opening into the main hall. The central feature of the hall was a huge circular hearth flanked by four columns supporting the roof. This arrangement was an elaboration of simpler Early and Middle Bronze Age Megaron house plans. Where the ground plans have been preserved, at Mycenae and Tiryns (and also at Troy), the most distinctive feature is the axial arrangement of the rooms composing the Megaron unit.

THE PALACE OF PYLOS
The remains on Epano Englianos hill, 17km (10½ miles) north of Pylos in the southwestern Peloponnese, gives us the most elaborate

Treasury of Atreus

and complete plan of a Mycenaean palace in the 13th century BC. There was no external protection apart from the steep sides of the hill itself. Many of the principal features used here are familiar from Minoan palaces – courts, ashlar masonry (limestone), staircases, exterior walls with offset rather than continuous sections, frescoes and painted floors, and elaborate drainage.

The richly painted interiors of Mycenaean palaces must have looked much like Minoan ones. There were large storerooms full of jars and organic containers stopped with decorated clay sealings, pantries full of delicate egg-shell thin cups and vases. Cult is the most difficult aspect to reconstruct. Snakes, double axes, offering tables and female figurines have been found in a shrine on the akropolis of Mycenae, along with frescoes portraying a divinity or worshippers, all rather reminiscent of Cretan religion. At the same time we know from Linear B tablets that many of the later "Olympians", Zeus, Hera, Athena, Poseidon and Apollo, were among the gods worshipped at Mycenaean sites. The tablets show that Pylos was the centre of an extensive network of interdependent subsidiary sites, with goods passing between them.

Tiryns 60km (37¼ miles from Korinth, 4km/2½ miles from Nauplia on the Argos road): impressive circuit and remarkable stone casemates built into the fortification wall on two levels; underground cisterns as at Mycenae and Athens; foundations of palace walls.
Korinth: archaic temple of Apollo, Roman theatre and Agora.
Nemea: site of ancient sanctuary of Zeus with associated buildings and installations connected with Panhellenic Games, recently excavated by the University of California.
Argos (48km/30 miles from Korinth): remains of the Archaic and Classical city walls, early 3rd-century BC theatre and Roman Agora. About 8km (5 miles) off the main road north of Argos town just beyond the village of Khonika is the famous sanctuary of Hera.

A Mycenaean suit of armour and frescoes from Mycenae and Tiryns are in the local museum of the Argolid region at *Nauplia*. Material from Schliemann's and later Greek excavations at Mycenae and Mycenaean sites in Attika and the Argolid, and the rich grave goods from Vapheio in Lakonia, form the core of Mycenaean exhibits in the *National Archaeological Museum, Athens*. Dressed carved stones and the column shafts from the entrance to the "Treasury of Atreus", Mycenae, can be seen in the *British Museum*, together with finds excavated by the British School in Crete and Cyprus.
Thebes Museum: prehistoric and Mycenaean pottery from Thebes and the nearby environs; Linear B and 14th-century BC cuneiform-inscribed tablets from the Levant, found at Thebes; Mycenaean plate corselet and gold jewellery; frescoes that were removed from the Theban akropolis.

Nauplia is the most convenient base for visiting the Argolid. Regular trains and daily coach tours from Athens to Mycenae, thrice weekly in winter; buses from Nauplia and Argos to Tiryns and Mycenae.

CHRONOLOGY

*c*2200–1900 BC
Emergence of Greek-speaking groups in central and southern Greece with distinctive new features, including long houses, pottery shapes (including Anatolian influences).

*c*1550 BC
Shaft Graves of Mycenae.

*c*1400 BC
Mycenaean administration of Cretan palaces.

*c*1300 BC
Destruction of Troy (VI).

*c*1200 BC
Destruction of many Mycenaean centres (and Troy VII A).

Treasury of Atreus

Temple of Hera

OLYMPIA

The sanctuary of Zeus at Olympia has its origins in prehistory. Local legend attributed the foundation of the Olympic festival to Pelops, after whom the Peloponnese is named. The first Olympiad (the four-year interval between festivals) was reckoned by the 5th-century BC scholar, Hippias of Elis, as beginning in 776 BC. The precinct, known as the Altis, lies on the eastern banks of the river Kladeos, just north of its confluence with the larger Alpheios.

THE OLYMPIC GAMES

The games, which were the most prestigious athletic event in Greece, were held in conjunction with a festival to Olympian Zeus. Three heralds were sent to all the Greek states to announce their date and declare the universal truce, under which all hostilities were suspended for one week. The games were brought to an end in AD 393, under an edict of the Emperor Theodosius which banned all pagan festivals. The temples were destroyed in AD 426.

The games and the

sanctuary were normally administered by elected officials from the local town of Elis, who met in the Bouleuterion (Council House) and lived in the Prytaneion. These buildings were all situated outside the precinct walls. The earliest competition was the footrace, to which were added the pentathlon (running, jumping, wrestling, throwing the spear and the discus), boxing, chariot and horse-racing, as well as boys' events. Only Greeks could compete, slaves and women being excluded entirely from the festival, though non-Greeks might attend. Poetry and prose works were also recited.

Winners were given a palm branch, and on the final day a wreath of wild olive. They were permitted to commission a statue; if successful in three events this might be a portrait.

WHAT YOU WILL SEE TODAY

The building foundations within the precinct and many outside it are visible, if not always easy to identify.

TEMPLE OF HERA

This is the oldest structure in the precinct, originally dedicated to Zeus as well as Hera, and gradually rebuilt from wood into stone (the development of styles can be observed from the column shafts). The walls were of mud-brick with a tiled roof.

TREASURIES

Lined up against the hill of Kronos in the north-east was a row of treasuries, most of which represent western Greek cities. The oldest belonged to Gela in Sicily (c600 BC), this was followed in the next 30 years by those of Metapontion and Megara. The Megarian treasury was decorated with a battle scene in the pediment, of which figures are preserved. Others belonged to Cyrene, Byzantion, Sybaris, Syracuse and Sikyon.

WHAT YOU WOULD HAVE SEEN

TEMPLE OF ZEUS

Erected between 470 and 458 BC, this was the largest contemporary Doric temple in Greece, 200 Olympic feet long

(27.68 × 64.12m). The foundations alone rose more than 3m (3¼ft) above ground level and 1m (1yd) below, made of huge coarse limestone blocks. The colonnade (6 × 13 columns) was made of the same local stone, smoothed with a coat of stucco. Only the sculptured figures in the two triangular pediments were made of marble. Those at the eastern (front) end represent one of the founding legends of Olympia – the chariot race of Pelops and Oinomaos adjudicated by Zeus. The battle of Thessalian Lapiths and centaurs at the western end symbolizes the triumph of human culture over animal barbarism. The Labours of Herakles were depicted on 12 Parian marble slabs (metopes) above the entrance to the main chamber. Within was the colossal gold and ivory statue of Zeus – one of the Seven Wonders of the ancient world – seated majestically on an ebony and gold throne, holding his sceptre in his left hand and a figure of Victory in his right. Both the black marble pedestal and the throne were decorated with figure scenes. The whole figure is said to have stood 12m (40ft) high.

ECHO HALL

Along the east side of the precinct are the foundations of a long, aisled hall, once decorated with famous paintings. The present layout dates from the later 4th century BC, when the east side was adjusted after rebuilding the stadium. An earlier 5th-century version lay further out.

STADIUM

This is a rectangular open space about 190 × 30m (208 × 33yd) with starting and finishing lines marked in stone at the western and eastern ends. The present track dates from a rebuilding in the 4th century BC. The umpires' seats were about halfway up the track on the southern bank of seats (estimated capacity 40,000). The track was surrounded by a stone kerb and there were water basins at intervals along it. The shortest race was the stadion, one length of the track; the diaulos and race in armour took two lengths and the dolichos ten.

Until the 5th century, the stadium extended right as far as the Pelopion, an enclosed grove of trees containing an altar to Pelops. Numerous terracotta and bronze offerings were buried here.

LEONIDAION

Outside the precinct on the south-west side was a high-class hostel built in the 4th century BC by Leontas, a citizen of Naxos. Originally there was an open peristyle court with 12 Doric columns in the centre and a continuous

Altis Sanctuary from Heraion
colonnade of limestone Ionic columns around the outside.

GYMNASIUM

Greek gymnasia were not just sports halls. The best-preserved unit at Olympia is the palaistra (wrestling school), which consists of an open square surrounded by Doric colonnades on four sides, behind which were various rooms, used for musical and intellectual pursuits as well as physical training. Only the eastern arm of the covered gymnasium parallel with the road as you enter the site has survived.

MUSEUMS

The *Olympia Museum* houses sculptures from the temple of Zeus, bronze armour, and bronze and clay dedications from the sanctuary.

HOW TO GET THERE

Coach tours from Athens and regular trains to Olimbia village (800m/½ mile).

CHRONOLOGY

8th CENTURY BC
Significant quantities of dedications begin to appear in the Altis (grove) or sanctuary, although legends suggest an older history too.

MID-7th CENTURY BC
Two cities closest to Olympia, Elis and Pisa, dispute authority over the sanctuary (held predominantly by Elis).

c600 BC
Building of first temple of Zeus and Hera and earliest civic Treasuries, continuing through 6th Century.

5th CENTURY BC
New, more ambitious building programme transforms the Altis; new temple of Zeus c470-58 BC, cult statue of Pheidias added c430; formal enclosure of Pelops' sanctuary.

LATER 4th CENTURY BC
Rebuilding and relandscaping of the Altis, to create more distinct separation between sacred and secular land.

DELPHI

Temple of Apollo and theatre from above

The historical origins of the sanctuary at Delphi are obscure, but according to legend the young god Apollo superseded an older female deity, Mother Earth, and killed her son, the serpent Python. In Homer the sanctuary is called Pytho, and oracles were given by the Pythia (priestess) between the Shining Rocks (Phaidriades) on the southern slopes of Mount Parnassos long before the cult of Apollo Delphinios was established there from Crete. Later Dionysos, who took over the sanctuary in winter, and Athena (whose precinct lay on a lower terrace 1km/⅔ mile to the south-east) were also worshipped there.

THE ORACLE

Greeks and non-Greeks, kings and commoners, came to consult the oracle on private and public matters. It was first necessary to sacrifice an animal, then to wait in the inner chamber of the temple. Nothing has survived of the arrangements associated with this process. In Classical times the priestesses (there were three altogether) were women over 50. They first cleansed themselves in the sacred spring of Kastalia and drank water from another spring. They then chewed bay leaves while seated on a tripod suspended over a cleft in the rocks. The vapours issuing from the cleft were supposed to give the priestesses a heightened consciousness and cause prophetic utterances. These cries would then be interpreted by a male prophet, usually in ambiguous verse. Personal ethics and social morality were given great importance, and the sanction given to overseas settlements enhanced the sanctuary's influence in the wider Greek world. Although the statements tended towards political conservatism and at times weakness, the oracle's reputation for truth-telling remained high.

WHAT YOU WILL SEE TODAY

The sub-rectangular precinct enclosed by walls occupies a steep slope west of the Kastalia spring. Above it to the west is the stadium, and on the lower slopes south-east of the main road are the gymnasium and sanctuary of Athena at Marmaria. The Sacred Way, whose pavement was made up from re-used architectural slabs in Roman times, begins near the south-eastern corner and mounts the terraces in zig-zag fashion, flanked by the foundations of famous monuments and city treasuries. Delphi has one of the most evocative settings of any Greek site and, with a copy of Pausanias' *Guide to Greece* in hand, it is possible to imagine how sumptuous and stirring this jewel-box of Greek achievements actually was. Some of the monuments mentioned by him have been identified, and some have been reconstructed with a fair degree of precision from the extant remains (the treasuries of the Athenians, the Siphnians and Sikyonians). Most of the earlier (6th and early 5th century BC) structures lie below the temple terrace, those of the later 5th and 4th centuries are near the entrance to the precinct, and the latest were either on the temple terrace itself or above it. The podium of the 4th-century temple of Apollo, (built after the earthquake of 373 BC) and one column have been partly restored, and only fragments of the pedimental sculptures belonging to the earlier stone version (a rebuilding following a fire in 548 BC) have survived.

WHAT YOU WOULD HAVE SEEN

Most Greek sanctuaries contain small rectangular buildings, usually with a twin-columned portico, known as treasuries. These housed the precious offerings dedicated by individual states. The earliest and richest of those at Delphi was that of the Korinthians, reputedly put up by the tyrant Kypselos (c600 BC), which also housed many of the gold bars, gold statues and precious vessels dedicated by Croesus. Other monuments were put up in thanksgiving for a piece of good fortune, such as the Siphnian treasury after a rich vein of silver was discovered, or the bronze bull of Kerkyra for a huge haul of tunny fish. Many were built from the spoils of war, thus serving an expiatory function as well as one of thanksgiving – the monument of the Arkadians, the treasuries of Athens and Thebes, of the Tarentines, Thessalians, Phokians, and many others.

There were numerous statues of Apollo, various bronze animals, the marble sphinx of the Naxians and the gilded statue of Phryne, one of the great beauties of the 4th century BC. This was made by one of her lovers, the artist Praxiteles, and dedicated by the lady herself. Further statues and dedications were housed in the temple (including the poet Pindar's iron throne).

Political nuances are clearly detectable in the deliberate

Temple of Apollo

juxtaposition of the Arkadian heroes on a 4th-century monument opposite one by the Arkadians' former oppressors, the Spartans (for the victory of Aigospotamoi, 405 BC, over the Athenians). Numerous individual dedications were made in many forms, including armour, statuettes and dress ornaments, usually of bronze. The greatest collective dedication was the Serpent Column, surmounted by a tripod, inscribed with the names of the 31 states which participated in the resistance against the invading Persians in 480-479 BC.

MUSEUMS

The *Museum at Delphi* houses sculptures from the precinct.

HOW TO GET THERE

Delphi (166km/103 miles from Athens) is one of the most popular tourist sites in Greece and there are numerous coach tours, buses and trains from the capital.

CHRONOLOGY

586 BC
First Pythian games held.

548 BC
Temple of Apollo burned down.

513-505 BC
Temple of Apollo rebuilt with help of Athenian Alkmaionid clan.

480 BC
Abortive Persian attack on Delphi.

373 BC
Earthquake destroys temple of Apollo.

279 BC
Attack on Delphi by Celts under Brennus repulsed by the neighbouring Aitolians.

189 BC
Romans take control.

88 BC
Roman general Sulla plunders precinct.

AD 385
Oracle and shrine abolished by edict of Emperor Theodosius.

Rotunda in the precinct of Athena Pronoia.

View from Acropolis, Eretria

LEFKANDI AND ERETRIA

The island of Euboia (Evvia) is separated from the mainland of central Greece by a narrow channel, the Euripos. At its narrowest point, roughly in the central southern part of the island, a cluster of ancient settlements arose on the borders of the fertile Lelantine Plain. On a broad promontory closest to the mainland was Chalkis, and a little way further south was another site, now called Lefkandi, which may have been either Old Chalkis or Old Eretria, abandoned c825 BC. Classical Eretria lies 10km (6 miles) further south, around a fine harbour. Both the Classical city and the putative predecessor have been excavated during the last 25 years.

Euboia came under the influence of Boiotia during the Mycenaean Age, but thereafter its ties with Athens were equally important. A famous war between Chalkis and Eretria occurred in the late 8th century BC, which was said to have divided all Greece. Both Chalkis and Eretria were among the most outward-looking of Greek poleis, trading with the Levant and planting new settlements as far afield as central Italy.

WHAT YOU WILL SEE TODAY

The most extensive Classical excavations on Euboia are at Eretria (8th century BC-1st century AD). The eastern end of the modern town partly overlies the ancient polis, but extensive parts of the ancient fortifications lie beyond to the north and north-east, between the ancient akropolis and the shore. Investigations have concentrated around the ancient West Gate, just north of the Museum, near a late 8th/early 7th-century BC shrine to a hero or founder. The range and character of the buildings identified so far gives a good idea of the amenities provided in a prosperous Greek city of the late 4th and 3rd centuries BC. The fortifications around the West Gate were built c400 BC, and about the same time, the first stages of two palatial buildings appeared together with a theatre, the temple of Dionysos, two gymnasia, and the inner harbour. There is a quarter that contains fine 4th-century BC houses with pebble mosaics and architectural ornaments, variously remodelled over the next 200 years.

WHAT YOU WOULD HAVE SEEN

The settlement on Xeropolis hill near Lefkandi had extensive trade links with Cyprus in the 10th century BC. Cypriot bronzework has been found in burials, and Cypriot copper was being used to make tools. About one third of contemporary burials contained some gold, and in the following century the quantity and quality of goldwork increased, as did the range of eastern imports, including Egyptianizing seals and faience beads. In 1981 the stone foundations of a large aisled hall were discovered, about 10m (11yd) wide and 45m (46yd) long, dated to the mid 10th century BC. This is the earliest example to date of a Greek temple-like structure surrounded by a portico. The

Streets and houses of 4th century Eretria.

HOW TO GET THERE

Regular trains and buses from Athens (89km/55¼ miles to Chalkis) and ferry via Arkitsa.

CHRONOLOGY

BRONZE AGE
Manika and Lefkandi settled.

850-750 BC
Chalkis and Eretria with first formal colonies in Italy and Sicily; their rivalry erupts in Lelantine War; demise of Lefkandi.

506 BC
Athenians defeat Chalkidians.

490 BC
Eretria sacked by the Persians.

5th CENTURY BC
Euboian cities join Delian League.

338-194 BC
Euboia under Macedonian control.

walls were made of mud brick and the columns were probably wooden.

Eretria was already occupied by c900 BC. It was clearly flourishing by the 8th century, although there is little to be seen of this stage apart from the heroic shrine and the slightly later plan of the temple of Apollo. This was refashioned in stone in the second half of the 6th century. It was damaged when the city was sacked by the Persians in 490 BC, and later rebuilt. In the 4th century the city was ruled by the "tyrants" Themison, Plutarch and Kleitarchos (to whom the palatial buildings may have belonged). In the Hellenistic period Eretria had close ties with the Macedonian kings. The painter Philoxenos created the masterpiece, "Alexander and Dareios at the battle of Issos", which was used as a model for a mosaic in Pompeii. The city was sacked by Lucius Flamininius in 198 BC and largely rebuilt.

MUSEUMS

Finds from the three cemeteries that have been excavated at Lefkandi (Skoubris, Palaia Perivola and Toumba) are exhibited at *Eretria Museum*, together with pottery, bronzes and other finds from Eretria. *Chalkis Museum* (damaged in an earthquake in 1987 and temporarily closed) houses Mycenaean pottery and marble sculpture from Chalkis, Eretria and Karystos.

Painted clay centaur (c. 900BC)

Façade of a Macedonian tomb near Vergina (Palatitsa)

AIGAI AND PELLA

Whether the Macedonians were really Greeks or close ethnic relatives does not much matter, although it did to the ancient Greeks. The Macedonians were different not just because they spoke an odd dialect, but because their social organization was based on villages, not on poleis. Ultimately this distinction rested on the overriding powers of local princes and kings as opposed to autonomous communities (poleis). Unfortunately, no Macedonian writer has survived to tell us what the other side thought about such distinctions. The enormous expansion of archaeological studies and excavations in Macedonia means that it is at last becoming possible to make some independent assessment of this controversial region.

WHAT YOU WILL SEE

PELLA
On either side of the main road from Salonika to Edessa, about one-third of the way from the former, lies Pella, the second capital of Macedonia, the birthplace of Philip II and Alexander the Great. King Archelaos (413-399 BC) moved his seat here from Aigai in c400 BC, and invited many prominent Greek artists to fill its halls with masterpieces, artistic, literary and theatrical. One famous artist, Zeuxis, responded, as did the poets Agathon, Timotheos and Euripides of Athens, though others instead listened to the southerners' jokes about an upstart barbarian king and his pretensions. Pella developed into a luxurious city during the 4th century BC, reached its zenith during the reign of Antigonos Gonatas (283-239 BC) and continued to flourish well into the 2nd century BC.

AKROPOLIS
The earliest structures here might date from the time of Alexander. Sections of the northern circuit wall lie immediately to the north of the newly excavated buildings. Parts of the southern wall, complete with a well-protected gate towards the town, have also been cleared.

TOWN HOUSES AND STREETS
The main residential areas, arranged on a spacious grid plan, developed south and east of the akropolis. Some of the paved streets were 9m (29ft) wide, with a raised pavement of 1.8-1.9m (5½-6ft), and were lined with clay water-pipes and stone sewers. The houses excavated so far, dating from the end of the 4th century onwards, are unusually spacious, with mosaic-decorated rooms surrounding a peristyle court. Extensive frescoes have also been recovered.

VERGINA
The old capital, Aigai, nestles in the foothills of the Pierian mountains south of the Haliakmon river. The site was long known for its tumulus cemetery and a palace of the early Hellenistic period at the nearby village of Palatitsa. Over 100 tumuli have been excavated, dating from the Late Bronze Age to the Hellenistic period, and another cemetery with Mycenaean imports is now known in the Petra Pass.

THE PALACE AT PALATITSA

Remains of a vast, rectangular structure (104.5 × 88.5m/ 343 × 290ft) lie less than 1.5km (1 mile) from the village of Vergina, on a low hill overlooking the plain, with the Pierian mountains in the background. In plan it consists of a large courtyard surrounded by a peristyle with square and circular reception rooms opening off it. There was a second storey above and a monumental entrance on the east side. Architectural features reflect the influence of the most advanced and innovative schools of the day, but are resolved in a highly individual manner.

THEATRE

Philip II of Macedon was murdered at the theatre of Aigai in 336 BC. In 1981 this theatre was rediscovered just below the Palatitsa palace. It consists of an unusually large orchestra (28.5m/93ft diameter, compared to 19.5m/ 64ft for Epidauros), and a row of stone seats, presumably for the king and his retinue, the rest of the audience sitting on the grassy ridges above.

THE CHAMBER TOMBS

There are now said to be 11 chamber tombs of the "Macedonian" type in the vicinity of Vergina alone, including the remarkable trio inside the "Great Tumulus" (110m/361ft in diameter, 12m/ 39ft high), the tallest man-made mound in the area. Rectangular stone burial chambers were not uncommon in northern Greece during the 4th century, but at some point in the second half of the century the stone barrel vault began to be used to cover the chamber. Vaulting was a constant problem for tomb architects, because of the difficulty of judging the soil pressure from the traditional earth mound used to protect the tomb. The barrel vault is a true self-supporting arch and was therefore technically superior to any of the previous methods applied. The entrance to the chamber(s) was usually through a long passage, later backfilled, but the façade of the tomb was often decorated with a false door and architectural moldings made from painted stucco.

SECONDARY SITES

Verroia (Verria): a city in Macedonia from the 5th century onwards. The remains are mainly Roman, but they include some rock-cut Hellenistic tombs.
Dion: seat of a major sanctuary of Zeus in the foothills of Mount Olympos, and a flourishing Hellenistic/ Roman city. Two cult buildings of megaron type have been discovered, with votives dating from *c*500 BC onwards.

MUSEUMS

Archaeological Museum, Thessaloniki: main regional museum of northern Greece, houses spectacular finds from Vergina and Sindos, representative material from the prehistoric to Byzantine periods of the region.
Kozani: important finds from 5th and 4th century tombs from this strategic location on the ancient road to Epiros.
Aiani: finds from a regional centre south of Kozani, Late Bronze Age to Hellenistic.
Dion: finds from sanctuaries and tombs.

HOW TO GET THERE

By air to Thessaloniki; 38km (23½ miles) to Pella on the Edessa road; 75km (46½ miles) to Verria, thence 11km (7 miles) to Vergina; 69km (43 miles) to Polygiros in Chalkidiki; regular train and bus links.

CHRONOLOGY

*c*700 BC
Perdiccas I founds Macedonian kingdom.

359–48 BC
Philip II becomes king.

336 BC
Philip II assassinated; Alexander the Great succeeds further.

334–27 BC
Alexander conquers Persian Empire.

323–01 BC
Wars of Alexander's Successors.

275 BC
New dynasty (the Gonatids) is established in Macedon.

168 BC
Gonatids deposed by Romans;

146 BC
Macedon annexed by Romans.

Lion mosaic from late 4th century house at Pella

167

Aerial view of Thasos

GAZETTEER

THASOS

Thasos was one of the richest and most powerful island states of the Aegean. Her wealth was based primarily on gold and silver mines, both on the island and on the mainland opposite. According to Herodotos, the Phoenicians were the first to exploit these resources on a large scale, at Ainyra and Koinyra. Parians migrated to the island in the 680s BC. They were opposed by the native Thracians, but the new Parian foundation flourished. In the 5th century BC Thasian wealth proved too great a temptation to the Athenians, who appropriated the city's mining revenues (between 200 and 300 talents annually) after a lengthy siege (465-463 BC). By the late 5th century, however, Thasos had not only won back her revenues and autonomy, re-established trading links with her daughter colonies and the Thracians on the mainland, but had begun to expand her export of wine. These trends continued into the Hellenistic period and are reflected in inscriptions referring to special legislation, a growing number of amphora production centres, and the wide dispersal of Thasian coins, from the 2nd century BC throughout the Balkans.

WHAT YOU WILL SEE TODAY

The modern town of Limenas lies to the west and north of the ancient city. Most of the excavated remains, enclosed by the fortification walls, form an archaeological zone. Good building stone is plentiful; gneiss (a coarse-grained rock with a layered appearance) was used for substructures and internal walls, the local white and grey veined marble for colonnades, steps and decorative work. The earliest structures were spread out within this area between the double harbour and the akropolis.

AKROPOLIS
West of the citadel itself (thought to have been the site of a sanctuary to Pythian Apollo) are the remains of a stone temple of Athena built in the 5th century BC. Nearby was a cave sanctuary to Pan.

The earliest structures at the sanctuaries of Artemis and Herakles date from the same period.

FORTIFICATION WALLS
The earliest walls were destroyed by order of the Persian King Dareios I (492/1 BC), and the postwar replacement was again demolished when the Thasians capitulated to Athens in 463 BC. The present circuit retains one of the most distinctive features of the earlier walls — the low-relief sculptured slabs which lined the gateways situated at intervals on the western and northern sections. One slab represents a vibrant Seilenos with his horse tail twitching, holding a wine cup. Another has Zeus and Hera on a chariot, a third Herakles on bended knee, stretching his bow. All the reliefs are associated with specific Thasian cults. The fabric of the present walls, which in many places are preserved to 2m (6½ft), belongs to the late 5th-century reconstruction. There were two ashlar faces, the

Gate of the Silenos (early 5th century BC)

intervening space being packed with rubble.

HERAKLES'S SANCTUARY

Herodotos claimed he had visited a sanctuary to the Phoenician Herakles (Melqart) on Thasos. The precinct was located on the lower slopes to the west of the city. Whereas in the 6th century this consisted of a conventional temple, entirely of marble but with an attractive clay gutter showing mounted archers chasing a hare, it was replaced in the 5th century by a suite of rooms and a new Ionic temple on the opposite side of an open square. The ensemble was approached by a flight of steps cut by a columned porch.

THE PASSAGE

In the 5th century BC a road ran between the Herakles sanctuary and the eastern side of the city. Just south of the agora was a monumental passageway, which in the 4th century had the names of the religious magistrates (theoroi) carved on its sides. A century earlier three magnificent

reliefs, showing Apollo crowned by nymphs, the Three Graces and Hermes (taken to the Louvre in 1863), were inserted into the walls.

RESIDENTIAL AREAS

A residential quarter excavated on the north-east side of the city has shown that houses were set out on a grid plan from the 6th century BC onwards, although some reorganization came about when the town walls were built.

AGORA

In the 4th century BC a more formal plan was introduced in the agora. The earliest monument there was the tombstone of Glaukos, a friend of Archilochos, the lyric poet, who was also the son of Telesikles, the founder of Thasos. A temple of Zeus Agoraios was built, around which arose the court surrounded by covered halls (stoas), between the 4th century BC and the 1st century AD. In the following century the main port was closed off with round towers and a

lighthouse, a scene building was added to the 5th-century theatre, and a semicircular loggia containing statues of Dionysos, Tragedy, Comedy and others was dedicated.

The material found in excavations shows that Thasos had close contacts with various parts of the Aegean. The availability of good marble meant that the standard of carving was high. In recent years more evidence has emerged of the pre-colonial Thracian occupation of the island and of wine amphora factories. A sizeable body of inscriptions has revealed a considerable amount about the leading families of the island and the kinds of public activities they participated in.

The *Museum* contains marble sculpture and reliefs, local and imported ceramics, jewellery and domestic equipment.

By ferry from Kavalla to Limenas at least 6 times daily (1½ hours), or by car ferry from Keramoti.

CHRONOLOGY

BRONZE AGE
Thracians from north Aegean coast established on island.

c680 BC
Telesikles, father of poet Archilochos, founds a colony from Paros on the island.

491–80 BC
Thasos subjected to Persian authority.

477–411 BC
Thasos joins Delian League led by Athens, though loses revenue as a result of revolt in 465-3.

4th CENTURY BC
Reorganisation of civil administration and continental possessions; foundation of Krenides (later Philippi) on the mainland (360).

Marble head (early 3rd century BC)

Theatre

PERGAMON

Pergamon was founded by Aiolic Greeks in the 8th century BC on a steep hill overlooking the rich valley of the river Kaikos, about 24km (15 miles) from the sea. It became prominent in the 3rd century BC when Philetairos, an officer of King Lysimachos of Thrace who was deputed to guard his treasure at Pergamon, made himself an independent ruler. In 280 BC there was no one to challenge his move. Three years later he succeeded in fighting off some bands of Celts who had crossed from Europe to Asia. When his nephew and successor, Eumenes I defeated Antiochos I of Syria in 262 BC, Pergamon truly became a separate principality.

Further assaults by Gauls in 228 and 201 BC under Eumenes' successor, Attalos I, brought lasting fame to the dynasty. Attalos began the policy of cooperation with the Romans against the Greek kings of Macedon and Syria, and was thus able to expand his territories as far as the Maiander after 190 BC. Ten years later Pergamene

territories had more than trebled. In the first half of the 2nd century BC Pergamon reached the zenith of its power and influence under Eumenes II and his brother Attalos II. In 133 BC, Attalos III died childless leaving his kingdom to the Romans.

WHAT YOU WILL SEE TODAY

The ancient site lies north of modern Bergama and has been extensively investigated. Explanatory boards have been provided at regular intervals. The principal civic area falls into two groups, the monuments around the royal palaces on the akropolis and the area around the gymnasia on the lower slopes. The whole city was carefully landscaped by constructing a series of terraces with powerful substructures to create a winding perspective culminating in the palaces and precinct of Athena.

GREAT ALTAR
A huge pi-shaped platform 34 × 36.5m (112 × 120ft) and nearly 5.5m (18ft) high

intersected by a marble stairway 21.3m (70ft) wide was built in the reign of Eumenes II on a square terrace overlooking the upper Agora. Around the upper edge of the platform was a figured frieze in high relief, depicting the battle of the Olympian gods against their predecessors, the Titans. About 70 over-life-size figures have survived, of which 14 have their names carved below. A smaller frieze, showing the story of Telephos, a son of Herakles by a Mysian princess, was set into the wall behind an Ionic colonnade on top of the platform. The altar was dedicated to Zeus and Athena and designed by Menekrates of Rhodes.

THEATRE
A theatre was cut into the western side of the akropolis in Eumenes' reign and the rows of seats are banked at an unusually steep angle. Supporting it from below was a series of retaining walls topped by a stoa and processional way, leading up to a temple of Dionysos.

PRECINCT OF ATHENA

The most prestigious precinct of the upper city was dedicated to Athena, bringer of Victory. It was approached through a monumental entrance flanked by four Doric columns topped with four Ionic columns. Between them was a balustrade carved with war trophies. The same mix of Doric and Ionic was repeated in the colonnades surrounding the court beyond. In rooms behind the north wall was the famous Pergamon library: the tiers of bookshelves could be made out from iron wall fixtures.

PALACES

Fragments of mosaics and wall plaster show how elaborate the decoration of these interiors must have been. Some rooms had marble veneering on the lower parts of walls. The prevailing plan is of a central peristyle or colonnade surrounded by rooms of varying size.

THE LOWER SLOPES

The lower agora, an open court 30.5 × 61m sq (100 × 200ft sq) with two storeys of rooms and shops on the north-west and eastern sides, formed the centre of a luxury residential area along the main road up the hillside. Above these was a huge complex of gymnasia landscaped on several levels. A long, narrow lower gymnasium buttressed with

arches formed the lowest retaining unit, above which was an open middle terrace. Against this an underground stadium had been built, together with even more substantial compartments retaining the upper terrace.

ASKLEPEION

Most of the remains date from the 2nd century AD, but the sanctuary came into being in the 4th century BC. The nucleus of the design was a rectangular court with a portico on three sides. On the south side stood the incubation and sleeping rooms.

WHAT YOU WOULD HAVE SEEN

Pergamene rulers developed the art of terracing by the use of underground passageways and multi-storeyed façades. They took a great interest in methods of water provision and storage facilities. They encouraged mining and stockbreeding, textiles and the manufacture of paper from cured skins (pergamena). They were also great patrons and collectors. Pergamon became a cultural centre second only to Alexandria. The library could accommodate 17,000 volumes. The copies of famous statues commissioned by the Attalids were complemented by bold new initiatives, such as the Great Altar and a number of separate groups commemorating the defeat of the Gauls.

Relief from Altar of Zeus

MUSEUMS

Berlin, Pergamonmuseum: apart from the Great Altar, there is a large collection of sculpture from the 19th-century German excavations. More fragments of the altar frieze are in the *Ashmolean Museum, Oxford, England* (Fawley Court relief) and *Worksop*.
Archaeological Museum, Bergama: finds from Pergamon and environs. Roman copies of statues of Gauls belonging to the Pergamene dedications are in the *Capitoline and Vatican (Chiaramonti) Museums, Naples (ex-Ludovisi Collection), the Louvre, Aix-en-Provence, Athens National Museum and Mykonos Museum* (both from Delos).

HOW TO GET THERE

Approximately 38km (24 miles) from Izmir by bus or *dolmus* (shared) taxis from Ayvalik to Bergama; site lies just north of Bergama, but taxi up the steep akropolis is recommended.

CHRONOLOGY

283 BC
Philetairos (283-263 BC), defects to Seleukos I of Asia.

281 BC
Death of Lysimachos and Seleukos I creates political vacuum in Asia Minor.

262 BC
Victory of Eumenes I of Pergamon and Ptolemy II of Egypt over King Antiochos I near Sardis.

238-7 BC
Attalos I defeats Gauls, at the Sources of the River Kaikos.

133 BC
Attalos III dies without issue, leaving Pergamon to the Romans.

Restored Altar of Zeus in Berlin

Reconstructed column from Temple of Hera, Samos

EPHESOS AND SAMOS

Around 1000 BC Ionian Greeks emigrated to the central part of the west Anatolian coastline between the River Hermos and the Halikarnassos (Bodrum) peninsula. The coastline forms a series of bays enclosing parallel river valleys separated by headlands. The offshore islands of Lesbos, Chios and Samos are extensions of these peninsulas, and their history interweaves with that of the mainland.

WHAT YOU WILL SEE TODAY

The greatest cities of Greek Ionia, Ephesos (Selçuk), Miletos (Milet) and Smyrna (Izmir), are today overshadowed by the extensive remains of their Roman successors.

EPHESOS
The principal early Greek settlement nestled up to the sanctuary of Artemis, or Artemision, south-west of the modern city of Selcuk. This is still the only significant Greek monument discovered. The site itself is marshy and excavation is not possible without special pumping facilities.

The podium belongs to the 4th-century BC temple, a rebuilding of the original stone construction burned down in 356 BC. The 4th-century structure retained certain features of the earlier design, with eight columns on the short ends and 21 on the sides. However, the new podium was larger than the original, so the spaces between the columns were widened. In both the original temple and its successor, the drums of the inner, lower row of columns were carved in high relief, a custom also found at Didyma and Kyzikos. The 4th-century carvings were by some of the most celebrated artists of the day – Skopas and Apelles, with the altar decorated by Praxiteles.

Unlike most Greek temples, which faced eastwards, the Artemision faced west, perhaps in response to native tradition. It seems clear from the temple's organization and the presence of the multi-breasted cult statue that the cult of Artemis was merged here with a local nature goddess.

WHAT YOU WOULD HAVE SEEN

SMYRNA
At the head of the Hermos valley lay Smyrna, settled by Aiolic-speaking Greeks c1000 BC, but later penetrated by Ionians. In the 7th century BC there was a prosperous walled town at Old Smyrna (Bayrakli, outside Izmir) that had a regular street plan but the Lydian attack c600 BC caused deterioration. The city was revived by Alexander the Great's Successors and moved to the area of Izmir.

SAMOS
Samos town (modern Pithagorio, formerly Tigani) was set around the best harbour of the island on its south-east side. The most flourishing period of the island's history began around the middle of the 6th century BC, when the first temple of Hera was built, and the engineer Eupalinos of Megara made a tunnel 1km (⅔ mile)

long and 1.75m (2yd) high to ensure a safe water supply for the akropolis. This flowering continued under the tyrant Polykrates (c540–522 BC), who developed the harbour, and encouraged arts, crafts and stockbreeding.

The temple of Hera, about 6km (3¾ miles) south-west of Pithagorio, stood on the banks of the river Imbrasos.

The most famous temple on this site was the mid 6th-century BC version, built by the local architect Theodoros and the artist Rhoikos. Theodoros, seems to have been the technical wizard on this marshy site. Pliny suggests that he invented a new kind of lathe to turn the immense number of stone column drums. The Samians, who had close relations with the Egyptian pharaoh Amasis at the time, may have been inspired by Egyptian temples

with their numerous columns. Theodoros' temple design used a simple though much enlarged platform with two steps, on which the columns were set well back and doubled on all sides. This building was burned to the ground in 530 BC.

SECONDARY SITES

Belevi About 3km (1¾ miles) north-east of Selçuk (55km/34 miles from Izmir) is one of the finest Greek funerary monuments in western Turkey (mid 3rd century BC).
Priene (37km/23 miles from Kuşadası to nearest village, Gullubahce): extensive remains of city built mid 3rd-2nd century BC.
Miletos (a further 16km/10 miles): most of the visible remains are Roman, but the temple of Athena and western Agora, Delphinion and

Curetes Street leading to the Roman state agora, Ephesos

stadium all belong to the pre-Roman city.
Sardis (nearest village Sartmustafa, 99km/61½ miles from Izmir): this extensive site includes remains of the Lydian, Hellenistic Greek and Roman cities; the temple of Artemis is on the southern outskirts.

MUSEUMS

Archaeological Museum, Istanbul: finds from archaic deposits at Ephesos, sculpture and metalware from various sites in Turkey.
Ephesos Museum, Selçuk: material excavated at Ephesos and surrounding regions.
The British Museum houses fragments from the first and second temples of Artemis at Ephesos.
Samos Museum, Vathy and Pithagorio Museum: sculpture and reliefs from Samos.

HOW TO GET THERE

Regular buses and *dolmus* (shared taxis) depart from Izmir for Ephesos (79km/49 miles). Samos can be reached by steamer (5 times a week, taking about 15 hours, to Karlovasi and Vathy) or by air from Athens (1½ hours).

CHRONOLOGY

*c*1000 BC
Migration of Ionian Greeks to Samos.

6th CENTURY BC
Tyrants rule the island.

479 BC
Samos among founder members of anti-Persian League of Greeks, after fighting on Persian side at Salamis.

440 BC
Unsuccessful revolt of Samos against the League.

411 BC
Samos becomes stronghold of democratic groups during the reactionary period at Athens.

Egyptian bronze statuette

View of Bodrum harbour

HALIKARNASSOS
AND RHODES

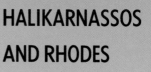

Halikarnassos (Bodrum), Knidos and Kos, with the three Archaic cities of Rhodes (Ialysos, Kameiros and Lindos) together composed the six Dorian settlements in the south-eastern Aegean. Dorian immigrants from Troizen in the Peloponnese reached the Dodecanese around the same time as the Ionians beached further north. Both geographical position and historical ties combined to link the affairs of these states. From the 7th century BC at least, the great neighbouring empires of the Babylonians, Assyrians and Persians attracted these Greeks to seek their fortunes as traders and mercenaries. Rhodes and Kos were stopping points on the sea route between the shores of the southern Mediterranean and the Aegean.

WHAT YOU WILL SEE TODAY

HALIKARNASSOS (BODRUM)
Little more than the base of the huge platform on which the famous Mausoleum stood survives today, though it was still unscathed in the 12th century AD, and was destroyed only in 1402. In a famous description Vitruvius compared Maussolos' city to a theatre; the Agora by the harbour formed the orchestra, while roads emanating from the centre, where the Mausoleum was located, resembled the *diazoma*, or passage, separating wedges of seating. The actual theatre lies further up the slope from the Mausoleum platform. A temple of Ares crowned the summit of the ascending slopes, while below, on either side of the horned harbour entrance was the royal palace to the east and the Salmakis fountain on the west.

KOS, AGORA
In the north-east part of the modern city are the remains of a stoa, the porticoes which once surrounded the agora, including a sanctuary of Aphrodite, some shops and houses. The stadium, first erected in the 4th century, lies west of the harbour. A covered gymnasium was located to the south.

KOS, ASKLEPAION
Work began on a sanctuary dedicated to Asklepios, about 4km (2½ miles) from the city, after the mid-4th century BC. The methods of healing practised by the followers of Asklepios here were specifically concerned with physical treatment. At first there was only an altar on what was to become the middle terrace, below a sacred grove. Around the turn of the 4th century BC, a small Ionic temple was built facing the altar. The whole area was reconstructed some time in the first half of the 2nd century BC, when a tall, narrow or pi-shaped portico with a monumental entrance was built below the temple to accommodate visiting pilgrims. On the upper terrace, a second temple was built as part of a complex intended to mirror the porticoes below – a pi-shaped stoa around an open court, with a monumental staircase linking the new temple to the middle terrace and a new altar that had the same form as the Great

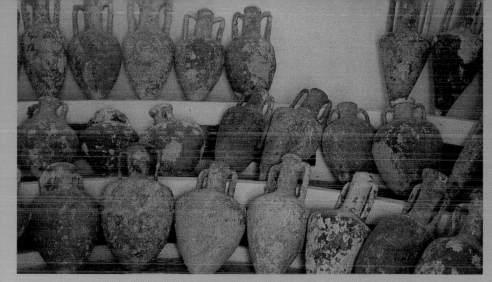

Amphorae (Hellenistic period) dredged from Bodrum harbour

Altar at Pergamon.

RHODES

The Classical city of Rhodes, whose appearance was also compared with that of a theatre, may have inspired the plan at Halikarnassos. Although the Mediaeval Old Town, built by the Knights of St John, effectively prevents exploration of the large harbour of the ancient city, aerial photography and subsequent fieldwork have revealed a grid plan extending right across the northern tip of the island. On the western side was the akropolis, with a stadium and theatre (now much restored) a gymnasium and two major temples, one to Athena Polias, the other to Pythian Apollo.

KAMEIROS

Despite the unification of the Rhodians in 408 BC, the older sites continued in use thereafter. At Kameiros 34km (21 miles) west of Rhodes city there was a great deal of new building in the Hellenistic period. A broad new terrace was created for residential buildings, above the sanctuary terrace, closer to the sea. The steep slope dictated the frequent use of steps. Many of the houses were rebuilt after the earthquake of 227 BC.

LINDOS

The cult of Athena on the akropolis at Lindos superseded a pre-Greek goddess whose worship modified the customs of the incoming Greeks. In 342 BC a Doric temple was built, together with a monumental gateway flanked by porticoes. Towards the end of the 3rd century BC, a broad flight of steps flanked by huge T-shaped wings fronted by a colonnade were added to create a series of terraces which focus on the temple above.

WHAT YOU WOULD HAVE SEEN

There are chamber tombs in Lykia and Karia that must have formed the models of the Mausoleum at Halikarnassos (p.71), but none approached the latter in size and splendour. Maussolos' city

became a model for the Pergamene rulers of the Hellenistic age, while Rhodian architects and artists were among the foremost creative spirits at the Pergamene court. Kos became famous in the 3rd century both for the Asklepaion and the poet Philetas, whose younger associate was the Sicilian pastoral poet, Theokritos, Rhodes, meanwhile, became a centre of philosophy second only to Athens.

MUSEUMS

Bodrum Museum, Castle of St Peter: architectural fragments from the Mausoleum. The over-life-size figures of Maussolos and Artemisia, with slabs from the Amazon and chariot-racing friezes; (some fragments are in the British Museum) *Rhodes Archaeological Museum in the Grand Hospital of the Knights*: houses sculpture, reliefs and pottery. *Kos Antiquarium* in the Castle of the Knights: sculpture, inscriptions; others in *Kos Archaeological Museum*.

HOW TO GET THERE

Bodrum: about 161km (100 miles) from Kuşadasi; Kos and Rhodes: by ship from Piraeus, Kavalla and Thessaloniki. Flights to Kos.

CHRONOLOGY

408 BC
Rhodian cities combine to create new democratic city of Rhodes.

377 BC
Maussolos, Persian *satrap* of Karia, moves his capital from inland Mylasa to Halikarnassos.

377-5 BC
Rhodes and Kos under Maussolos power after their revolt from Athens.

366 BC
Communities of Kos unite to create new city around Mandraki harbour.

353 BC
Artemisia II, wife and sister of Maussolos, repels attack of Rhodians on Halikarnassos and captures Rhodes after his death.

305-4 BC
Rhodes besieged by Demetrios 'the Besieger'.

3rd CENTURY BC
Golden age of Rhodes as mercantile city, Kos as cultural centre.

167 BC
Rhodes eclipsed by Delos, which had been declared a free port by the Romans.

Avenue of Lions, outside the precinct of Leto

G A Z E T T E E R

DELOS

The sacred island of Delos, a mere 4km (2½ miles) across and little more than 1km (⅔ mile) wide, is virtually barren. Yet it became the centre of a cult of Apollo and Artemis, both reputedly born there, which spread from the islands to involve mainland Greece in the 8th century BC. There was Mycenaean activity here. At first strongly influenced by neighbouring islands, Delos came under the Athenian political dominance in the 5th and 4th centuries. During the 3rd century BC Delos gained a measure of independence and, in her capacity as treasurer of the League of Islanders, was lionized by the Successor kings of Alexander the Great. The island became a corn exchange and banking centre, with a growing immigrant population. Delos' fortunes were dramatically improved when it was declared a free port in 167 BC.

WHAT YOU WILL SEE TODAY

A wide range of structures have been unearthed in the excavations of the French School, which give a vivid picture of Delos at the time of its greatest expansion in the Hellenistic age.

EARLY DELOS

Between the 7th and early 5th centuries a series of small buildings appeared within the precinct of Apollo and Artemis in the area north of the port on the island's southern shore. Following a burst of Cycladic dedications in the 7th and 6th centuries, the Athenians set up two temples to Apollo. Further west was a processional way lined with statues of lions, and in the mountainous centre of Mount Kynthion are a cave and complex of stairs and passages of special ritual significance.

HELLENISTIC PERIOD

Around and between these zones arose the Hellenistic monuments.

STOAS

The Ptolemies and Antigonids struggled to control the new League of Islanders during the 3rd century and both dynasties had festivals organized in their honour. Three stoas were commissioned by Antigonid rulers around three sides of the precinct.

AGORA OF THE ITALIANS

Further west, on the eastern shore of the Sacred Lake, a purpose-built agora was set up for Italian merchants through the munificence of some of their number, towards the end of the 2nd century BC. It consists of a ground floor colonnade on four sides, backed by shops

Aphrodite and Pan (2nd century BC)

Agora of the Italians mosaic

and offices, with an upper Doric-pilastered storey.

Between the agora and a hypostyle hall built towards the end of the 3rd century there was a temple dedicated to 12 gods, probably the 12 Olympians, in front of which there were 12 altars.

THE POSEIDONIASTS

South of the Lake, the establishment of the votaries of Poseidon from Berytos (Tyre), merchants, armourers and entrepreneurs, was sited. As in the case of the Italians, this cult centre, hostel, meeting-place and bank for native Tyrians illustrates the tendency of visitors from different ethnic communities to take up common residence. Other such groups are known to us from inscriptions.

RESIDENTIAL QUARTERS

In the same quarter there were luxurious houses built around a peristyle court and named after their finest mosaic floors (such as the House of the Comedians and the House of the Tritons). Apart from abstract and figured pebble

mosaics in many colours, both in dining-rooms and the peristyle court, these houses were adorned with statues, particularly copies of popular Classical or Hellenistic works.

Further towards the northern shore of the island was a well-appointed gymnasium and stadium of the late 2nd century BC, together with a synagogue founded about a century later. But the bulk of the built-up area extends eastwards of the precinct of Apollo and Artemis towards Mount Kynthion. Most of the Hellenistic houses are in this quarter, between the precinct and the theatre halfway up the hillside (House of the Masks, House of Dionysos), and on the northern side of the theatre (the four-storey House of the Hermes).

FOREIGN CULTS

This is also the area where the newer cults had their sanctuaries – the three-roomed complexes in honour of Serapis, or the courts, dining-rooms and theatre of two Syrian deities, Atargatis and Hadad.

Temple of Isis

MUSEUMS

The *Delos Museum* contains important sculptures, dedications from the precinct, portraits and a great variety of Hellenistic decorative pieces. There is also a collection of inscriptions that provide much information on the cosmopolitan community and the administration of the sanctuary.

HOW TO GET THERE

From Athens by air to Mykonos or by steamer from Piraeus several times daily (about 5–8½ hours). From Mykonos *caiques* take ½ hour.

CHRONOLOGY

*c*1500–1200 BC
Mycenaean settlement.

10th–8th CENTURIES BC
Principal cult centre of the Ionian Greeks.

478–404, 394–314 BC
Athens dominates the sanctuary.

314–166 BC
Delos nominally independent. Numerous public buildings erected.

166–69 BC
Development of private, social, commercial and religious buildings to suit a larger cosmopolitan population. Delos sacked in 88 and 69 BC.

West magazines passageway, Knossos

KNOSSOS AND THE MINOAN PALACES

During the Middle Bronze Age (2000-1550 BC) Crete was the centre of a wealthy and innovative civilization based on a series of palaces, of which Knossos was the most important. Cretans in this period settled on the islands of Rhodes, Kythera, Melos and Thera. They also maintained lively contacts with Attika, the Peloponnese, the west Anatolian seaboard, Cyprus and Egypt. Minoan art styles, architecture and cult practices were incorporated into contemporary mainland (Mycenaean) culture.

WHAT YOU WILL FIND TODAY

ROYAL PALACES
The major palaces of the Minoan period are still visible in outline today. The restoration of Knossos began while Arthur Evans was still excavating. This, the largest and most thoroughly explored of the palaces, Phaistos and Mallia in central Crete (both c1700-1450 BC and Zakros in the east (preserved outlines c1550) all share the same essential plan, including a

central court surrounded by rooms arranged in uneven blocks around it. The former three also have a western court and a western monumental façade. Public and private rooms, bathrooms, kitchens, storerooms and cult rooms are present in each case. Individual features include the stepped theatre at Phaistos, the staircase and altar facing the main court at Mallia, the "shrine-treasury", stone-built well and circular pool at Zakros. Knossos had two storeys below ground level, reached by the Grand Staircase in the Central Court, and at least one upper storey.

HOUSES AND VILLAS
These were usually situated in small towns with narrow, winding streets. Knossos itself is encircled by a series of smaller but still ostentatious residences (which are not open to the public). Those on the south side of the palace were connected to it by a viaduct crossing the Vlychia stream. At Phaistos a paved and stepped road led up to a

series of stone granaries and downwards probably to the town. Nearby is one of the finest country villas, Ayia Triadha. The largest coastal town is Palaikastro. Town and country houses often might have as many as 20 rooms, the ground floor usually being reserved for storage area and workrooms, the upper floors being used for residential purposes.

WHAT YOU WOULD HAVE SEEN

The palaces and mansions were airy buildings with plentiful water supplies, variegated façades, brightly painted halls and dark recesses. Storage rooms were packed with ordered rows of every kind of vessel and tool, inlaid treasure chests and ornaments, as well as documents sealed with clay stamps. In the recesses of the palaces, as well as in towns and on hilltops, were shrines dedicated to the snake goddess containing horned altars packed with sacred vessels. On the coast there were paved quays and roads,

The Queen's apartments, Knossos

and columned halls like that found at Kommos.

Tylissos (13km/8¼ miles south-west of Herakleion): three large Late Minoan villas contemporary with the final stage of the Palaces, with well-preserved interiors.
Arkhanes (19km/11¾ miles south-east of Herakleion): remains of palatial structure, contemporary with last phase of the Palaces, in quality on a par with Knossos alone; the nearby villa at *Vathypetro*, of the same period, has some of the best evidence of Minoan crafts (potting, weaving, wine and oil presses).
Gortyn (near Ayioi Dheka; 45km/28 miles south of Herakleion): largest city of the Classical and Roman periods.
Ayia Triadha (61km/38 miles south-east of Herakleion): extensive remains of Late Minoan villa overlying a Middle Minoan predecessor, surrounded by contemporary and 14th/13th century BC houses, with stone-built tombs on hillside above.

Thera (Santorini), the largest of the southern group of Cycladic islands (known as the Sporades), has extensive remains of the Classical and Hellenistic Greek city 12km/7½ miles from the modern capital, Fira, as well as the well-preserved and finely decorated Late Minoan houses on Akrotiri, about the same distance from Fira.

North entrance, Knossos

The *Archaeological Museum, Herakleion* houses the largest and most comprehensive collection of Cretan antiquities. There is a temporary exhibition of finds from Akrotiri in the *National Archaeological Museum, Athens*. Finds from Sir Arthur Evans' private collection and material excavated by D.G. Hogarth and others are in the *Ashmolean Museum, Oxford* and the *British Museum, London*.

For Crete by air to Herakleion, or by ship from Piraeus to Herakleion. There are regular buses from Herakleion to Knossos (5km/3½ miles), Phaistos (61km/38 miles), and Mallia (37km/23 miles) for eastern Crete, Chania for the west. On Thera (Santorini), buses and taxis go from Fira to Pirgos and Kamari for ancient Thera, and Akrotiri village.

CHRONOLOGY

MIDDLE MINOAN II 1900 BC
First palaces built.

MIDDLE MINOAN III 1700 BC
First palaces destroyed, rebuilt.

LATE MINOAN IA 1500 BC
Flowering of second palaces, towns and villas.

LATE MINOAN IB 1500 BC
Destruction of Thera.

LATE MINOAN II 1450 BC
Widespread destruction of Minoan and Cycladic sites.

LATE MINOAN IIIA 1400 BC
Mycenaean domination of Crete.

LATE MINOAN IIIB 1200 BC
Destruction of many Mycenaean centres.

LATE MINOAN IIIC 11th CENTURY
Late continuity on older sites.

Harvesters' vase

Temple at Paestum

METAPONTION, HERAKLEIA AND SOUTHERN ITALY

The earliest evidence of Greek contacts with Italy after the Bronze Age is in the Bay of Naples (from 770 BC onwards), when Euboians began to trade with Etruria. However, Greek settlement of a more systematic kind began in the foot of Italy, with Rhegion (Reggio) and Sybaris founded by Achaians in the 720s BC and Kroton and the Spartan colony at Taras (Taranto) in the late 8th century BC. More Achaians went to Metapontion (Metaponto) in the following decade or two, and a few disparate outsiders followed in the 670s BC – Lokrians from central Greece to Lokroi, Epizephyrioi and Kolophonians to Siris (Siri). The Greek presence became significant enough for the whole region to be called Magna Graecia (greater Greece). Native sites, frequently on hilltops or promontories, were sometimes taken over by the incoming Greeks. Elsewhere the natives prospered: in the 4th and 3rd centuries BC they proved more durable than the Greek cities.

SOUTH ITALIAN POTTERY

Local versions of Greek pottery designs were being produced from the end of the 8th century BC onwards. However, from the late 5th century, when groups of Athenian potters founded their own workshops at Taras and Herakleia, high-quality colonial production drove out imports from the Greek mainland. At least three major schools can be identified, made in the three regions of Apulia (south-east), Lucania (south) and Campania (south central) with offshoots in Sicily and Paestum. Greek influences in Etruria were longer lived, subtler and more varied.

WHAT YOU WILL SEE TODAY

The quantity of Greek material found in southern Italy has increased enormously during the last 30 years. In most cases we can detect contacts with local peoples (Oinotrians, Messapians) both before the establishment of formal Greek immigrant foundations as well as afterwards. The foundations were located in fertile river valleys, which provided good access routes to the Tyrrhenian coast or made useful stopping points for ships going to Sicily.

TARAS (TARANTO)

Apart from one 6th-century BC Doric temple, there is little to see of the Spartan immigrant community which settled on the peninsula around the best harbour of southern Italy (Mare Piccolo). There are impressive finds from cemeteries, and figure-decorated chamber tombs were a local speciality. The popularity of Spartan bronzeware, pottery and other products in southern Italy is usually associated with Taras, although Achaians may have preferred Spartan products and styles.

METAPONTION (METAPONTO) AND HERAKLEIA (POLICORO)

The street plan and public buildings of both Metapontion and its near neighbour, Herakleia, can be seen today, although the modern shore line is now more than 1 km (²⁄₃

View of street and houses, Heraklia

HOW TO GET THERE

Paestum is 95km (60 miles) south of *Naples* on Highway 18. *Taranto* is 292km (181 miles) from *Naples* by road; there are also rail services. *Metaponto* is 48km (30 miles) from *Taranto,* and *Policoro* 21km (13 miles).

mile) further out. At Metapontion the sanctuary area contained temples dedicated to Apollo Lykeios, Hera and Athena, plus one unidentified temple. North-east of the town stand 15 columns belonging to another temple of Hera.

Native burials at L'Incoronata and S. Teodoro in the Basento valley, and Alianello in the Agri, contained Italian bronze ornaments, iron weapons and *impasto* pottery. Seventh-century Greek pot cremations at L'Incoronata are quite distinct from the local extended inhumations, some of which are aristocratic warrior tombs.

PAESTUM

Some of the finest surviving Greek temples are at Paestum (Poseidonia), an early colony of Sybaris, which has also produced many painted tombs in the cemeteries north-east of the town. A Doric temple to Hera was built near the mouth of the river Sele in *c*500 BC and decorated with sculptured reliefs in a distinctive local style. The city itself was situated on a plateau about 13km (8 miles) inland, laid out in a chequer-board plan and surrounded by a polygonal well in the 6th century BC. The temple precinct lay to the west of the main northsouth road.

MUSEUMS

Taranto, Museo Nazionale is the major museum of the south-east with sculpture, pottery and jewellery from the archaic to Hellenistic periods. The *Museo Nazionale della Siritide at Herkleia-Policoro* has architectural and votive

Mirror support (5th century BC) found near Rome

terracottas, bronzes and vases from tombs.
Paestum Archaeological Museum contains sculptured decorations from the "treasury" and from Heraion at the mouth of the Sele, painted slab sarcophagi, local and mainland Greek ceramics and eight splendid bronze jars from the "underground shrine".
Museo Nazionale di Reggio Calabria contains Greek material from the south-west, as well as two magnificent full-size bronze statues of warriors found in the sea near Riace in 1972.

CHRONOLOGY

706 BC
Taras founded by illegitimate Spartans.

c475 BC
Democracy replaces traditional autocratic rule at Taras.

433/2 BC
Colony founded at Herakleia, becomes headquarters of a Greek League in southern Italy.

4th CENTURY BC
Golden age of Taras under leadership of Archytas, philosopher and mathematician.

334 BC
King Alexander I of Epiros and Tarentines defeated by Lucanians.

282 BC
Romans establish protectorate over Thourioi.

280-275 BC
King Pyrrhus of Epiros joins Taras against Lucanians and Rome; at first remarkably successful, later defeated. Tarentine Livius Androncius becomes dramatist for the Romans.

213 BC
Taras sacked by Hannibal.

209 BC
Retaken by Romans.

SYRACUSE AND SICILY

The Euryalus fortress, Syracuse

Sicily was the most intensively hellenized area of the Mediterranean outside Greece itself. The colonists were mainly Peloponnesians, and Doric architectural styles prevailed, as well as Dorian cults and institutions. However, throughout Sicily there was a more significant admixture of Ionians, principally Chalkidians. Different connections were fostered by the joint Rhodian-Cretan foundation of Gela. Sicilian temple architecture shows Ionian influences, while painted terracotta roof tiles and gutters, though Korinthian in origin, have non-Dorian elaborations.

According to the Athenian historian Thukydides, there were three different ethnic groups in Sicily before the Greeks arrived: Sikani in west-central Sicily, of Iberian origin; Italian Sikels in the east; and "Trojan" Elymi in the west. Current archaeological research suggests that this ethnic multiplicity is plausible. Although Greek architecture and domestic goods penetrated the island, the native cultures were by no means extinguished and this is perhaps the most interesting area of recent investigations. The nature of Carthaginian occupation in the north of the island has also been reconsidered. Although historical sources emphasize military conflict between Greeks and Carthaginians, archaeology presents the complimentary aspects of coexistence and cooperation.

WHAT YOU WILL SEE TODAY

Traces of Greek occupation are visible at most settlements, but the following deserve special mention.

SYRACUSE

Korinthians settled here on the island of Ortygia within a year of the earliest Greek colony in Sicily at Naxos (734 BC). The harbour is the finest on the island. Recent excavations have revealed a grid plan of streets on Ortygia as well as on the mainland, with Greek structures immediately succeeding native ones, without any evidence of destruction. There were two early stone temples on Ortygia, one dedicated to Apollo *c*575 BC, the other to Athena in the 5th century (still preserved in the fabric of the *Duomo*), although they both had earlier clay predecessors.

The mainland received colonists very soon after Ortygia, and a causeway was built to the island later in the 6th century. Near the causeway was the Agora and major civic sanctuaries, joined in the early 3rd century by a magnificent theatre and stoa (in the time of Hieron II). The main cemeteries at *Fusco* (west of the city) and at *Grotticelli* (east of the theatre), with a variety of rock-cut and built monuments, reflect the wealth of Syracuse during its greatest days. The plateau is dominated by the fortifications of *Epipolai*, which were consolidated and strengthened by Dionysios I.

GELA

The excavated city lies on a low hill, which later formed the akropolis on the west bank of the Gelas estuary. The earliest foundation was probably much smaller than the total area of the Classical city. Late in the 7th century BC a sanctuary of Demeter arose on the eastern (Bitalemi) bank. There was another sanctuary, of Athena, east of the citadel, and a third on the north side.

AKRAGAS (AGRIGENTO)

This foundation was one of the most ambitious on the island. The akropolis on the north side and the lower town enclosed by walls, probably before the end of 6th century, on the south, covered about 388.5 hectare (1½ miles). There had been a native settlement here and quite a bit of contact with Greeks before the main influx from Gela c580 BC. The most spectacular surviving remains are the temples ranged along the inner wall or scarp, beginning c550 BC and continuing into the 5th century. The largest was that of Olympian Zeus, and an original feature was the use of colossal supporting male figures (telamones) on the outer sanctuary walls.

SELINOS (SELINUS, SELINUNTE)

Even more impressive visually is Selinos. As in most Greek foundations, the city is situated on a low hill close to an estuary (River Hypsas), with the walled akropolis facing the sea and the residential quarter running out behind it. The sanctuary precinct within the akropolis walls contained four temples, two of which (C and D) were erected in the 6th century BC, and two in the 5th century (A and O). There are further temples west of the river (at the sanctuary of Demeter) and landscaped on a hill east of the town (E, F, G), which had sculptured decoration. Temple G was almost as large as that of Zeus at Akragas.

WHAT YOU WOULD HAVE SEEN

Greek immigration to Sicily took the form of two major currents – the Peloponnesian and the Chalkidian. At first these coexisted, with Syracuse (Peloponnesian) expanding into the southern part of the island, and the Chalkidians, based on a good harbour at Naxos, spreading to Leontinoi and Katane, whilst others who had made a foothold at Kyme (Cumae) in central Italy turned to Zankle (Messina), and later Mylai (Milazzo) and Himera. Megarians who had founded Megara Hyblaia (named after the native king Hyblon, were caught between the hammer of the Syracusans and the anvil of the Chalkidians.

Art and architecture flourished in the second half of the 6th and throughout most of the 5th century BC, before tension between Greeks and Carthaginians became endemic. Apart from the distinctive architectural variants on Greek practice

Colossal Atlas figure, Agrigento

displayed by Sicilian temples, the majority of Sicilian cities have now been shown to have been built on a grid plan, probably from the start. Sicilian sculpture in stone and clay, painted pottery, terracotta and coins show a mixture of styles drawing on mainland and East Greek sources, often producing original and technically highly competent work.

MUSEUMS

The *Museo Archeologico Regionale "Paolo Orsi"* is at Syracuse. Regional museums are at *Agrigento, Gela, Sciacca, Himera, Marsala, Marianopoli, Enna and Aidone*. The *Museo Nazionale Archeologico* at Palermo houses the oldest collection of Greek sculpture and pottery on the island.

HOW TO GET THERE

The Palermo – Trapani motorway (A29) runs just below the Greek temple at Segesta (75km).
Palermo – Selinunte, A29 motorway (107km); there is a rail and bus link (2½-3hrs.). Palermo-Agrigento: 129.5km following the N121 and N189; (2¾-3hrs. by rail). Route N115 (216km to Syracuse) passes through Gela (73.5km). There are good road, rail and bus links between Syracuse and Catania (ancient Katane). Route N114 crosses the road to Megara Hyblaia at 27km, 45km for Lentini (Leontinoi).

CHRONOLOGY

734 BC
Syracuse founded by Korinthians.

*c*490 BC
Gelon, tyrant of Gela, takes power in Syracuse.

466-406 BC
Democracy at Syracuse.

427-424, 415-413 BC
Wars with Athens.

406-367 BC
Dionysios I tyrant.

317-289 BC
Agathokles, becomes tyrant, later king of most of Sicily.

213-211 BC
Romans capture Syracuse.

Pompey's Pillar and sphinx

ALEXANDRIA

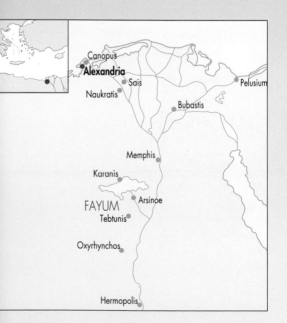

The most famous of Alexander the Great's foundations, Alexandria in Egypt, was intended from the start (332 BC) to be more than just a military colony and harbour combined. Alexander personally selected the site, on a peninsula west of the Nile Delta, between the island of Pharos and a lake, Mareotis. Whereas the Egyptian pharaohs had had their seat at Memphis, south of the Nile Delta, Alexander laid the foundations of the Macedonian empire in Egypt on the coast, so as to receive maximum benefit both from Mediterranean seaborne trade and from goods passing down the Nile.

WHAT YOU WILL SEE

Ptolemaic remains in Egypt today are but modest reminders of a splendid past. Apart from Ptolemais, Ptolemy I's only official colony, Greek settlers, who came in their thousands during the first century of Ptolemaic rule, flocked to Alexandria and the district

around lake Moeris in the Fayum, just south of Memphis, where their rubbish tips have proved to be of the greatest interest. The Ptolemies continued the Pharaonic tradition of monumental building at regional sanctuaries – at the temple of Ammon at Karnak, the temple of Horus at Edfu the temple of Isis at Philai and elsewhere. It is these, rather than any of the royal monuments of Alexandria, that have endured to this day.

At Alexandria the most extensive remains from the Ptolemaic period are the underground cemeteries in the former suburbs. At Anfushi the earliest tombs were rectangular rock-cut chambers approached by a staircase. More complex catacombs with multiple chambers and even underground peristyle courts are known from Wardian, while at Shatby these more advanced forms were often highly decorated in a style partly reminiscent of Macedonian tombs and partly reflecting Egyptian themes.

WHAT YOU WOULD HAVE SEEN

Alexandria was the greatest city of the Hellenistic world, with a large cosmopolitan population, Alexander had put Egypt into the hands of an extremely able administrator, Kleomenes of Naukratis, who redirected the pharaonic tribute into Macedonian coffers and used these revenues to lay the foundations of what was to be the most beautiful Greek city in the world. Alexandria was designed by Deinokrates of Rhodes, a flamboyant personality. It had exceptionally broad streets (the two largest, crossing at right angles, were said to be 30m/98ft wide and a sumptuous Royal Quarter near the eastern harbour to which each of the Ptolemies made additions.

STRABO'S ALEXANDRIA
The best description we have of Alexandria in the Ptolemaic age is the geographer Strabo's (25 BC). The Pharos island, with its lighthouse, built under Ptolemy II, was attached to the

concave bay opposite by a sea wall, the heptastadion, which thus created two harbours, the Greater (eastern) one and the western Eunostos harbour (of happy return). There was also a private royal harbour along the eastern promontory of the Great Harbour, leading directly to the palace quarter: the Mouseion, with its comfortable arcades and dining hall, and the royal cemetery, where the Ptolemies lay close to Alexander's tomb. Ptolemy I instituted a cult to the divine Alexander.

Another small harbour, "the chest", and a number of subsidiary canals provided access to lake Moeris, which became a giant inland harbour for trans-shipment. Strabo describes two libraries, a theatre, a splendid gymnasium along the main west-east highway, as well as municipal buildings, including the lawcourts, a stadium, hippodrome, parks and gardens, a viewing tower for panoramas of the city, and the sanctuary of Serapis, a new Greco-Egyptian divinity, in the south-western quarter.

THE WEALTH OF THE PTOLEMIES
In Strabo's day many of the city's buildings were falling into disrepair. For a more imaginative account of the Ptolemaic style we must go to the compendious *Table Talk* of Athenaios of Naukratis (*c* AD 200), which quotes from a treatise, *On Alexandria*, by the Hellenistic writer Kallixeinos of Rhodes. The passage related describes a procession in honour of Ptolemy II Philadelphos ("sister-loving") staged in 271/0 BC, in which took part many hundreds of cattle, scores of exotic beasts (including bears, leopards, lions, panthers, a giraffe and a rhinoceros), floats carrying gold statues of gods, Alexander and Ptolemy I, together with gold tableware, gold and silver ritual ornaments, and women in expensive clothes in gold crowns representing Greek *poleis* in Asia and the islands, and a vast army of infantry and cavalrymen all fitted out in splendid uniforms. Kallixeinos only mentioned the most expensive floats; there were many more besides, as well as the numerous gold crowns with which individuals were honoured in the subsequent games, to a total of 2,239 talents.

MUSEUMS

Graeco-Roman Museum, Alexandria: contains sculpture, architectural ornament, terracotta and pottery from excavations in Alexandria.
Pelizaeus Museum, Hildesheim: important collection of plaster casts from metal objects, found at Mit Rahineh.
Other important collections of Graeco-Egyptian art and artefacts are to be found in the *Musée du Louvre, Paris; British Museum, London; Ashmolean Museum, Oxford; the Burrell Collection, Glasgow; Antikenmuseum Preussischer Kulturbesitz, Berlin; Metropolitan Museum of Art, New York; Brooklyn Museum; J. Paul Getty Museum, Malibu; Kelsey Museum of Archaeology, University of Michigan* (late Ptolemaic and Roman material from Karanis).

HOW TO GET THERE

By air to Cairo; Nile cruises from 5 days, style and comfort to suit all tastes.

The Rosetta Stone (196BC)

CHRONOLOGY

331 BC
Alexandria founded.

323 BC
Alexandria Ptolemy's capital.

c300 BC
Library is founded.

c260 BC
Pharos, world's first lighthouse, is completed at harbour entrance.

30 BC
Egypt annexed by the Romans.

AD 270
Alexandria sacked.

AD 640
Egypt taken over by Arabs.

Graeco-Egyptian god Serapis

GLOSSARY

Agora
Open space within cities where most civic and commercial business was conducted.

aiolic
Dialect group, originally from Thessaly and Boiotia, which migrated to the north-west coast of Turkey.

akropolis
Fortified hilltop serving as stronghold and refuge; often also an important cult centre.

amphora
Two-handled, narrow-necked wine jar.

Black Figure
Technique used in fine pottery during the period *c.*625-525 BC. The pot is first painted with a coloured slip, then the graphic details are incised.

Blegen, Carl W (1887-1971)
Great American archaeologist. He excavated at Korakou, Zygouries, Prosymna, Troy and Pylos.

Caskey, John L.
American archaeologist who worked with Blegen at Troy. His excavations at Lerna and Agia Eirene on Kea have made fundamental contributions to the study of the Bronze Age in the Aegean.

Caylus, Anne-Claude-Philippe de Toubières, Comte de (1692-1765)
Served in the French army before becoming French ambassador to Constantinople, from where he visited western Anatolia, exploring ancient sites. In 1717 he returned to Paris to devote himself to the study of antiquities. His *Recueil d'Antiquités égyptiennes, étrusques, grecques, romaines et gauloises,* in seven volumes, appeared between 1752 and 1767, and was the first major compendium of ancient art.

cella
Main hall of a Greek temple, housing the cult statue.

Choiseul-Gouffier, Marie-Gabriel Florent Auguste, Comte de (1752-1817)
Member of the French Scientific Expedition to the Mediterranean in 1776, Louis XVI's ambassador to Constantinople (1784-93), patron and collector of antiquities; his *Voyage pittoresque en Grèce* I-III (1782-1812) contains interesting data about 18th-century Greece.

cist grave
Rectangular earth-cut grave, lined and roofed with stone slabs.

Cockerell, Charles Robert (1788-1863)
British architect and archaeologist, visited Greece, western Asia Minor, Italy and Sicily in 1810-16. His mature work as an architect (notably in the Ashmolean Museum, Oxford, and the Fitzwilliam Museum, Cambridge) was greatly influenced by his close study of Classical Greek architecture.

Conze, Alexander (1831-1914)
Professor of Archaeology at Halle and Vienna in the 1860s. Following his excavations at Samothrace in 1873 and 1875, he became Director of the antique sculpture galleries in Berlin, from whence he supervised the early investigations of Pergamon.

Curtius, Ernst (1831-1914)
Having spent two decades researching the ancient history and geography of Greece, Curtius became Professor of Classics at Berlin (1872). He actively supported moves to turn the Archaeological Institute into a full state institution and likewise to establish a new branch at Athens. From 1875 he directed excavations at Olympia, for which he had campaigned since 1852.

Cyriac of Ancona (1391-1455)
Full name, Ciriaco de' Pizzicolli; Italian merchant who travelled to Greece and the eastern Mediterranean between 1418 and 1448. His drawings of Greek antiquities and copies of inscriptions were the chief source of western knowledge of Greek artefacts during the Renaissance.

Dodwell, Edward (1767-1832)
British artist and traveller who toured Greece in 1801 and 1805-6, making sketches and watercolours of ancient sites and remains. His detailed descriptions, including some less well-known sites, as well as remarks on contemporary inhabitants, are still valuable.

Dorian
One of the three principal Greek dialects. The Dorians lived in the Peloponnese, Crete and their colonies in the south-east Aegean, as well as in parts of central Greece. A strong though not altogether historical tradition links them with an armed invasion of the Peloponnese early in the 1st millennium BC.

Gell, Sir William (1777-1836)
British traveller, first to Greece alongside Dodwell in 1801 and 1806, and in 1812 to a number of Greek sites in western Asia Minor, this time as the leader of a professional expedition sent by the Society of Dilettanti. His *Itineraries of Greece* were published in 1810 and 1817. After 1820, he settled in Italy and devoted himself to Italian antiquities.

Geometric
Decorative style composed of regular geometric patterns. This kind of ornament was particularly characteristic in the period *c.*1050-700 BC, which is therefore often referred to as the "Geometric" period.

gerousia
"Council of Elders", a term often used for the executive bodies in aristocratically governed Greek states, the best known being that at Sparta.

gymnasion
Not just an exercise yard for athletes;
more often a sports complex
including a running track with
changing-rooms, bathrooms and
dining-rooms grouped around a
central yard. In the Hellenistic age
libraries and lecture rooms became
regular features, too.

herm
Cult statue of the god Hermes,
consisting of a sculptured head and
phallus mounted on a pillar. They
were located at roadsides,
crossroads and in the *agora*. Perhaps
derived from an older cult connected
with stones.

Hellenistic
Term used, from the 1st century BC
onwards, to describe the "decadent"
art of the period from *c.*300 to 31 BC,
and applied by modern historians to
the age of Alexander the Great's
Successor kings.

Hogarth, David G. (1862-1927)
British archaeologist and Director of
the British School at Athens. He
excavated Minoan town houses at
Knossos and Zakros, and ritual
deposits in the Diktaian Cave near
Psychro. He is best known for his
investigations of the earliest phases
of the temple of Artemis at Ephesos.

insula
From the Latin, meaning island, and
borrowed from Roman archaeology.
One of a series of land plots within a
grid plan of streets, divided into
house units.

Ionian
One of the three major Greek
dialects. It apparently has an older
history in the Greek mainland than
Doric, although its relationship to
Arkadian (the dialect closest to
Mycenaean Linear B) is unclear.

kantharos
Deep drinking cup on a high foot with
upswinging handles.

kore
Votive statue of a young woman.

kouros
Votive statue of a youth.

krater
Wine mixing bowl with several
variants: *bell* (bell or bucket-shaped);
column (shouldered bowl with
horizontal rim supported by
colonnettes); *kalyx* (two-piece bowl
with flaring mouth); *volute*
(shouldered urn with high volute
handles).

kylix
Commonest form of drinking cup – a
shallow bowl on a high stemmed
foot, often richly painted.

Leake, William Martin (1777-1860)
British army officer who made
substantial contributions to the study
of ancient Greek topography, both in
the mainland and in Asia Minor.

Mackenzie, Duncan (1859-1935)
Scottish archaeologist who took part
in the first major British excavations
of the prehistoric Aegean (at
Phylakopi, Melos), and became Evans'
principal assistant in the excavations
of Knossos palace. He has been
called one of the first scientific
workers in Aegean archaeology, and
his Daybooks were a principal source
for Evans' publications on Knossos.

megaron
Common house form in the Bronze
Age Aegean, consisting of a porch,
main room and storage room at the
back, which might be rectangular or
curved in shape. This basic plan was
extended and elaborated in
Mycenaean palaces.

metopes
Square slabs, either plain or
sculpted, alternating with smaller,
corrugated *triglyphs* to make up the
standard frieze on Doric temples.

metroon
Sanctuary of the Mother of the Gods,
often also used as a depository for
official documents.

metropolis
Literally a "mother city" – the
community which sent out colonists
to a new location.

palaistra
Exercise yard for athletics.

pediment
Triangular space between the
horizontal and sloping cornices at
either end of a Greek temple roof. In
buildings of the Doric order, it was
traditionally filled with sculptured
figures.

polis
A self-governing community of Greek
citizens; neither complete autonomy
nor an urban focus were essential
features.

Red Figure
Technique of vase decoration used
mainly in the period between *c.*525
and 300 BC. It involved first sketching
the outline of a design with a brush,
and then covering the rest of the vase
with black glaze.

satrap
Regional governor of a province in
the Persian Empire.

skyphos
Broad, flaring, stemless cup.

stele
Stone slab used for public and
private inscriptions and dedications.

stoa
Elongated hall, walled on three sides,
with an open, colonnaded front. More
elaborate plans might have two or
more storeys and a series of rooms
or shops behind the facade.

sphinx
Mythical winged monster with a
female bust and lion's body.

Spon, Jacob (1647-85)
French doctor who preferred to
pursue his antiquarian interests, first
at home in Lyons, later (1675 and
1676) in Greece, in the company of an
English botanist, George Wheler
(1650-1723), and a member of the
Royal Society, Francis Vernon
(1637-77). Spon produced one of the
most useful and sophisticated early
accounts of Greece.

tell
Settlement site forming a man-made
mound, with new structures built
directly over collapsed older ones.

tholos
Circular building often surrounded
by a colonnade, used either for
secular or religious purposes.

Tournefort, Joseph Pitton de
(1656-1708)
French Professor of Botany, sent by
King Louis XIV in 1700 to study the
geography, history, commerce,
customs and flora of Greece and
Asia. A great collector as well as a
keen observer.

INDEX

Note: page numbers in italic type denote captions to illustrations; page numbers in bold type denote main entries in the gazetteer.

BIBLIOGRAPHY

ACKNOWLEDGMENTS

Quarto Publishing would like to thank the following people and organizations whose photographs appear in this book. Although we have made every effort to acknowledge all copyright holders, Quarto would like to apologize should there be any omissions.

General

ANDREWES, A., *The Greeks* (London, 1967).

BOARDMAN, J., GRIFFIN, J. & MURRAY, O., *Oxford History of the Classical World* (Oxford, 1986), reprinted in paperback in two parts (1988) as *Greece and the Hellenistic World* and *The Roman World*.

HASKELL, F., & PENNY, N., *Taste and the Antique. The Lure of Classical Sculpture, 1500-1900* (New Haven & London, 1981; corr. repr. 1982).

TALBERT, R., ed., *Atlas of Classical History* (1985; repr. Routledge 1989).

Prehistoric Greece

BARBER, R.L.N, *The Cyclades in the Bronze Age* (London, 1987).

BUCHHOLZ H.-G., & KARAGEORGHIS, V., *Prehistoric Greece and Cyprus* (London, 1973).

DOUMAS, C., *Thera. Pompeii of the Ancient Aegean* (London, 1983).

HOOD, M.S.F., *The Minoans* (London, 1971).

PENDLEBURY, J.D.S., *The Archaeology of Crete* (London 1939; repr. New York 1965).

WACE, A.J.B. *Mycenae. An Archaeological History and Guide* (Princeton N.J., 1949).

WARREN, P., *The Aegean Civilizations, from Ancient Crete to Mycenae* (Phaidon, 2nd ed. 1989).

Greece – from the Archaic to the Hellenistic Age

ANDRONIKOS, M., *Vergina* (Athens, 1984).

ARIAS, P., & HIRMER, M., *A History of Greek Vase Painting* (London, 1962).

BERVE, H., GRUBEN, G., & HIRMER, M., *Greek Temples, Theatres and Shrines* (London, 1963).

BOARDMAN, J. *Greek Art* (rev. ed. 1973; new ed. 1991). *The Greeks Overseas* (2nd ed. London 1980).

COLDSTREAM, J.N., *Geometric Greece* (London, 1977).

CRAWFORD, M., ed., *Sources for Ancient History. Studies in the use of historical evidence* (Cambridge, 1983).

HUMPHREYS, S., *Anthropology and the Greeks* (Routledge 1978; repr. 1983).

LING, R., *Classical Greece* (Oxford, 2nd ed. 1988).

MURRAY, O., & PRICE, S., eds., *The Greek City: from Homer to Alexander* (Oxford, 1990).

OSBORNE, R., *Classical Landscape with Figures: the ancient Greek city and its countryside* (London, 1987).

ROBERTSON, C.M., *A Shorter History of Greek Art* (Cambridge, 1981).

2 (tl) Roger Wilson (tr) British Museum 3 (cr) British Museum (bl) Ecole Française d'Archeologie, Athens (cr) Roger Wilson 10 (l) Ecole Française d'Athènes 11 (b) C.M. Dixon, (l) Peter Clayton 12 (l) Peter Clayton 14 (t) American School of Classical Studies: Agora Excavations 14 (l) Deutsches Archaeologisches Institut, Athens 15 (c) Roger Wilson 16-17 Roger Wilson 18 (r) Kunsthistorisches Museum, Vienna 19 (t) collection of the J. Paul Getty Museum, Malibu, California (b) Alan W. Johnston 20 (t) Alan W. Johnston (b) American School of Classical Studies: Agora Excavations 21 (b) C.M. Dixon 22 (c), 23 (c) Raymond V. Schoder S.J., © 1989 Loyola University of Chicago 23 (b) Roger Wilson 24 (t) C.M. Dixon (c) reproduced by courtesy of the Trustees of the British Museum (b) Peter Clayton 25 (t) Roger Wilson (c) British Museum (b) Peter Clayton 26 (l) collection of the J. Paul Getty Museum, Malibu, California 27 (r) Roger Wilson (l) Uffizi Gallery, Florence/Scala 28 (l) Ekdotike Athenon (t) Roger Wilson 29 Vatican Museum/Scala 30 (l) British Library 31 (t) ET Archive (b) Mark Cator/Impact Photos 32 (l) Ecole Française d'Athènes (b) by courtesy of the Wedgwood Museum Trustees, Barlaston, Stoke-on-Trent, Staffordshire, England 33 (t) British Museum 34 Museo Pio Clementino, Vatican/Scala 35 (t) Ashmolean Museum (c) C.M. Dixon 35 (b) Museo Pio-Clementino, Vatican/Scala 36 (l) British Museum 36 (b) Ecole Française d'Athènes 37 (l) Ashmolean Museum (r) Museo Capitolino/Scala 38-9 reproduced by gracious permission of Her Majesty the Queen 40 (b) Mansell Collection 41 (t) Wedgwood Museum 41 (l) British Museum/Bridgeman Art Library 42 (l) National Portrait Gallery 43 (bl) Victoria & Albert Museum 43 (c) British Museum (tr) Raymond V. Schoder S.J., © 1989 Loyola University (cr) Roger Wilson 44 (l) C.M. Dixon 45 (t) Staatliche Antikensammlungen und Glyptothek, Munich 45 (b) ET Archive 46 (l) Bridgeman Art Library 47 (tl) British Museum 47 (c) Hulton Picture Company 47 (tr,br) C.M. Dixon 48 (l) His Grace the Duke of Norfolk K.G. 48 (l) British Museum 49 The Tate Gallery, London 50 (t) C.M. Dixon 50 (l), 51 (t) ET Archive 51 (b) Charles Robert Cockerell, from C.R. Cockerell, The Temples of Jupiter Panhellenius at Aegina and of Apollo Epicurius at Bassae near Phigaleia in Arcadia, London 1860 52 (l) Audrey Petty from Helen Waterhouse, British School at Athens: The First Hundred Years 53 (t) West Yorkshire Archaeological Service 53 (b) L & R Adkins 54 (tl) 55 (bl) Alan W. Johnston 55 (t,r) C.M. Dixon 56 (l) Mansell Collection 57 (tl) Roger Wilson 58 (l) C.M. Dixon 58 (b) Raymond V. Schoder S.J., © 1989